Military Gec

MW00643565

RGS-IBG Book Series

The *Royal Geographical Society (with the Institute of British Geographers) Book Series* provides a forum for scholarly monographs and edited collections of academic papers at the leading edge of research in human and physical geography. The volumes are intended to make significant contributions to the field in which they lie, and to be written in a manner accessible to the wider community of academic geographers. Some volumes will disseminate current geographical research reported at conferences or sessions convened by Research Groups of the Society. Some will be edited or authored by scholars from beyond the UK. All are designed to have an international readership and to both reflect and stimulate the best current research within geography.

The books will stand out in terms of:

- the quality of research
- their contribution to their research field
- their likelihood to stimulate other research
- being scholarly but accessible.

For series guides go to http://www.blackwellpublishing.com/pdf/rgsibg.pdf

Published

Military Geographies
Rachel Woodward

A New Deal for Transport?
Edited by Iain Docherty and Jon Shaw

Geographies of British Modernity
Edited by David Gilbert, David Matless and Brian Short

Lost Geographies of Power
John Allen

Globalizing South China
Carolyn L. Cartier

Geomorphological Processes and Landscape Change: Britain in the Last 1000 Years
Edited by David L. Higgitt and E. Mark Lee

Forthcoming

Domicile and Diaspora
Alison Blunt

The Geomorphology of Upland Peat
Martin Evans and Jeff Warburton

Fieldwork
Simon Naylor

Putting Workfare in Place
Peter Sunley, Ron Martin and Corinne Nativel

Natural Resources in Eastern Europe
Chad Staddon

Geographies and Moralities
Roger Lee and David M. Smith

Military Geographies

Rachel Woodward

Blackwell
Publishing

350 Main Street, Malden, MA 02148-5020, USA
108 Cowley Road, Oxford OX4 1JF, UK
550 Swanston Street, Carlton, Victoria 3053, Australia

First published 2004 by Blackwell Publishing Ltd

Library of Congress Cataloging-in-Publication Data

Woodward, Rachel.
   Military geographies / Rachel Woodward.
      p. cm. – (RGS-IBG book series)
   Includes bibliographical references and index.
      ISBN 1-4051-1053-8 (hardback: alk. paper)––ISBN 1-4051-2777-5 (pbk.: alk. paper)
      1. Military geography. 2. Militarism. I. Title. II. Series.
      UA990.W663 2004
      355.4'7–dc22   2003021517

A catalogue record for this title is available from the British Library.

Set in 10/12 pt Plantin
by Kolam Information Services Pvt. Ltd, Pondicherry, India

For further information on
Blackwell Publishing, visit our website:
http://www.blackwellpublishing.com

Contents

Figures

Acknowledgements

The map of the defence estate at Figure 2.1 is Crown Copyright, reproduced with permission from HMSO. The lyrics of *Shipbuilding* at Figure 3.1 is reproduced with permission from BMG Music Publishing Ltd. and International Music Publications. Figure 5.1 is reproduced with the permission of the Army Training and Recruiting Agency. Figure 5.2 is reproduced with the permission of Joe Painter.

The research on which this book is based was undertaken during my time as Runciman Research Fellow at the University of Newcastle's Centre for Rural Economy, and more recently as Lecturer in the University of Newcastle's School of Agriculture, Food and Rural Development. Some of this research was funded by grants from the Nuffield Foundation, from the University of Newcastle's Small Grants Committee, and from the Faculty of Agriculture and Biological Sciences Research Committee, and I am grateful for this support.

My thanks to my colleagues at the Centre for Rural Economy, the School of Agriculture, Food and Rural Development, and the Centre for Gender and Women's Studies, all University of Newcastle, for advice, help, support and encouragement during the completion of this book, in particular Katy Bennett, Eileen Curry, Philip Lowe and Hilary Talbot. Nina Laurie, Trish Winter and David Wood kept me company during some of the fieldwork and offered their own insights into the military geographies that surround us. My thanks also to the staff on the Inter Library Loans desk at the University of Newcastle's Robinson Library for their tireless help in tracking down some of the more obscure literature used in this book. I am grateful also to my academic colleagues beyond the University of Newcastle who have shared their thoughts with me about military geographies, particularly Celia Clark, David Doxford and the members of the COST A10 network. Nick Henry (the Series Editor), Joe Painter, Neil

Ward, Trish Winter and David Wood all commented on various drafts of this book, and I'm thankful for their suggestions.

My biggest debt of thanks goes to my family, Joe, Ruth and Patrick Painter, for their love, their support during the preparation of this book, and for their companionship during fieldwork. I'm grateful for their patience, good humour and tolerance of my military geography obsessions.

Series Editors' Preface

The RGS/IBG Book series publishes the highest quality of research and scholarship across the broad disciplinary spectrum of geography. Addressing the vibrant agenda of theoretical debates and issues that characterise the contemporary discipline, contributions will provide a synthesis of research, teaching, theory and practice that both reflects and stimulates cutting edge research. The Series seeks to engage an international readership through the provision of scholarly, vivid and accessible texts.

Nick Henry and Jon Sadler
RGS-IBG Book Series Editors.

Abbreviations

AAG	Association of American Geographers
ACP	Arms Conversion Project
ADF	Australian Defence Force
AFB	Air Force Base
AFTC	Army Field Training Centre
AS90	Artillery System 90
BBC	British Broadcasting Corporation
BICC	Bonn International Centre for Conversion
BRAC	Base Realignment and Closure Commission
CAAB	Campaign for the Accountability of American Bases
CCTV	Closed Circuit Television
CMS(R)	Common Military Syllabus (Recruits)
CND	Campaign for Nuclear Disarmament
DASA	Defence Analytical Services Agency
DE	Defence Estate
DEO	Defence Estates Organisation
DERA	Defence Evaluation and Research Agency
DETR	Department of Environment, Transport and the Regions
DoD	Department of Defense
DU	Depleted Uranium
GDA	Gun Deployment Area
Ha	Hectares
HCDC	House of Commons Defence Committee
MGSG	Military Geography Speciality Group
MLRS	Multiple Launch Rocket System
MoD	Ministry of Defence
MOOTW	Military Operations Other Than War
MP	Member of Parliament

NAAFI	Navy, Army and Air Force Institute
NAO	National Audit Office
nd	no date
npn	no page number
NoPD	Notice of Proposed Development
OPAG	Otley Peace Action Group
OP	Observation Post
OPI	Otterburn Public Inquiry
OTA	Otterburn Training Area
PAC	Public Accounts Committee
PCBs	Polychlorinated biphenyls
PX	Post Exchange
RAF	Royal Air Force
RN	Royal Navy
SDR	Strategic Defence Review
SSSI	Site of Special Scientific Interest
SSVC	Services Sound and Vision Corporation
TNT	Trinitrotoluene
UK	United Kingdom
US	United States
USAF	United States Air Force

Chapter One

Military Geography, Militarism's Geographies

Military Geographies are Everywhere

I stood at the fence and looked in through the wire. On the other side lay a broad strip of grass. A little further on and to the left, sat red-and-white-painted wooden baffle boards, mounted with lights. Further on from that, the dull, grey strip of runway stretched off into the distance. At the far end huddled a collection of structures and objects in shades of green, grey and black, unidentifiable from this distance. Occasional pops from rifle fire, perhaps, competed with the traffic noise from the road beside me. Crows hopped around on the empty runway. I poured a cup of coffee from my vacuum flask, watched and waited. Engine noise grew louder and then a dark blue pick-up truck with US-style police lights and a foreign number-plate came driving swiftly up the service road alongside the runway, slowing as it rounded the end, and then halting, to my right. I'd been seen, a coffee-toting speck beyond the perimeter fence at the bottom of the runway. The pick-up drove right to left in front of me, 30 m distant, two beret-topped heads swivelled in my direction, watching me as I watched them. The truck drove on to the baffle boards, executed a quick three-point turn and came back, left to right. It paused, watching. Another three-point turn, another traverse in front of me, another pause, engine running. I drank my coffee and ate a chocolate bar, wrapper stowed carefully in my pocket (the sign in a nearby lay-by, where I had parked, warned 'Civic Amenities Act 1967 No Litter Penalty £100'). My focus swam with the effort of switching, from watching wire 30 cm from my nose and buildings 3 km distant. I refilled my cup, balancing it on the final post of a smaller fence perpendicular to the wire barrier ('MoD Keep Out') mindful of the sign on the larger fence ('Ministry of Defence (Air) Anyone Attempting to Enter will be Detained and Arrested'). My movements sparked activity; the truck did another sweep, left to right, three-point turn, right to left, pause, engine idling, watching me as I watched them, drinking my coffee. They watched, I watched, and I realized that this was a stand-off; they were waiting for me to do something. This is their job; waiting for people do to things. Well, this is my job. I watched back as I finished my coffee, capped flask with cup, turned and walked back to my car, feeling their eyes on my back.

As I sat taking off my boots, a police car passed me, turned next left and appeared to double back through some bracken. I drove off and followed it, past another fence and another sign ('Wildlife Protection Area; Please Don't Park on Verge') ending up in an aircraft viewing area at the far edge of the runway ('MoD accepts no responsibility for loss or damage to property') beyond the boundary marked out by the perimeter fence. The carpark was half-filled by the cars of a collection of middle-aged male aviation enthusiasts on a Sunday outing, who clustered around the police car. I parked, got out my road atlas, and wound down the window so that I could hear what the policeman was saying. 'Anyone near that fence line is suspect...' he was telling the plane spotters; their expressions mixed worry that they'd strayed over the line, with concern for the fight against whichever evil infiltrator might dare to stand near the fence in a suspicious way.

This Sunday lunchtime security encounter could have happened anywhere; Tom Vanderbilt and Richard Misrach describe similar events during their travels around Nevada (Vanderbilt, 2002; Misrach, 1990). In fact, it was at RAF Lakenheath, home of the United States Air Force 48th Fighter Wing, a base for F15 jets and the 5,000 US military personnel and 2,000 US and British civilians who service them, located on the A1065, 80 km or so north-east of Cambridge, England. A place where looking through fences causes Sunday lunchtime security jitters amongst those charged with the defence of this military space. Where every fence, every road, every boundary bears a sign marking out this military territory. Where the US Air Force works, rests and plays (a golf course is strategically placed between the main road and important structures), endlessly rehearsing to perfect its fighting capabilities, a little piece of America in the middle of the Cambridgeshire countryside. Where the British police close public highways with concrete blocks by military order. Where a church stands forlorn and isolated in a field of maize, broken belfry windowframes waving in the wind, the roof sagging, deconsecrated by military order. Where wildlife is protected by military order. Where military orders create their own geographies, where these geographies of military activity are writ large on the physical and social landscape, where these geographies exert webs of moral control and where I, for a fraction of time, caused a security alert, because I violated this order by standing on a scrap of grass, next to a public highway, looking through a fence.

This book is about the military geographies of places like Lakenheath. It is about how militarism and military activities create spaces, places, environments and landscapes with reference to a distinct moral order. It is also about how wider geographies are touched and moulded, more indirectly, by militarism and the activities of military forces. This book is about how military geographies are constituted and expressed. Its central theme is that militarism and military activities in nonconflict situations exert control over space in ways and through means which frequently render this control invisible, in contrast to the more obvious controls exerted by military forces during and following armed conflicts. This control is both material and discursive.

The definition of militarism used here is of militarism as 'an extension of military influence to civilian spheres, including economic and socio-political life' (Thee, 1980, p.15). Militarism at its most extreme is an ideology which subordinates civic or governmental ideals to the military, and promotes a policy of aggressive military preparedness, but militarism may not necessarily be manifest in these ways. Militarism as the extension of military influence into economic, social and political life is culturally, locationally and temporally specific. The intention of this book is not to define typologies of militarism from which different geographical conse-quences can be read, or systematically to document militarism's geograph-ies in states around the world. Rather, the intention is to describe and explain how some specific geographies – configurations of entities and social relations across space – are shaped by militarism, with a view to explaining how the controls exerted by militarism operate across a range of contexts. Militarism and the controls it exerts is essentially geographical, in that it is expressed in and constitutive of space, place and landscape, and those outcomes are variable, nuanced and fluid, rather than uniform in cause and effect and immutable in consequence. Military geographies are everywhere. They – and their study – are inherently political, in that they are about the imposition, negotiation and (sometimes) the challenging and checking of control over people, place and space. Understanding the pat-terns of entities and social relations across space – across the globe – requires taking account of military power and its role in shaping these patterns. Militarism's geographies are about the control of space, about creating the necessary preconditions for military activities.

Military geographies are everywhere; every corner of every place in every land in every part of this world of ours is touched, shaped, viewed and represented in some way by military forces and military activities. Military geographies are made by a bewildering range of actions – a soldier's foot-print, a landowner's custody, an invader's force, an occupier's presence. The manufacture of weapons, the destruction caused by armed conflict, the construction of military facilities, and the pollution of conventional and nuclear weapons all mark the earth. Military activities, an endless cycle of preparations for waging war, and war itself, define countless lives. People fight, flee, defend, work, live, conquer, celebrate, suffer and die, scratching their progress and their demise onto place under circumstances defined by militarism in its various national guises. Castles and bastles, forts and ports, depots and silos, bases and training spaces are built, used and relinquished. Military geographies are representational as well as material and experiential. Military maps and information systems name, claim, define and categorize territory. Infantry and artillery and armoured regiments analyze terrain. Spy planes and satellites scan from above, watching. Military geographies surround us, are always with us.[1]

Yet this is not a book about war and geography. War – an increasingly catch-all term for the active, direct engagement between armed forces in conflict – is the most obvious manifestation of military activity and militarism. It is the culmination of these. It is the most visible and destructive of a range of military activities inspired or guided by militarism. It is the end product of these military activities and expression. This book is not about the geographies of armed conflict, or military operations other than war, or the logics, motivations and explanations for warfare. Rather, it looks at how the continual preparations which states make in order to be able to wage war and engage in military operations shape wider economic, social, environmental and cultural geographies, and produce their own ordering of space. This choice is deliberate, guided by an interest in the geographies of those activities which make armed conflict possible. This is not to imply that the geographies of armed conflict are not of significant concern to warrant study, but instead to argue that a wider set of geographies shaped by preparations for war and by militarism and military control merit consideration in their own right. Furthermore, given the rich contemporary literatures emerging in critical geopolitics, given political geography's long engagement with the causes and consequences of struggles over territory and sovereignty, and given an even older fascination amongst some geographers with matters of terrain and tactics, I have been reluctant to revisit the well-trodden ground of war and its geography.[2] War and its geography constitute the apex of a pyramid; this book is concerned by the imprint marked by that pyramid's base.

The Invisibility of Military Geographies

This book focuses on the geographies constituted and expressed by the material practices of military activities and the discursive strategies of militarism. These are the baseline and backroom activities which structure and facilitate armed conflict. They have received far less sustained scholarly attention than conflicts themselves. As Ó Tuathail (1996) remarks, contemporary geography rarely gives militarism the attention it deserves, despite the profound and destructive influence of militarism on the twentieth century.

The absence of 'military geographies' within standard introductory undergraduate texts in human geography would seem to bear this out. Early on the life in this book, restless in my University's library, I browsed through some definitional geography texts and their indexes in search of my favourite keywords – 'war', 'military', 'defence' and 'army' – and anything else that took my fancy. This impulsive and nonscientific exercise was revealing in its own way.

The Student's Companion to Geography (Rogers and Viles, 2003) contained nothing. This 'essential resource for those studying geography at university... [with] contributions from leading geographers from around the world provide[s] a whole range of information on what today's geography is all about...', judging by the blurb on the back cover. It certainly looks like a really useful book. But not if you're looking for geography's disciplinary engagement with militarism and its consequences. My keywords are absent. The second edition of *The Dictionary of Human Geography* (Johnston, Gregory and Smith, 1986) contained no military anything – no armies, navies, airforces, soldiers. One index reference for 'defence, national' referred back to an entry on 'public goods'. 'Air space and concept of boundary' referred back to the 'boundaries' entry (which also includes territorial waters). 'War, representation of demographic consequences' referred back to a population pyramid for France in 1984 showing clearly the low birth rate following the end of the 1914–18 war. In the fourth edition of *The Dictionary of Human Geography* (Johnston, Gregory, Pratt and Watts, 2000), military geography still doesn't get its own entry; we move straight from migration to mimesis. From the index, 'War: boundary dispute as cause' leads us to 'sovereignty'; 'war: geographers' role during' leads us to 'Applied Geography' and a discussion about geographers' roles in military intelligence activities; 'war: and sense of place' leads us to battlefields and 'war memorials' leads us to 'monuments'. I'm more lucky with *A Feminist Glossary of Human Geography* (McDowell and Sharp, 1999). There between migration and mimesis, sits 'military/militarism', which outlines the arguments for understanding the gendering of militarism through the construction and representation of gender identities and potential enhancement or limitation of women's roles that this brings. In *Geographies of Global Change: Remapping the World* (Johnston, Taylor and Watts, 2002) I find even more: 'military Keynesianism', 'military, technoscientific', 'war memorials', 'weapons', 'armaments industry', and a whole section on geopolitical change. It's a start.

This exercise is indicative of the peripherality of militarism and its geographies within the disciplinary structures which define academic geography. It is there, within the spaces defined by political geography and its concerns with territoriality and sovereignty. It is there in feminist critiques of the social construction of gender relations. But military geographies as the object of sustained scholarly interest within the discipline appear to be absent.

Appearances are deceptive. The connections between geography as an academic discipline concerned with descriptions of the world, and military issues, are drawn explicitly in Military Geography. Military Geography has disciplinary status primarily in North American geography, via the Association of American Geographers' Military Geography Speciality Group (MGSG).[3] For the MGSG, Military Geography is '. . . the application of geographic information, tools, and techniques to military problems', focussing on the range of military scenarios from peacetime to war (Palka and Galgano, 2000, p.xi). It is concerned primarily with how military activities and armed conflict are shaped by terrain and environment. Military Geography has a long history, its roots tangled up with the imperial ambitions and military requirements that late-nineteenth-century Geography emerged to serve. Yet as an academic discipline, Military Geography has failed to evolve. The application of topographical and environmental knowledge to the conduct of military campaigns, and the strategic and tactical considerations to be taken into account, were set out by T. Miller Maguire in 1899 (Maguire, 1899). Over the twentieth century and into the twenty-first this understanding of Military Geography held fast (see Peltier and Pearcy, 1966; O'Sullivan and Miller, 1983; O'Sullivan, 1991; Winters et al, 1998; Palka and Galgano, 2000; O'Sullivan, 2001).

What explains this evolutionary stasis? Palka and Galgano's lament is telling:

> The demise of military geography among universities and academics coincided with the widespread social and political unrest that occurred in America during the mid-1960s and early 1970s. During that era, anti-war sentiments and a general mistrust of the federal government prompted geographers to become increasingly concerned with being socially, morally, and ecologically responsible in their research efforts and professional affiliations with government agencies. Contributing to the war effort in Vietnam came to be regarded as irresponsible by many members of the AAG. The controversy surrounding the Vietnam War cast a persistent shadow on military geography as an academic discipline throughout the 1970s. (Palka and Galgano, 2000, pp. 3–4)

Controversy surrounding US military engagement in Vietnam was essential in shaping contemporary Anglo–American geography. Opposition to the war politicized a small group of geographers working in (primarily) British and American universities in the late 1960s and early 1970s. 'Radical

Geography' as a disciplinary marker for a politicized Leftist human geography emerged as a movement bent on transforming the scope of the conventional discipline. This group criticized the discipline as irrelevant to pressing political issues of the time such as the movement for civil rights, opposition to the Vietnam War and protest at the irreversible consequences of environmental pollution (Peet, 2000). Suggestions for the politicization of Military Geography were there; an influential collection of essays on Radical Geography (Peet, 1977) includes a chapter by Lacoste (1977) on the need to link geographical discourse with political and military interests, an argument which forms the basis of his analysis of the links between topography, environment and military campaigns in North Vietnam. It is an essay of its time. 'Many geographers today honestly consider their "science" as detached knowledge', notes Lacoste, an observation hardly possible in the contemporary discipline with its concerns about relevance and political engagement. The discipline of Geography has gone on to embrace radical and critical approaches, informed by structuralist and poststructuralist social theory. The study of armed conflicts and their geographies has moved on from topographical and environmental concerns, via the concerns of political geography to the critiques of critical geopolitics. Military Geography has been left standing, the subdisciplinary label indicative of an applied, largely atheoretical spatial science, unconcerned with a wider conceptualization of the geographies constituted and expressed by militarism and military activities, and bounded closely by US military and state discourses of state, nationhood, sovereignty and security.

Does any of this matter? Are dictionary entries and the disciplinary framework of the AAG important here? On the one hand, no, they are not. The disciplinary name-tags which we give to scholarly endeavour are just that, labels to stick on for ease of identification. Within a social science that is increasingly inter-disciplinary (or even post-disciplinary), the content and intent of scholarship is more important than the demarcation of artificial boundaries with which we can categorize that scholarship. Yet labels are useful, sometimes. Naming things is a political strategy. Naming things makes them visible, draws attention to the content and intent of that scholarship. So, on the other hand, the identification tags and disciplinary definitions are useful. 'Military geographies' is, for me, a useful label, and one which will be used throughout this book. It is useful because it grants visibility to the geographies of militarism and military activities which are traced in this book, geographies which, in my view, should form a more central part of the contemporary geographical project as currently researched and taught in Anglophone Geographic communities. It is useful because it provides at the very least a brand name with which to market this scholarly enterprise within the discipline. The label is useful also because it makes military geographies an issue. As I go on to argue in subsequent chapters, discourses of militarism legitimize and naturalize the activities undertaken by the state in preparation for armed conflict. This naturalizing obscures their geographies and consequences from critical gaze, and facilitates the military control of space. This normalizing legitimizes secrecy about land uses in the name of national defence and national security. Talking explicitly about military geographies makes these things an issue.

Doing Military Geography

This book, then, is about the geographies of militarism and military activities – their impacts on space, place, environment and landscape. The ideas driving the analysis are straightforward.

In the beginning, there is description. In doing geography, we write about the earth, and that writing necessarily requires us to document what is there and what is where. This is an important task in its own right, but also has its limits. Description of what is where doesn't automatically bring with it an explanation of what happens as a consequence of things being where they are. Explanation follows from description – the 'why?' of 'where?'. This involves explanation of location and explanation of process and change. So far so good; as far as writing these military geographies is concerned, this would involve choosing places or themes to look at, describing the material form and lived experience of those military geographies, and seeking explanations for these geographies with the help of the insights from contemporary social scientific research and social theory.

In doing this, my attempts to think through and write out military geographies kept getting snagged and held back by military explanations of its own geographies. Each journey through a particular theme stumbled into arguments originating in military organizations and armed forces. These were insistent arguments, about why military geographies appear as they do. They were often very seductive justifications as to why these military geographies should be so, and had to be so. Representation seemed to be an important theme in military geographies, as the means by which the mechanisms and strategies of military control were explained, normalized and naturalized. Representation as a strategic military act emerged as a central problematic to the writing of military geographies.[4] These military representations constitute some of the many discursive practices of militarism. Writing military geographies seemed more and more to be about understanding representation as a practice of militarism, and less and less about explanation rooted in more abstract structural conceptions of militarism as an ideology.

Three observations follow from this. The first observation is that this focus on representation brings the situated nature of knowledge to the fore.

I don't look down the wrong end of the barrel of a gun on a regular basis. This fact about my situation or positionality seems to me significant in my prioritizing representation as I do. The second observation is that this representational approach emphasizes the specificity in time and space of militarism and its geographies. Military geographies are always shifting and changing; the ones I focus on are contemporary, reflecting research and fieldwork conducted from 1996 to 2002. The third observation is that this understanding of military geographies as changeable brings with it possibilities for negotiation and challenge. This makes the writing of military geographies less concerned with just understanding geographies of militarism and more aware of our responsibilities to think coherently and critically about the moral authority on which military geographies are based. Ultimately, the study of military geographies involves a moral decision. If we study the ways in which military activities inscribe themselves onto space, place, environment and landscape, should we ignore or accept unquestioned the politics of that process? There are those, I'm sure, who would argue for the possibility of objective, politically neutral military geography. I am not one of them. Studying military geographies means making a moral judgement about the need to think critically about militarism. It involves questioning the moral authority of militarism, the rights and wrongs of the use of violence in pursuit of political and economic ends, and the morality of the consequences of military preparedness. Whether the outcome of that critical analysis is to our collective liking, and whether we agree with this moral understanding of the forces shaping military geographies, is a different matter. The point, to me, is that military geographies are not politically neutral, and our study of military geographies should not pretend otherwise.

These observations influenced the themes that I chose for study in this book. The themes are geographies of control over space, military economic geographies, military environmentalism, militarized landscapes, and challenges to military geographies. They were all chosen for what they could illustrate about the influence of militarism on the patterning of material entities and social relations, and for what an examination of those patterns and relations (i.e. those military geographies) could tell us about the controls exerted by military power. The themes were also chosen because in some respects, although they spoke in general terms to many of the central concerns of contemporary geographical scholarship, the military specificities have been either ignored or underexplored within this body of work. Also relevant were issues such as the availability of information from military and nonmilitary sources; the range of available literature within primarily but not exclusively the social sciences; the resources (time, money) available to me for fieldwork; and my own interests and curiosity. Also very relevant were the competing requirements between writing a book with international appeal which included consideration of European, North American and Australasian examples, and my requirement to write authoritatively about what I know and resist the pressures to write extensively about cultures and situations which I know less about. The British materials won, in the end, because they provide the context and culture and raw data which I know best and have most ready access to, but I have also tried where possible to provide comparative examples which either reinforce or unsettle my analysis. This should not be taken to imply some inherent applicability of the British case to other contexts; to restate, my purpose is not to provide broad theoretical explanations of how militarism's geographies look and work, but to indicate strategies by which militarism makes its geographies through material and representational practice. In terms of the scope of this book, as I have already explained, I did not want to revisit much of the political geography and critical geopolitics literature which talks into the spatiality of armed conflict and the exercise of political power. Nor have I considered themes such as the links between militarism and urban form, surveillance, and the mapping of space through intelligence; others are better qualified than me to discuss these particularly military geographies.[5] The themes that I consider here all relate to the military control of land in some way, not as the occupation of sovereign territory as the direct and immediate result of military aggression or armed conflict, but the often more prosaic military act of just being there. I am interested in the military geographies that this 'being there' produces, and in understanding the power relations and strategies for control inherent in these geographies.

Chapter 2 considers military space. It looks at the domestic military control of space by armed forces, and the foreign control of sovereign territory, as the primary mechanism for the assertion of military control in nonconflict situations. The chapter highlights one of the key difficulties in assessing the scale and nature of military control via occupancy – that of the absence of reliable, available data on the military use of land. The chapter then goes on to look chronologically at the debate in the UK about the size of the defence estate relative to military needs. The chapter concludes by suggesting that the intricacies of military control are discernible when one looks at the ideologies underpinning land management, the practices of governance which filter through to defence lands management, and the discursive strategies which are developed to explain the military control of space.

Chapter 3 considers military economic geographies. It looks at the controls exerted over places by the economic impacts of a military presence. The chapter marks out the difficulties inherent in assessing the level of these impacts, but draws on a range of studies to examine the measurable and nonquantifiable impacts, in economic and social terms, of military control. The chapter then looks at the conversion of military sites, advocating the study of conversion not only as an issue in its own right, but also as a means of assessing the extent and permanence of military influence.

Chapter 4 considers militarized environments. The impact of military activities on the natural environment is a tricky issue, politically contentious and often underexplored because of military sensitivities. The chapter looks at environmental pollution, the risks posed by nuclear, chemical and biological contamination, and environmental modification. The policy responses developed in response to concern and criticisms about environmental impacts are explored, with reference to the caveats which policies provide for military activities. The chapter then goes on to look at discourses of military environmentalism, defined as strategies developed by military authorities in order to give meaning to environmental impacts and by so doing to legitimize the military presence.

Chapter 5 considers military landscapes. I discuss military ways of seeing landscapes, ways of reading the iconography of military landscapes, and the use of representations of landscapes as a strategic military act. The chapter then goes on to consider issues of landscape and identity, looking at the construction of gendered and national identities with reference to military landscapes. The chapter argues that military control, as well as being a material practice, is discursive, in the sense that power is mobilized through the development of explanatory narratives about military legitimacy and place in the landscape.

Chapter 6 considers challenges to military geographies and the military control of space, looking at attempts to contest the manifestations of military control and efforts to challenge militarism itself. The chapter starts by examining challenges which have pitted the state against the concerns of local governmental and nongovernmental organizations in debates over military training at the Otterburn Training Area in the UK. The case study is used for what is it indicates about civil–military relations and about the nature of contemporary militarism. The chapter goes on to assess direct challenges to militarism and militarism's geographies from antimilitary protests where military land use practices are contested as part of a wider critique of militarism. The chapter concludes with a discussion of the reimagination of military spaces, places and landscapes and the challenges that this brings to military control.

Chapter 7 concludes the book by considering explicitly the issue of military control. Military control driving military geographies, I suggest, flows from four things: physical presence, controls over information, the state's practices of governance, and the discursive construction of ideas about national security. My concluding point concerns the pervasiveness of military geographies in the contemporary world, and the moral imperatives to develop the study of these geographies more thoroughly in geographic research and teaching.

Chapter Two

Military Space

The Military Control of Land

The Otterburn Training Area in Northumberland is vast. From a high point on a crest in the centre, one can see for miles across a panorama of hill, valley and moor. Everything in view is under military control. Unique in what it contains, though not in what it represents, the training area at Otterburn epitomizes a basic fact about military geographies, that they are about land and its control, at a most fundamental level. Physical occupancy counts. The Otterburn Training Area (OTA) epitomizes that, in its assertion of the fact of military presence through the signs, flags and marks across its landscape, and in its assertion of the essential contribution this place makes to the pursuit and consolidation of British military power. The soldiers who landed on the Falklands in 1982 could not have yomped across those islands unless they had been trained to do so at the OTA, a constituent part of the base of the military pyramid.

The military occupancy of land is at face value a rather prosaic issue. In the nonconflict situations on which I focus, it does not involve obvious displays of military might and military hardware, immediate action or visible force. The military occupancy of land is a critical issue almost *because* of its relative invisibility. That which is taken for granted may relish obscurity. It is also a critical issue because the themes that follow in subsequent chapters – military economic geographies, militarized environments, military landscapes and challenges to the military presence – are all predicated on a basic fact of military occupation of space. The control of space is fundamental to understanding military geographies.

This chapter is about the military control of land. I start by reviewing some of the facts about military occupancy by looking at the military control of domestic space by armed forces, and the foreign control of sovereign territory for military purposes. I then focus more closely on the UK in order to examine how the control marked by military occupancy has been justified during the course of debates on the size of the UK defence estate versus justifications for the need of an estate of that magnitude. The course of this debate over the past 30 years is traced with a view to picking out the salient points from the intricacies of military land use debates. These, I argue, relate to the power and significance of physical presence, the controls exerted on information about military land uses, the controls which practices of governance put into place, and the controls which the rhetoric of defence and national security exerts.

The military control of domestic space

Most developed economies devote large areas of land to military purposes. Westing estimated that 1 percent of land was used for military purposes in a study of 13 advanced economies (Westing, 1988). In the United States, the Department of Defense (DoD) controls around 12 million hectares (ha), of a federal estate of around 274 million ha; the DoD is the fifth largest federal land management department. The majority of these land holdings are in the 12 states of the Rocky Mountain and Pacific regions of the US (Cawley and Lawrence, 1995). In France, training areas cover around 110,932 ha, and the French also make use of French dependent territories overseas, most famously for nuclear testing in the Pacific. The Swiss Army have about 21,000 ha of land at their disposal for training (Doxford and Judd, 2002). The Australian armed forces have about 3 million ha available. The Canadian armed forces use about 20,000 sq. km (Canadian National Defence, 2000).

In the UK, military land and foreshore holdings (freehold and leasehold) cover a total of 241,000 ha. The UK defence estate is (reputedly) the second largest single land holding in the UK (also large are the estates of the Forestry Commission and the National Trust); wood, country estates and preparations for war all use large amounts of land. The total surface area of the UK is 241,600 sq. km, so about 1 percent of the UK is owned by the Crown for military purposes and the UK fits well with Westing's average figure. The UK Armed Forces have training rights over a further 124,900 ha. These neat statistics hide considerable variation, of course. In terms of land and foreshore, both leasehold and freehold, England has 190,200 ha (79 percent of military land), Wales has 20,700 ha (8.5 percent), Scotland has 27,100 ha (11.2 percent) and Northern Ireland 3,200 ha (1.3 percent). Training rights are unevenly distributed; rights to train over private land cover 88,100 ha in Scotland, 34,000 ha in England, 2,200 ha in Wales and 100 ha in Northern Ireland (DASA, 2002).

Accurate information on the distribution of sites in the UK at county or regional level is hard to come by. Comprehensive information is not published by the MoD as a matter of course, so statistics on military lands and establishments have to be cobbled together from disparate sources which themselves may rely on unpublished methods of data collection and analysis. Figure 2.1, published in 1994 in response to a House of Commons Defence Committee inquiry, shows an anticipated uneven distribution. Compare, for example, the 41,388 ha in Wiltshire (southern England) with County Durham's 377 ha in northern England (all figures for May 1993). In this bland map, the reader has to do the work, using knowledge of geographies of production (agriculture, industry, services) reproduction (population location) and consumption (culture, lifestyle) as mental overlays to understand the disparity in military distribution across Britain and Northern Ireland. The Wiltshire/County Durham disparity is explained by the presence, in the former, of the huge Salisbury Plain Training Area (38,000 ha) and key army headquarters functions at Upavon and Tidworth, and in the latter by the small Bowes Moor training area and Light Infantry and Territorial Army barracks. The location of these key sites is a function of successive rounds of military investment and locational decision making, but the map doesn't tell us this or about other explanatory features such as the power of functions contained in a place or the consequences of a concentration of military establishments for local economies. The map is a snapshot of a distribution at one moment in time.

At the time of writing, this 1993 data on the county-by-county distribution of military lands in the UK is all that is available; more recent statistics showing the distribution of defence lands at a scale below that of country are not published by the MoD, and although we could speculate that the distribution shown would be broadly similar in the early twenty-first century there may well be significant differences in detail. However, there is no way of knowing. There is a remarkable absence in the UK of reliable and detailed data on the distribution of military land holdings. This makes questioning the extent, contents and changes in the defence estate a difficult task. Control by military establishments over land becomes far easier to sustain when little information about those establishments is placed in the public domain.

Information about the scale, distribution and contents of military establishments in the UK is available only at a very broad level. MoD and armed forces publicity literature and corporate documents describe the estate by distinguishing between the built and rural estate. The built estate in the UK is listed as covering a total area of 80,000 ha and comprising three naval bases, 64 airfields, 140 storage depots, 213 barracks and camps, 47 research and development installations, 17 major communications facilities, 63,000 married quarters, 147 town centre Career Offices and 668

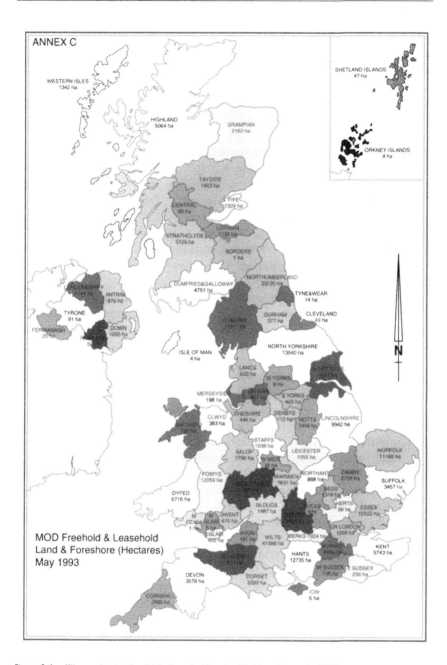

Figure 2.1 UK map showing the distribution of military land holdings by county, 1993.
Source: HCDC, 1994. Crown Copyright.

protected buildings. The rural estate is described as being 160,000 ha, comprising 60 training areas, 36 small arms ranges, 7 major test and evaluation ranges, 7 aerial bombing ranges, 196 Sites of Special Scientific Interest and 598 Scheduled Ancient Monuments (MoD, 2000a). The Australian defence estate is similarly presented for publicity purposes in broad terms. Covering around 3 million ha with 25,000 facilities and 370 properties, the whole has a value of about A$15 billion. The Australian defence estate contains areas such as the Woomera training area (at 127,000 sq. km, larger than Portugal and ideal for weapons testing and space launch), Bradshaw training area (18,710 sq. km) and smaller training areas at Yampi (5,560 sq. km), Shoalwater Bay (4,545 sq. km), Delamere (2,112 sq. km) and Mt Bundy (1,170 sq. km) (Trinder, 2002). Canada's defence estate is also represented in this way, with defence documentation listing the Canadian armed forces' 27 land, naval and air bases and stations, 449 individual properties and 550 leased properties, containing 11 million sq. m of office space, which is about 45 percent of the federal government's total floor space (Canadian National Defence, 2000).

For the UK estate, descriptions according to function are available: 68 percent of the estate is occupied by training areas and ranges, 10.3 percent by airfields, 7.3 percent by research establishments, 4.5 percent by barracks and camps, 4.7 percent by storage and supply depots, 2.3 percent by telecommunications stations, 2.1 percent by miscellaneous activities and 0.4 percent by naval bases (DASA, 2002). The *UK Defence Statistics*, an annual publication, as well as giving data on ha/use, also provides information by service (the Army uses more lands than the Navy, for example). But where is the detail which would facilitate a closer analysis of the distribution and contents of the defence estate?

The lack of information available on the defence estate is problematic. There is a lack of information on the properties (land and buildings) owned for military purposes. This data problem has been a source of embarrassment for the MoD; in 1994, for example, the House of Commons Defence Committee berated the MoD for 'sadly lacking the essential pre-requisite for effective estate management: an accurate, detailed and up-to-date list of the properties held and their functions' (HCDC, 1994a, p.xxxviii). Subsequent National Audit Office (1998), House of Commons Defence Committee (1998) and Public Accounts Committee (1999) reports have reiterated the criticism. The data problem is an issue of public accountability. Statistics make things visible (the word 'accountable' means precisely that, describing the rendering of information in a form that is auditable). Entities appear as issues for public debate through the provision of data and statistics about them; the absence of data will obscure an issue. Furthermore, once domains of life are rendered into statistical representations, they become amenable to forms of intervention, forms which themselves both depend upon and bring into being the representations yielded by statistics. Statistics on military land are important because they help constitute the ways in which intervention, in the form of mechanisms for control, are developed. Forms of intervention depend on the story told with the statistics. Poor data leads to poor management. Data presented in a particular way will consolidate a particular vision being promoted through statistical information. Entities are brought into being, thought into being, by governments, through the collection of statistical data (Murdoch and Ward, 1997).

One way in which the military control of land is enabled, then, is through the techniques of production of statistical information about that land. There is a lack of information also on the location of military properties. Public information is limited in its detail, and this is telling because of the inference we can draw that military lands are secret places. The defence estate remains invisible because its precise extent and details of its location are not revealed. Furthermore, by controlling the information available on military lands, that land immediately becomes labelled as solely for military purposes; the possibility for multiple purposes (multifunctionality) of that land, the idea that it can serve more than one purpose, is removed.

The logic of this secrecy is sustained, we could assume, by arguments about the security needs of the defence estate. Revealing precisely the location and extent of all military holdings could be presumed to constitute a security risk, even in peacetime. This argument, however, fails close scrutiny for two reasons. First, that information *is* actually available publicly, albeit scattered through a host of government and parliamentary documents and websites. An individual with the time, resources and tenacity could eventually piece together the jigsaw quite readily using documentary sources and dogged fieldwork.[1] The only reason that this hasn't been done is lack of time and resources.[2] Second, the discourses of national security which wrap around many governmental statements on the defence estate lose their force once it is recognized how readily they are applied to all eventualities. Yes, these are military places and require a level of security. But that security is applied in physical form on all sites, in any case. Making public the extent and locations of the defence estate as a whole does not alter that requirement. The 'security' arguments are insecure, but they constitute a powerful discourse which operates against public interest concerns about the accountability of the management of military lands.

Foreign military control of sovereign territory

The control over sovereign territory exerted by foreign military powers is also a significant issue here. Before the end of the Cold War, in 1989, over

525,000 US military personnel were deployed in military establishments worldwide, with 230,000 in Germany, 125,000 in other European counties, 48,000 in Japan, 44,000 in South Korea, and 50,000 in other Asian, Pacific, Caribbean and Latin American countries. The occupation of Soviet troops of foreign sovereign territory was notable too, with 627,000 Soviet troops deployed in 19 nations including 380,000 in the former German Democratic Republic and 185,000 shared between Hungary, Poland and Czechoslovakia (Gerson and Birchard, 1991).

Whilst the scale and pattern of foreign military residence on overseas bases may have changed with the end of the Cold War, the issue of the control of space has not. For example, USAF bases in the UK occupy around 2,686 ha of land in places such as RAF Lakenheath in Suffolk (764 ha), RAF Mildenhall in Suffolk (477 ha), RAF Molesworth, Cambridgeshire (271 ha), RAF Fairford, Gloucestershire (470 ha), RAF Upwood, Cambridgeshire (9 ha), and small parts of RAF St Mawgan in Cornwall, RAF Spadeadam in Cumbria and RAF Oakhanger, Hampshire. US forces in the UK also occupy some off-base housing and there are also unmanned USAF sites. Sites are made available under the general provisions of the Status of Forces Agreement (SOFA) of parties to the North Atlantic Treaty; the NATO SOFA places a responsibility on the UK to make suitable arrangements to make available to the visiting forces the land, buildings and associated facilities and services it requires (Defence Estates, 2001b).

The US has a chain of military establishments around the globe. Since the end of the Second World War, overseas sovereign territory has been occupied by US forces in, for example, Kuwait, Guam, Japan, the Philippines, Diego Garcia, Spain, Germany, the Azores, Korea, Honduras, Saudi Arabia, Turkey, Iceland, Greenland and Italy; there are 29 US airbases (used by the US Air Force, Army and Navy) alone (Pilot Shack, 2002; see also Evinger, 1998; Navy Advancement, 2003). In 1999, 37,000 US military personnel were stationed in around 95 bases in Korea. 60,000 were based in Japan, and over half of these in Okinawa, the largest island in the Ryukyu chain in southern Japan. Okinawa has 39 bases, home to around 30,000 US military personnel and an additional 22,500 family members. About 83 percent of the population of the city of Kadena are US military personnel (Euler and Welzer-Lang, 2000). Another historically key location for personnel are bases in Germany, where about 70,000 US military personnel are stationed (Carson, 2002). Major US bases in Latin America and the Caribbean include Guantanamo Bay, Cuba (780 personnel), Soto Cano, Honduras (500), Roosevelt Roads (3,000) and Fort Buchanan (2,635) and personnel at the Vieques bombing ranges, all in Puerto Rico, Manta in Ecuador (475), Aruba (300) and Curaçao (300) (Lindsay-Poland, 2001; the numbers are maximum permitted personnel, although many are sceptical about adherence to these limits). The Australian Anti-Bases Campaign (2003) lists 34 US bases in Australia, but notes that this list is not exhaustive because of secrecy about uses and locations. The most famous (or infamous?) is Pine Gap in central Australia, a communications and listening station linked to Menwith Hill in the UK, a key National Security Agency installation (Australian Anti-Bases Campaign, 2003). The withdrawal of US forces from major bases in Panama in 1999 and the Philippines in 1992 (Subic Naval Base and Clark Air Base) should be seen as a reflection of temporary shifts in geopolitical influence, rather than a fundamental downsizing of the US military's global presence. As Grossman (2002) notes, the establishment of overseas bases by the US military – for example, in Saudi Arabia or Kosovo – is best understood as an opportunistic response and outcome of strategic military interventions.

The UK also has a number of bases overseas, with a military presence in Belize (used primarily for military training in jungle operations), Brunei (another jungle operations training area) and Kenya (another training area). There are two Sovereign Base Areas in Cyprus, at Akrotiri and Dhekelia, covering 98 sq. mi. in total. There are bases in Germany, at Bergen-Hohne, Osnabruck, Gutersloh, Rheindalen and Paderborn, home to around 20,000 UK military personnel, and major training areas at Sennelager and Haltern, the former covering 120 sq. mi. The British Army Training Unit Suffield (BATUS) in Alberta, Canada, provides a huge area for artillery training on the North American prairie. There are bases in Bosnia, the Falkland Islands and Gibraltar, all previous locations of military engagement. In Northern Ireland, technically part of the United Kingdom, around 12,500 troops are garrisoned as part of the military response to Irish republican activities, although an on-going peace process promises to reduce this number. France, India and Pakistan also have military bases outside their own bordered territory, although to a much lesser extent than the USA or UK.

The control of sovereign territory by a foreign power – however willing a nation state might be to play host – is, as we would expect, is a contentious political issue. It is contentious on a different scale and for different reasons than the domestic use of space for military purposes. For Gerson and Birchard, writing at the end of the Cold War (1991), US foreign policy had targeted new enemies in part to justify the continued forward deployment of US military forces in order to maintain US global economic and political dominance. Duncan Campbell, a staunch critic of the US presence in the UK, has termed Britain an 'unsinkable aircraft carrier' for the US, to highlight the military ambitions served by the forward deployment of US Forces personnel (Campbell, 1984). The British Campaign for the Accountability of American Bases (CAAB) nearly two decades after Campbell argues vigorously on the same point, viewing the UK as at risk from retaliatory strikes because of the uses to which American bases located on British soil are put. Motivated by a moral objection to military violence, the CAAB is critical not only of the activities undertaken at such establishments as Menwith Hill Station and Fylingdales, both in Yorkshire (nuclear weapons control, commercial and military espionage through communications surveillance), but also to the lack of democratic parliamentary accountability and oversight of such US stations. (I'll return to challenges to the military presence in Chapter 6.) The politics of opposition to foreign military bases, be they protests at Manta in Ecuador, Okinawa in Japan or Gibraltar on the southern tip of Spain, revolve around concerns about forward basing as expressions of (primarily US) military power, about the (in)ability to bring accountability to a foreign power for what it does in military terms on that land. In the following chapters, I'll discuss the economic, social and environmental impacts of a foreign military presence. In the remainder of this chapter, we return to the UK to unpick the issue of the extent of military land use and to examine the mechanisms of control in more detail.

Mantras and Bromides: Size Versus Needs in the UK

Armies need land in peacetime in order to prepare for military operations. But how much do they need? The debate about size versus needs is an on-going one in the UK with its roots in the establishment of a regular army with training needs in the mid nineteenth century. Armies can never have enough land to train, it seems; despite the size of the defence estate in the UK, the Armed Forces and MoD have argued consistently that defence holdings are barely adequate in size for the purposes of military training. Armed Forces are always reluctant to relinquish their lands (Brzoska, 1999). Many amenity and conservation bodies have argued equally consistently that the need for military training land is to be proven, rather than accepted as fact. The size versus needs issue is a tricky and complex one. It is highly political, in that it sets up for critical examination some fundamental issues about the need for the Armed Forces and the prioritizing of military needs over other concerns. In this debate over size and needs, the estate as a whole becomes visible, as do the philosophies which provide the basis for its management. It is also a highly technical issue, requiring calculations based on areas, functions and personnel. But at what point does the portrayal of technical difficulty become a strategy for excluding nonmilitary input into discussions about land use? The portrayal of military land management strategies as a technical and specialized task prompts questions as to whether civilians without experience of military training, let alone warfare, could have the requisite knowledge and 'intelligence' to make sense of complex military planning decisions and land use requirements.[3] The size versus needs issue is also a mechanism for the legitimation of intervention; it renders the estate visible in such a way as to prioritize certain forms of management over others. It can be viewed as discursive, in that it involves a portrayal of both an estate and its measurement which, through its very construction, begs questions about the purpose behind most military portrayals of the defence estate. The size versus needs debate is also highly emotive, in that it brings together events (such as the preparation for war) with entities (such as valued landscapes) which excite strong feelings.

Who is bothered by this issue? There are those who simply wish to see less military activity, be that in town or country, who would resist the militarization of space and who object to large areas of the countryside being used for preparations for war. There are also those concerned about the transparency (or otherwise) of the decision-making process. There are those concerned with the efficient use of scarce resources. There are those who see inefficiencies and inadequacies in the allocation of training lands for specific purposes as having a detrimental impact on valued landscapes. These various motivations have, over the years, prompted a number of calls for some sort of independent public review of military training lands.

This call has become something of a mantra, a devotional incantation, amongst certain amenity societies, countryside campaigners and pressure groups, and has been used frequently in media reporting and parliamentary inquiries into military land issues (the two public fora where military land use issues have most frequently been debated). The call for an independent public review is significant both for its intrinsic meaning and for the purposes which its repetition serves. The arguments behind this call merit examination for what they tells us about the way in which military training is constructed and portrayed by a prominent group of organizations which have set much of the agenda for the public debate about military training lands. The government and military responses in turn tell us much about military attitudes towards land ownership and use. In this (fairly polarized) debate over the need for an independent review, the mantra-like call for an independent review of military land use has been portrayed in some military quarters as unrealistic, unreasonable and unnecessary. However, the House of Commons Defence Committee (HCDC) was critical of this dismissive view:

> ... the public needs to be convinced to a far greater extent than before of the requirement for the [defence] estate, and [we] look to MoD to develop mechanisms both locally and nationally to meet public concern, not with bromides but with information. (HCDC, 1994, p.x)

This section charts the debate chronologically to show how arguments and counter-arguments have unfolded within their wider political and social contexts.

Military assessments in the 1970s and 1980s

The origins of the current debate over size versus needs lie in the aftermath of the 1939–45 war. Demands for the release of lands should always be viewed within their political and economic contexts. So, for example, in 1948 a (one-day) local public inquiry was held to discuss the proposals being put forward by the War Office to extend the training lands at Otterburn in Northumberland, England. The Northern Group of Labour MPs objected to these proposals, wanting a reduction of the ranges to the smallest possible dimensions in the interests of food production (Ministry of Town and Country Planning, 1948). After the 1939–45 war, although vast areas of land requisitioned during wartime were returned to their original owners, much was kept and used for the training and maintenance of the standing Armed Forces of the Cold War. In general, the Armed Forces have always been reluctant to release lands in their ownership. As Childs (1998) notes, the doctrine that it is a false economy to sell defence lands, even if demand appears low, dates from early in the century.

The policy debate on the defence estate was effectively established in the early 1970s, with the inquiry of the Defence Lands Committee chaired by Lord Nugent of Guildford, which published its findings in 1973. The political liberalism of the 1960s had spawned a range of environmental and ecological pressure groups. In John Childs' analysis, these groups found an obvious target for campaigning in the military occupation of the countryside (Childs, 1998). However, we should remember that these groups were driven by reformist rather than radical strategies at this time (Carter and Lowe, 1998), and this coloured responses to the Defence Lands Committee's inquiries. The Nugent report recommended the release of 40 sites totalling 19,000 acres and the possible disposal of a further 57 sites totalling 12,000 acres, plus the release of coastline areas; these figures are equivalent to around 12,500 ha (Defence Lands Committee, 1973). The recommendations were only partially implemented.

There are two points to make about the Nugent inquiry. First, as Childs has argued, the recommendations were not implemented in full, reinforcing the point that the prevailing social and political context is a key factor in military land use debates. Nugent's recommendations were based in no small measure on a desire to meet the demands of conservationists and environmentalists, but the recommendations were overturned by an obverse movement which argued that the Army was central to the local economy of areas such as Dorset, one of the localities examined by Nugent, and that a military presence should thus be maintained. 'Jobs and employment were victorious over lovers of the countryside' (Childs, 1998, p.207). Second, although the implementation of the Nugent recommendations was problematic, over the years the Defence Lands Committee set the bench-mark for contemporary debates about the need for, and appropriate mech-anisms to undertake a review of the ownership and use of military lands. As the first attempt to conduct a national review, it established what was feasible within the review process, and what obstacles were likely in the implementation of recommendations. The then Government's response to the Nugent report summarized this in its comment on the ever-present dilemma between the military need to train and the public requirement for alternative uses on lands with a high amenity or landscape value (Depart-ment of the Environment, 1974).

After Nugent, there have been no public attempts to conduct any sort of national appraisal of the use of military lands, particularly the training estate. A site-specific study of military live firing on Dartmoor (a National Park) was conducted by Baroness Sharp in 1977. It came out broadly in support of the military's need to train there, but provided an observation that military use was 'discordant, incongruous and inconsistent' with na-tional park purposes despite there being a need for it (Sharp, 1977). An internal MoD study was undertaken in 1984 by one Lt. Col. R.E. Barron into requirements for training lands. It concluded that the Army needed an additional 50,000 acres (about 20,400 ha) of training land. The Barron Report also reviewed the organization, management and potential for ra-tionalization of the built estate (HCDC, 1994). The Barron Report was never published, remaining classified despite questions in the House of Lords in March 1987 and House of Commons in March 1988 berating the MoD for this degree of secrecy. A further internal review, the Defence Costs Study, was conducted in 1992. The findings of this review were not published either. The secrecy surrounding the Barron report and the De-fence Costs Study was justified by the government on the grounds of national security. However, the closed nature of both reports could just as easily be interpreted as a mechanism to avoid public scrutiny of inadequate internal management processes in operation over defence lands (see the criticisms of the National Audit Office and the Committee of Public Ac-counts below). Civilian input was not welcomed at this point. This reluc-tance to allow wider consideration of military land use issues is a feature of military control over lands.

Parliamentary scrutiny: Value and efficiency deficits

During the 1980s and early 1990s, the assessment of military land use issues lay primarily with Parliament, through the work of the House of Commons Committee of Public Accounts, and through the assessments of the National Audit Office, which audits government expenditure. The reports produced by these bodies are useful for what they tell us about the military understanding of arguments about rationalizing the size of the defence estate in the 1980s and early 1990s. This documentation also tells a story about the changing mechanisms for military land management, with the gradual shift of responsibilities from the centre of government in the early 1980s, to a more peripheral outside agency two decades later.

The Public Accounts Committee (PAC) has had a long-standing interest in military land matters. For example, it produced two reports in 1983 and 1984 on energy efficiency in MoD properties, and one in 1984 on military lands in the Falklands (PAC, 1983, 1984a, 1984b). The nineteenth report (PAC, 1984b) endorsed the need to release surpluses promptly and expressed the Committee's disappointment that long delays were still occurring. These parliamentary inquiries during the 1980s were concerned less with the matching of defence estate size to military needs, and more with the efficiency of the management of these lands and the administration of disposals. For example, a National Audit Office (1987) report on the control and management of the defence estate examined the effectiveness of the organizational structure for defence estate management, the means for controlling the size of the estate and for ensuring the cost-effectiveness of expenditure on it, the adequacy of management information systems and the management of service housing. At this time, management of the defence estate was divided between the Property Services Agency (PSA) and the MoD. The report noted a 1984 study undertaken of possibilities for the disposal of properties and other internal reviews of MoD holdings, and concluded that the reviews had either resulted in, or might lead to, proposals for rationalization or disposals, 'but MoD have recognized that they are still maintaining an estate which, excluding training areas, is too large for its purpose' (NAO, 1987, p.2). The report emphasized the point, already noted above, that the changing nature of military requirements would have long-standing implications for the estate, with a likely increased demand for training lands and reduced demand for buildings. The NAO report concluded that although the arrangements for managing and maintaining the estate were 'adequate', they were not as efficient as they could be. These inefficiencies had resulted in a dispersal of responsibility and accountability, a risk of uneconomic use of estate assets and failure to get best value in expenditure on the estate. The NAO recommended that more discipline was required in the management of military lands. The NAO also made the point that 'MoD's initial reaction was that such arrangements might be inconsistent with their general management structure' (NAO, 1987, p.5), indicative of the extent of administrative and cultural changes needed in the administration of the estate. The NAO also suggested the production of a strategic plan for the whole estate, specific site plans, a regular review of holdings, performance monitoring and better management information.

The House of Commons Public Accounts Committee inquiry in 1987 drew directly on the NAO study (PAC, 1987). This report examined the controls over the size of the defence estate, the cost-effectiveness of expenditure on it and the effectiveness of arrangements for management. The MoD admitted to the Committee that it 'still maintains an estate larger than was required and that in the past there had been no regular or systematic approach to assessing the continued need for holdings' (PAC, 1987, p.vi). The Committee criticized the MoD's progress in conducting a survey of holdings as unsatisfactory and partial, and urged a planned, regular and systematic approach to reviewing the need for all holdings, based on clear guidance and standards. 'We are not impressed by MoD's argument for a piecemeal approach to developing a strategy for the Estate as a whole', the report concluded, and urged strategic planning and establishment of central function within MoD to make progress towards rationalization. The Committee were also dissatisfied with the pace of disposal of surplus land and buildings. The MoD had argued that the redeployment of functions to different sites in the name of rationalization was viewed as a rare and long-term action because of the cost. The Committee found this difficult to accept, urging more radical solutions to ensure that military uses occupied and used more intensively lands of low commercial value (consistent with military need) and pointing out that any potential for savings wouldn't be realized unless there was a positive strategy to do so. In summary, this particular investigation was concerned with value for money and efficiencies in rationalization; environmental, amenity and heritage issues were not on the agenda. Overall, the Committee was critical of the management practices for the defence estate, as undertaken by the MoD.

In 1989, the House of Commons Committee of Public Accounts had another go at scrutinizing the management of military lands (PAC, 1989). The Committee noted that it was pleased to see the MoD and its property managers adopting a more constructive approach in the management and control of the estate, but still identified potential to speed up improvements, enhance performance and realize the subsequent potential substantial savings. There were still delays on disposals of surplus sites and disappointment about rationalization (north-west London was highlighted as a place where rationalization was possible). The Committee remained 'convinced that [MoD] should have a more positive relocation strategy', and didn't accept MoD arguments that comparisons between itself and the greater efficiencies shown in the commercial sector in the management and disposal of land were invalid and misleading (PAC, 1989, p.v).

Military training – in National Parks?

The scrutiny of military land use issues by Parliament in the 1980s was entirely concerned with achieving optimal efficiency in the use of public money by the MoD and Armed Forces. During the 1990s, environmental arguments about military land uses, first made to the Nugent committee, reappeared. This reappearance was due in no small measure to the increasing strength of the environmental movement as a political force, and the development of a feminist and green critique of militarism from its origins in the peace camps at Molesworth and Greenham Common.

An important study, kick-starting much of the 1990s debate on environmental impacts of military land uses, was that into military live firing in National Parks, commissioned by the Council for National Parks, the Council for the Protection of Rural England, the Dartmoor Preservation Association, the Open Spaces Society and the Ramblers' Association. Written by Susan Owens from the University of Cambridge under the auspices of the UK Centre for Economic and Environmental Development (UKCEED), this detailed study examined experiences in Dartmoor, the Pembrokeshire Coast and Northumberland within the wider contexts of countryside impacts of military training, the costs and the benefits (Owens, 1990a). The study concluded, amongst other things, that 'a strategic framework for land requirements for military training should be prepared by the MoD and subjected to independent public scrutiny' (p.73). 'A problem with the argument about "need"', said Owens, 'is that it has never been the subject of independent scrutiny' (p.67). She also made the point that it had consistently been a powerful tenet of conventional wisdom that the needs of the MoD were not (and had never traditionally been) open to question.

The UKCEED study made an explicit call for independent scrutiny of military training land requirements, the basis of which should be a strategic framework for land requirements. The aim of such an inquiry would be to define the irreducible minimum need for land, and to provide a framework to justify land acquisitions and the continued use of valued landscapes for live firing. Such an inquiry would have to be both independent and public, be it by parliamentary committee, independent commission or nonstatutory public inquiry. Such an inquiry, based around a strategic framework, would amongst other things identify realistic objectives for the estate for the short to medium term, such as the phased withdrawal of some or all live firing from national parks. Susan Owens stressed elsewhere that above all, the debate would have to be conducted at a different level than that which it hitherto had been, dealing with the fundamental issue of the need for military land for live firing (Owens, 1990b).

National Parks Review Panel (NPRP) took up the call. Chaired by Professor Ron Edwards, it was established in 1990 by the Countryside Commission (the government's statutory adviser on landscape and protection) to examine the future of the National Parks in England and Wales. The Panel's wide-ranging remit included consideration of military training in National Parks (NPRP, 1991). The NPRP argued that the current pattern of military training lands reflected patterns of historical acquisition rather than modern training requirements. The NPRP came out strongly against the use of National Parks for military training, seeing military use as 'discordant, incongruous and inconsistent' with national park principles, echoing Baroness Sharp's 1977 conclusion without the caveat. It recommended the removal of live firing ranges from National Parks in the short term, and the cessation of military activity in the long term. Again, the call was made for a national strategic review of military training requirements, conducted through the auspices of an independent Commission of Inquiry. Again, the recommendation was that this should be public, with opportunities for cross-examination and submission of public evidence. It would also require an objective assessment of details such as personnel days, logistical requirements, the area of land needed and its location. The NPRP's findings were endorsed by the Countryside Commission.

The end of the Cold War: Options for change

The UKCEED and NPRP reports became public at a time of profound geopolitical change in Europe, with the collapse of the Soviet Union and the demise of totalitarian governments across central and eastern Europe. The military threats perceived by both West and Eastern Europe dissipated. In 1991, the British Government published details of its 'Options for Change' programme for the restructuring of the Armed Forces following these geopolitical shifts. Options for Change heralded major restructuring within the Armed Forces, including an overall reduction in Forces size and the return of personnel from Germany (MoD, 1991). As part of this process, the National Audit Office undertook a study in 1992 into the management and control of Army training land (NAO, 1992). (Note that it was training lands under scrutiny here, and not the entire defence estate.) The aim of this examination was to look at how needs and use for training lands were determined, to study land acquisition and disposal, and to inquire into public safety, conservation and environmental issues. Clearly, in contrast to its scrutiny in the 1980s the environment appears as an issue for concern, a consequence not least of the pressures brought to bear by the findings of the NPRP. The main finding of the NAO study was to argue

that the MoD needed better procedures for quantifying training requirements, assessing training land capacity and demonstrating optimum usage
of the training estate. The MoD resurrected the findings of the 1984
Barron report, apparently updated in 1990, to argue for a shortfall in the
amount of training land. However, the NAO study dismissed this argument
on the grounds that the procedures for assessment of this finding were
inadequate – returns from Regiments and Corps in the Army, which would
have provided proof for this argument about the need for more land, had
not been retained for subsequent independent (NAO) scrutiny. Again,
there appears to have been a problem with the provision of data by the
MoD. The NAO study suggested that the capacity of existing lands was
underutilized and urged the MoD to undertake better analysis of Army
needs and land usage to give a more accurate view of current and future
training land requirements. This comment in turn raises an interesting
point about assessing land capacity for training. John Childs (1998) argues
that the statistics for this depend on the assumptions informing the calculations: the NAO saw that training areas and ranges were only used for 66
percent of the available time. The Army divided its training areas into
subsections, and units booked a single subsection for a day's training. A
booked subsection counted as a reservation of the whole training area. The
NAO declared unbooked subareas as unused capacity. Depending on
which set of statistics was employed, a very different assessment emerged
of current use and future demands. The point which follows from this
observation is a constant one: demands by the Army for more land on
which to train were matched by the arguments of nonmilitary organizations
seeing the poor management of existing resources as the cause of the
problem.

A House of Commons Committee of Public Accounts inquiry followed
on from the NAO report (PAC, 1993). Restating the NAO's findings, it
signalled the necessity, in order to manage the use of available training land
efficiently, for there to be available reliable management information on
availability, bookings and utilization. The Committee noted that improvements were being made but were 'concerned that it has taken the [MoD] so
long to be able to monitor such basic data as that relating to the utilization
of training land and the level of cancellation of bookings' (PAC, 1993, p.v).

The House of Commons Defence Committee, 1994

By 1993, then, we have a parliamentary committee, the government's
auditors, an independent government-appointed review panel and an um-
brella group of amenity and conservation organizations, all calling for an
independent inquiry into at the very least, military training lands, and at

most, the defence estate. We also have by this time the consequences of Options for Change, growing interest in environmental issues both on and off the defence estate, the introduction of more complex and powerful weapons systems and a continual squeeze on defence budgets. The House of Commons Defence Committee bit the bullet. An extensive inquiry into the defence estate was undertaken in that year, and published in 1994 (HCDC, 1994).

The Committee's report is something of a treasure trove for those with an interest in the defence estate. Covering two volumes and totalling more than 300 pages, with oral evidence from 21 witnesses and written evidence from 46 individuals and organizations, it provides a wealth of information on the estate. Its scope was wide-ranging, including general issues facing the estate, questions of disposal, the management of the estate and its natural and built heritage. Its recommendations were similarly wide-ranging. Here, I want to concentrate on just one – that which deals with the call for an independent review of military lands.

A range of bodies made their case. The Countryside Commission called explicitly for the Government to conduct a full public review of defence land needs and the appropriate size of the defence estate. At issue where the size, location, use and management of the estate. A review along the lines of the Nugent report was needed, in order to be able to respond in a strategic rather than ad hoc way to the demands imposed by Options for Change. Military sensitivity (to change? to revealing its workings? to security issues?; it is unclear what the Countryside Commission meant here) should not be used to prevent legitimate public discussion. (This call was also made in the Commission's advice to the Government on the MoD's development proposals for the Otterburn Training Area. It urged the MoD to participate in an independent national review of military training needs, but gave no details on the possible scope, remit and composition of such a review, beyond endorsing the NPRP's recommendations (Countryside Commission, 1994)). The Council for the Protection of Rural England (CPRE) recommended a comprehensive environmental audit of the MoD estate to update that carried out by the Nugent Committee. It also called for a strategic assessment of the environmental implications of current land requirements for military purposes, to be subject to independent public scrutiny and which would aim to secure the release of land no longer necessary. The Royal Society for the Protection of Birds (RSPB) recommended a strategic national review of training land, to enable conservation objectives and military training needs to be integrated on the estate. The Association of National Parks suggested 'a very thorough review'. The Council for National Parks recommended that an independent body should undertake a national, strategic review of training needs to determine whether any surplus of land across the estate could be available for release.

Such a review, which would follow along the lines suggested by the NPRP report, would be 'both popular and timely'. The Dartmoor National Park Authority argued that in the absence of a review, it was impossible for it to quantify the scope for reduction of military lands on Dartmoor, a National Park. The Ramblers' Association asked the Committee to recommend a public review of defence land requirements, involving public consultation and Parliamentary debate, rather than 'continuing with the current piece-meal approach which leaves a legacy of sometimes bitter local conflict in its wake'. The Open Spaces Society submitted that there should be an independent, wide-ranging review of all military land holdings in the UK, calling the military acquisition of lands 'opportunistic' and 'piecemeal'. The Royal Town Planning Institute asked for an overall defence land strategy, part of which would entail an overview of the entire land holdings owned by MoD. The Royal Institute of Chartered Surveyors requested better management of lands to open up transparency and to help the fit between need and usage. The County Planning Officers' Society stated that better availability of information on site resources was essential. A firm of architect planners asked for a better strategic assessment of the process of disposals.

These calls for some sort of review at this point in time raise three points. First, these calls are broadly based in nature, making a point of principle rather than detailed recommendations on exactly how a review could proceed. Of course, the formulation of detailed recommendations was not within the overall scope or aims of these organizations. In submitting evidence to the Committee, they were making a public declaration of position, rather than acting as MoD advisers. The second point is to draw attention to the connections between the groups calling for a review. These are either statutory or voluntary sector amenity or conservation groups, an indicator of the significance of environmental issues in the management of military land use. Many of these have a long history of campaigning for the protection and enhancement of the conservation and amenity values of rural areas. Some of these bodies are mass-membership organizations; an implication of this is that their statements within a public domain such as a parliamentary inquiry come with the endorsement of a broader public, rather than just representing the views of specialist organizations within an elite debate. The third point is to highlight the level of detailed expertise evident in the witness statements and memoranda submitted by all the above groups; many show a detailed and comprehensive grasp of military land uses and its consequences. This is indicative of the wider constituency with concern for military lands; these groups made clear that discussion of the defence estate was no longer the sole preserve of the MoD, however much representatives of the MoD or Armed Forces might argue otherwise. Clearly, the military's right to absolute control was being challenged at this point.

Unsurprisingly, the MoD opposed the idea of a review at Committee hearings, on the grounds that it would follow on too closely to the Defence Costs Study, the recommendations of which required time to implement. Lord Cranborne, the Under-Secretary of State for Defence at that time, made plain the MoD's resistance to a public, participatory review of defence lands needs:

> We think that it is important, once we have decided internally what that overall strategy is, that we should go out and explain our position and gain acceptance for it.... It seems to us that it would be sensible for the sort of debate that is necessary for us to gain acceptance for what we need to take place in the context of our own plan and then the consultation process which we have to continue to undertake anyway, rather than for somebody who has not got responsibility for the day-to-day management of the defence estate to take a snapshot which may very rapidly become out of date and dictate from outside what our priorities should be. (HCDC, 1994, Vol. II, p.36)

This is a paternalistic argument, in that it is based on an assertion that the military not only has the expertise to make a judgement about its use of land, but also that it is the sole body with the authority to do so. This paternalism in land management is surely a mechanism for reinforcing military control. The 'public interest' here is both defined and represented by the landowner, claiming both authority over the land and authority to determine which set of interests should be prioritized.[4]

The Committee report endorsed this view, arguing that current changes in planning and environmental protection regimes would in any case allow greater public scrutiny of the defence estate. This was despite the fact that many other recommendations made clear the Committee's disappointment with the existing provision of information of various aspects of the defence estate to the public. It concluded that a major public inquiry into the defence estate as a whole would not be productive at that time, but noted that such an inquiry would become necessary by the end of the decade if there was continued evidence of shortcomings in the MoD's estate policy and practice. (As of March 2003, no such inquiry has yet been announced.) Overall, however, 'we are confident that [the estate] should be reduced in scale, driven not by targets for one-off capital gain but by military requirements and assessment of particular sites' (HCDC, 1994).

The government response to the Committee's recommendation was to publicize its latest initiative for the management of information training lands. This would allow the MoD 'to achieve the most efficient use of the training estate and provide a quantifiable method of demonstrating to the public the reasons for which it is retained' (HCDC, 1995, p.iv). The origins of this land reconciliation study lay with the pressure put on the MoD following the publication of the 1992 NAO and 1993 Committee of Public

Accounts reports. The study was billed by the Army as 'important as a practical means of making the best use of the Army's training estate' (HQ Land Command, 1997, p.12). This covered the training requirements of all UK-based formations, units and establishments with a military training requirement. It identified a theoretical deficit of training lands of around 83,000 ha and an effective shortfall of 39,000 ha, or about 21 percent of the Army's total requirement. This was certainly not the type of review requested or result expected by the groups making a call for an independent review. Doxford and Hill (1998) call the study part of a 'make do and mend' approach to military training areas, which itself had postponed a radical rethink of the use of military training lands. Nor was the study, by its nature, a process in which wider public participation (through amenity groups and statutory bodies) could be facilitated. The study was a modelling exercise using sophisticated computer software, not a public debate.

The Strategic Defence Review and the *Strategy for the Defence Estate*

The final significant event in this story was the publication of the Strategic Defence Review in 1998. This, the new Labour Government's assessment of defence capabilities and organization, as well as setting out financial targets for estate disposals (see Chapter 3) set in motion the production of the *Strategy for the Defence Estate*, which appeared in June 2000. This set out the strategic objectives for the estate's management (MoD, 2000a). Media reaction to this significant document was nonexistent; military land use issues in the main present long-burning problems rather than immediate news. It is important for this story, however, for the extent to which it put into place mechanisms to meet past criticisms of defence land management practices. The *Strategy* made explicit note of the calls which had been made for an independent review of military lands, but it noted that 'we do not believe that this is either necessary or appropriate', given that the *Strategy* would demonstrate transparency over need and include processes to ensure that the estate is no bigger than it needed to be (MoD, 2000a, p.1).

Defence Estates presented the Strategy as 'major change' and 'a blueprint' for the future management of the defence estate. It is certainly a significant document. The defence estate is vast; whatever happens on it affects not only the military capabilities of the UK, but also a number of groups of people who live on it, or use it, or have some other interest in its function and future. It is also a diverse estate, requiring increasingly complex management systems in order to meet the needs of its users. The Strategy constituted part of a wider process of overhaul of the function and workings of Defence Estates, and was intended as the reference point to improvements in land management systems five, ten and even twenty years in the future.

The Strategy set out a broad strategic framework for the ways in which land use policy on the defence estate would operate, opening with a 'Charter for the Defence Estate' (there are echoes here of the Citizen's Charter programme established by the previous Conservative government). The Strategy set out the framework for the future management of the estate, revolving around 12 specific objectives. These objectives were geared towards maximizing cost efficiencies and improving the general competence of the organization. Initiatives to achieve these objectives included a 'core sites' policy (which would link long-term military requirements to specific core sites on which future use and investment would be focussed), the increased involvement of the private sector, the use of 'smart construction' procurement measures, the deployment of management incentives and training, improved management information, and the use of the environmental appraisal process. The Strategy also listed the performance indicators in place to assess achievement of these objectives. Accountability and performance assessment would be delivered through annual Stewardship Reports prepared by the Chief Executive of Defence Estates for public scrutiny.

A considerable proportion of the Strategy was devoted to explaining its implications for different stakeholders, identified as groups with a use for or interest in the defence estate and including the Armed Forces, planning authorities and local communities, cultural heritage bodies, access groups, and tenant farmers. The Strategy promised delivery of improved accommodation and facilities to the Armed Forces, underpinned by an improved planning framework. It promised to take full account of regional planning issues in decisions affecting the Strategy. It promised the release of resources through efficiency initiatives, and promised to take into account the interests of wider stakeholders. An appendix listed in more detail a set of management objectives for the rural estate, including considerations concerning the use of 'private' land for training; promises about the conduct of the relationship with agricultural and other tenants, local communities and the public in respect of access and recreation; commitments to landscape, nature conservation and cultural heritage issues; and aspirations regarding MoD actions during the disposal and acquisition of sensitive property.

This is certainly not the independent review which groups ranging from the Countryside Commission to the Open Spaces Society had requested. The question is: did it come anywhere near to recognizing the concerns voiced as part of that broader call for an independent review? The Strategy provided several important things. It promised the publication of an annual stewardship report on activities and the achievement of indicators. This is significant in that by publication it opened up for wider scrutiny the workings of Defence Estates; this amount of transparency should be compared to the comments made, for example, to the 1994 Defence Committee on the Army's assumption of its prerogative to make assessments prior to and independent of external consideration. The Strategy is also significant because it sets up a mechanism for an on-going process of review of defence lands. One of the criticisms of the idea of a once-off national review was that it would only provide a snapshot picture, and whilst this might have been valuable in itself, a snapshot is by its very nature a static thing. The significance of the Strategy also lay in the integration of environmental policy goals and concerns within the management policies of the estate. This is a reflection of several things, including the 'Greening Government' initiative (an attempt to integrate environmental agendas into government policy and practice), and the concerns of a wide constituency regarding the environmental impacts of military activities, particularly in areas benefitting from statutory protection such as National Parks and Areas of Outstanding Natural Beauty.

Ultimately, the Strategy has not provided the type of independent assessment of military land needs demanded by the MoD's critics. What it has done is side-stepped these calls by putting in place management systems that would appear to meet many of the criticisms of military land use management, whilst still maintaining military control over the estate. The bromides offered a decade previously have dissipated. The mantra-like call for an independent review has also faded, at least for the time being. There has been a growing 'civilianization' of management, with responsibility shifting from inside the MoD and Property Services Agency, to the Defence Estates Organisation, to the renamed Defence Estates as an agency external to government, to a private company contracted to provide key land management services for the Army Training Estate.[5] These changes should be understood within the context of wider changes central and local government, with the emergence of new practices in public management (the 'new public management' – see Ferlie, Ashburner, Fitzgerald and Pettigrew, 1996). This shift in governance in general has involved features such as greater managerial emphasis and greater responsiveness to the market. Defining features have included an emphasis on performance indicators, audit systems, resource-based systems of accounting and monitoring. The influence of new styles in public management in the case of the MoD is revealing for what this says about control. It has been problematic; for example, Gillibrand and Hilton (1998) argue that the use of Resource Accounting and Budgeting has been difficult within the MoD because of the problems of assessing the value of the MoD's asset base. It has also been progressive; the principles of new practices in public management rest very much on auditability, rendering things visible through their reduction to statistical data. Things become accountable, primarily in the sense that they can be made visible or understandable through accounting proceedings. This is not necessarily a bad thing; making things accountable to accountants may not constitute the opening-up of the decision-making process for full public scrutiny, insisted upon by some bodies, but it certainly provides some visibility. The *Strategy for the Defence Estate*, with its language of performance targets and stakeholders provides a degree of external accountability, even if it doesn't provide any external or independent assessment. And the MoD still makes the final decisions, couched in discourses of national security (MoD, 2000a; Woodward, 2001a). The UK Armed Forces are like any other in their reluctance to relinquish their control of military lands, even if there is little military justification for keeping them (Brzoska, 1999b).

The Military Control Of Space

This chapter has ranged widely over varied terrain, from the salient facts of military occupancy of both domestic and foreign space, to the intricacies of land management systems developed by the UK Government (via the MoD) in response to internal and external criticisms. At the start of the chapter, I noted how occupancy and land management issues are fundamental to the ways in which militarism and military activities assert control over space, and thus to the constitution and expression of military geographies. I want to conclude by drawing out four key features of this military control over space which seem to me to be critical in understanding how that control works.

The first feature is the fact of physical presence. As I have argued, this is foundational to understanding the pattern of militarism's geographies. Mapping military land ownership and occupation, particularly the small-scale and domestic, may seem prosaic, a 'so what?' issue. But military control, over economies, social structure, environments and landscapes flows directly from this very fact of being there. We cannot understand how militarism and military power are geographically constituted and expressed without an understanding of the patterns and consequences of the fact of physical military presence.

The second feature of control is information. Military control over space is reliant in part on controlling data or information about military occupancy. To reiterate an argument made earlier in this chapter, there is, in the UK at least, a basic lack of reliable, accessible information on patterns of land ownership and use by the Armed Forces. There may be clear reasons for this (whether these are 'good' reasons or not is a different matter), but the point remains that the provision – or absence – of information about the military occupancy of space is a feature of military control. I return to this point in subsequent chapters, as it provides a common thread running through my attempts to unpick militarism's geographies.

The third feature of the military control of space is the practices of governance in the management of armed forces and the management of civil-military relationships. Understanding militarism's geographies and the geographies of military activities means understanding the practices of governance – the policies and ideologies – which mediate the control of space. In the UK, for example, the military control of land is underpinned by paternalism in land management. Paternalism justifies restrictions on the uses of space, and restricts challenges to the control of that space, by arguments which in themselves are well-meaning but which are ultimately restrictive. Paternalism is an ideology which determines that the freedom of individuals can be restricted in order that their interests may be better served. Moreover, those interests can be legitimately defined by an elite authority, rather than by popular expression. The arguments that justify the maintenance of the defence estate rest very much on paternalistic notions about the moral authority of the Armed Forces and MoD to control space. These arguments are often presented as the actions of a responsible land-owner, serving the needs of the people – see, for example, the Government responses to arguments about the need for greater transparency in the land management process. We should note, too, that practices of governance are changeable and malleable. The military control of lands is not necessarily immutable or steadfast.

The fourth and final feature of the military control of space is that it is a discursive as well as a material practice. For example, implicit in many of the military responses to challenges about the size/needs issue has been an argument emphasizing the primacy of 'national security' in the management of the defence estate. This emphasizes national security and national defence as the single most important factor in determining the management of lands. This in itself would naturally be expected. What is notable, however, is the way in which appeals to the primacy of national security are made with reference to land. Shaw (1991) argues that a 'national military myth' underpins the ideologies of military practices in the UK, the terms of reference of which include the idea of a constant threat to the security of the island nation from hostile overseas forces. This is an idea which draws for its potency on ideologies evolving during two World Wars to consolidate the morale of the British population. It is an idea which, Shaw argues, resonates in contemporary attitudes towards the Armed Forces, granting power and control to military activities over and above any identifiable risk. Challenges to military control over lands are met, as we have already seen, with arguments which draw implicitly on this discourse. The precise nature of the discourses which legitimize the control of military lands will vary with national context. What is certain is that the control of space is as much a discursive as it is a physical act, in that control is wrapped up in arguments about defence and security in order to legitimize military claims to space.

Chapter Three

Military Economic Geographies

The Imprint of Military Money

Catterick, in North Yorkshire, has long military associations. The economy of this locality cannot be understood without first seeing the controls exerted by militarism and military activities. Cataractonium, a Roman settlement, had a strategic location on Dere Street, the Roman road which crossed the wide, flat plain between Roman York and Hadrian's Wall, the northern border of the Empire. The *Gododdin*, a seventh-century Old Welsh epic poem, mourns the slaughter of 300 nobles here at Catraeth, a strategic point between the strongholds of Celtic-speaking peoples of South Scotland, the Angles of North-East England and the British of South West Britain.[1] A medieval castle dominates the skyline on the bluffs above the River Swale at the neighbouring market town of Richmond. Catterick Training Area covers 23,500 ha of upland above the plain, a military site since before the First World War. Barracks and airfields (Marne, Leeming, Dishforth, Topcliffe) have lined the A1, the Great North Road, for over 50 years. And nestling on the edge of the plain, on the lowest reaches Swaledale on the edge of the Yorkshire Dales National Park, sits Catterick Garrison. The imprint of the garrison's economy is stamped across the settlement.

The visible signs of military occupation are obvious immediately on entering the garrison area; everywhere one looks there are high wire fences, low institutional buildings, swept tarmac covered with tidy rows of jeeps and trucks, khaki tractors and camouflaged diggers, neat green grass verges, checkpoints, men with guns. The road signs confirm this as military space: 'Tanks turning', 'Report Suspicious Activity to the Police: CCTV in Operation', 'Caution, military training'. Placenames such as Helles, Somme and Vimy Barracks hark back to battles in 1915, 1916 and 1917 respectively.

Names like Gaza and Jaffa exoticize this location. Signposts everywhere carry strange combinations of letters and numbers – ABRO CATTERICK or 521 SQU 11 EOD REGT RLC seem like a specialist code. Men wearing military berets sit behind the wheels of Ford Escorts. Pale faces streaked with brown camouflage cream peer out of the back of army trucks, on their way up to the training area in the hills behind. This is military space, obviously and visibly. Catterick Garrison is where the British Army's Infantry Training Centre is based, providing combat infantryman training for Phase II recruits who've completed their initial basic (CMS(R)) training, and trained soldiers with continuation training. A Gurkha company is based here, as are the 19th (Mechanized) Bridge, Royal Artillery with their Multiple Launch Rocket Systems. Catterick Garrison is home to 12,000 military personnel behind heavily guarded perimeter fences. The only military force outside the wire is the Salvation Army. The place has an atmosphere that is simultaneously mundane and highly unsettling.

If the militarization of space is immediately obvious to the visitor to the Catterick Garrison area through such signs, so is the structuring of social and economic relations by the military presence in the surrounding streets and settlements. Outside the wire which surrounds the garrison we find Le Maginot restaurant, the John Bull café, The Scorpion pub (a cavernous beer hall), 'Pulse: Designer Clothes for Men', a tattoo parlour, takeaways, newsagents and other types of retail outlets where money is spent in small quantities by large numbers. The housing is uniform, much of it recently refurbished. Women with toddlers in buggies walk by in the afternoon. The shiny new outpost of Darlington College of Technology, offering training in information technology skills in a new 'Telematics Learning Centre' targeted at women returning to work, sits in the middle of a parcel of land still raw from construction. These are the outward, visible signs of an economy shaped by a military presence, geared towards servicing the soldier and the military family, and a military presence which creates its own idiosyncratic geographies.

Militarism and military activities control space and economies. War is the violent means of exerting control over space in service to territorial ambitions, and these are almost always about resources. Wars are waged often as economic acts. War boosts and destroys production and consumption. Wars determine the control and use of natural resources. War determines trade patterns and distributions, manufacture and sale, divisions of labour and circulations of capital. War creates economic geographies. In this chapter, I will not look at this economic geography of war directly, but will cast an eye to one side, to nonconflict situations. This chapter looks at what I term military economic geographies, the shaping of space by economic forces exerted by the military presence and its activities, and the consequent impact on social relations. A key argument of this chapter is that military control is not just a physical presence of men and women in khaki, navy or airforce blue. Military control is not necessarily even a dangerous, exciting, secret, sexy thing; it can actually appear quite mundane, quite 'normal'. Military control can be an economic act on localities because of its influence, for good or ill, on local economic and social relations. Military control can be about the seemingly mundane, the routine exertion of control over space by an economic entity. It requires attention just as much as big dramatic events like armed conflict, because of its potential influence over the lives of so many.

The analysis of the economic geographies of military establishments and activities has not been a common feature of Military Geography, or of economic geography, nor even of economics. Those interested in the economic geographies of militarism have focussed primarily on the defence industry (and I discuss this body of work below). Military establishments, in contrast, have not been overburdened with scholarly interest in their economies and economic geographies. A popular economic geography reader (Bryson, Henry, Keeble and Martin, 1999), for example, mentions neither defence or the military in its index. Yet the economic geographies of military establishments are significant for what they say about the impact of military activities in shaping economic space, and for what they reveal about the political economies of contemporary militarism.

This chapter focuses on the economic controls exerted by military establishments; how military establishments control and shape the localities in which they sit through their influence on economic geographies. The chapter starts by outlining the key economic features of the occupation of land by military establishments, and the geoeconomics of location. It goes on to examine the economic geographies of military activities in terms of their measurable and nonmeasurable impacts, and the economic geographies of the defence industry. I then look at the conversion of military establishments to civilian uses; the emphasis in this chapter on conversion enables us to see how the economic impacts of militaries change over time. It also reflects an explanatory conundrum; because of the paucity of accurate data on military establishments (for reasons I go into), it is very hard to get an accurate picture of the contribution of a military establishment to its surrounding economy – to map military economic geographies – until establishments close. By seeing what remains and what changes as a result of closure, we can get a clearer picture of the impact of military presence as well as of departure. The chapter discusses how conversion can be conceptualized before moving on to consider the scale of military base conversion as an issue, the effects (positive and negative) of military base conversion for affected localities and regions, how 'success' might be measured, the specificity of military base conversion as a land use issue, and the policy responses in the UK and USA to the question of base conversion.

The Geoeconomics of Location and Origin

The term 'military establishments' encompasses a great variety of types and functions of places – bases, barracks, depots, training areas, dockyards, airfields, rifle ranges, naval bases. I use the term to denote spaces occupied and used by the Armed Forces, for whatever purpose. They vary hugely in terms of scale. Aldershot, 'The Home of the British Army', on the Surrey/ Hampshire border, is an established military base of 533 hectares, head-quarters of the Army's 4th Division, with over 8,000 military personnel based there. Hampshire County Council estimated that in 1996, 47 per-cent of jobs in the locality were defence related. Farnborough, the 'home of British aviation', Sandhurst (home of the Royal Military College for officer training) and Pirbright (a location for both selection and training centres for the Army) are nearby. The Army is embedded in the local economy, and like Catterick this is visible everywhere:

> there are everyday markers . . . , such as the occasional soldier in uniform at a bank machine in Aldershot, the dry cleaners with the sign in the window reading 'Specialists in Forces Uniforms and Mess Dresses', or roundabouts in the town named 'Ordnance Roundabout' and 'Naafi Roundabout'. (Tivers, 1999, p.309).

RAF Boulmer on the Northumberland coast is tiny in comparison, comprising a sea rescue and communications centre between the beach and the village of Longhoughton. The village displays its Air Force pres-ence through little more than a stream of cars between base and village at lunchtime and the occasional Sea King helicopter overhead. Fort Knox, Kentucky USA, as well as being home to the US Bullion Depository, is the base for the US Army's Armour Centre and the US Army Recruiting Command. Around 14,000 military personnel, 4,500 reservists and 4,000 civilian personnel, plus retired personnel, plus families of serving person-nel, work here in a city of 33,000 total. Contrast this with the US Army's Yuma Proving Ground in Arizona, USA, where a vast 1,300 sq. mi. of the Sororan desert is home to 1,700 workers engaged in weapons testing activities. Big and small, urban and rural, secretive or public, spybase or runway; the point here is the diversity of types of places and their functions, and the range of possible military influences on social and economic net-works. Military establishments are where they are because of basic strategic and logistical needs for land, sea and air. Its an obvious point that location follows basic geography, hence in Britain the Royal Navy's requirement to site ports in places like Portsmouth with deepwater moorings and easy access to access to open sea, the RAF's use of the escarpment above the wide Trent valley in Lincolnshire and its favourable air currents blowing in from the west, and the Army's need to practice infantry and artillery manoeuvres out on Salisbury Plain away from areas of concentrated habitation and industry.

But the economic geography of the distribution of military establishments is, of course, much more complex and subtle than this basic geography suggests. It is a truism of economic geography that local economic differentiation is endemic under capitalism. Location isn't just about the availability of physical resources or natural attributes, but is also about successive rounds of decision making, over decades or even centuries, concerning the investment of resources (money, labour) in specific places. It follows that the contemporary distribution of military establishments is not necessarily the consequence of the planned distribution of such establishments according to military requirements and physical resources, but the consequence of a more complex, changeable and cumulative interplay of planning and decision making, land availability and chance. As Barney Warf observed (1998, p.544), drawing on a metaphor used elsewhere in both economic and cultural geographies, the geography of military facilities is best conceptualized as a palimpsest; just as the shadows of previous inscriptions show through on reused parchment, so do military landscapes reflect the multiple layers of base openings and closures which are the result of the successive accumulation of strategic locational decisions made over time and under varying political and economic circumstances. Uses change, locations shift in significance, and the remnants remain in the economic landscape.

A broad typology of military establishments according to locational origin illustrates the range of economic geographies shaped by military establishments, and provides a basic explanation of how successive rounds of decision making and investment work to establish military control over space. First, there are those establishments reflecting through their current location historical assertions of state power. In London, the centrality of military planning (through the Ministry of Defence in Whitehall) and of the Army (through the parading soldiers outside Horseguards and Buckingham Palace) is the visible and symbolic manifestation of the long association between the military and the state. Second, there are those establishments which reflect by their location more contemporary geopolitical ambitions of hegemonic states – the British and US (and formerly Soviet) bases in Germany, US bases in Japan and Korea and central America, British bases in Belize and Cyprus, for example. Third, there are those establishments which reflect through their location changing priorities over land use and shifting values ascribed to landscapes. For example, the British Army trains in areas which were deemed otherwise unproductive in the nineteenth century (and which today have acquired an altogether different set of values) – places such as Dartmoor in Devon, and on the chalk downland of Salisbury Plain. The US Army's use of the south-western desert lands is another example. Fourth, there are those establishments now unwanted or unused, the cause of their establishment having disappeared, a hangover of previous rounds of investment and geopolitical ambitions. The point here is military control in the present can be understood not only in terms of what it contributes to local economies now, but also in terms of the economic and political impacts of past histories.

Military establishments, then, comprise a variety of types of place and function, and generate their own diverse economic geographies. The point is not a trite one about how everything is different, and nor is it about the reduction of complexity to a few universal laws or variables. The point about the geoeconomics of location is about the need to study the origins, entrenchment and withdrawal of military establishments because it helps us to understand how economic control operates.

The Economic Geographies Of Military Establishments

Military control over space is exerted both by physical presence, and by the economic influence of military establishments on a locality. These economic relations exert control over space at levels beyond the obvious visible fact of presence signalled by barracks and barbed wire. The shaping of economies and localities, and the influence of these economic relations on local political and social life, are a feature of military control. Armed forces everywhere are aware of that, of course; consider these two rather self-conscious statements from the British and US Armies about their economic roles in Catterick Garrison and the Yuma Proving Ground respectively:

> As the Army's largest base, embracing 7,500 regular soldiers, 1900 recruits and 2,000 civilian contract staff, Catterick Garrison is the standard bearer for the changing face of the modern British Army, strengthening ties with the local district and developing commercial opportunities within an integrated community. (Army, 2003)

> US Army Yuma Proving Ground plays a vigorous role in the economic stability of Southwest Arizona and contributes significantly to the economic health of the entire state. The proving ground is an active consumer in the Yuma County economy through its purchase of standard goods and services and its requirements for high technology items and services related to its mission. (US Army, 2003)

In this section, I examine how this relationship between military control and local economic relations operates.

Measurable impacts

Investigating how economic control operates means initially looking at the measurable economic or financial contribution of military establishments to the localities in which they sit. The first point to make concerns the difficulty of establishing that contribution with any precision. There has been a basic lack of economic research on this.[2] The huge diversity of types of military establishments that exist render simple models meaningless and make the development of more sophisticated modelling techniques extremely complex. There is a basic lack of easily accessible data on the economic and financial contribution of military establishments to their localities. What we know about the economic impacts of military establishments is often derived from studies conducted with reference to specific policy considerations (for example, base closure, which is discussed later in this chapter), rather than from a more abstract set of research questions (Parai, Solomon and Wait, 1996). Furthermore, military establishments and their economic impacts emerge onto policy agendas as a result of the political concerns of individuals in policy elites, and disappear just as rapidly once those political concerns have been addressed. With these caveats in mind, a review of available research data on the economic impacts of military establishments is still helpful in sketching out how the military control of space operates through economic activities.

Military bases can have a substantial economic input to and impact on their surrounding localities. In a study of the impact of the Royal Australian Airforce's Richmond Air Base in Greater Western Sydney, an estimated A\$106 million value-added was contributed to the regional economy of the Hawksbury, even after allowing for leakage and flow-on. Some 6.5 percent of the workforce of the municipality was engaged in defence-related employment; 2,050 in direct employment, and 628 in indirect employment. The figure of 6.5 percent reflects adjustments after taking into account nonresident workers and resident nonworkers on the base. Most of the economic contribution came via wages and salaries, but benefits were spread across local businesses (retail and services). A few businesses had more than 6 percent of their turnover from base-related expenditure (PricewaterhouseCoopers, 2002). At the Yuma Proving Ground, the statement above on local economic linkages came from a wider set of estimates about the economic contribution of the 1,654 personnel located there in 2001. The 183 military personnel, 601 civilian employees and 706 contractors were paid a total of US\$84,938,911. Contracts and direct spending were valued at US\$13.7 million, and expenditure at the commissary, PX (Post Exchange) and on health services was valued at US\$ 26.4 million (US Army, 2003).

Military patronage may be directed to local shops, bars and restaurants, which may in turn depend solely or almost entirely on military personnel for their custom (Le Maginot restaurant and the John Bull pub in Catterick, mentioned above, are examples with their equivalents the world over). Support to local business and services generates profits for firms and wages for employees. Military establishments support local labour markets through the provision of employment opportunities to civilians. In 1989, prior to their respective closures, Subic Naval Base in the Philippines generated 15,881 direct and 21,300 indirect jobs for local Filipino labour, and Clark Air Force Base generated 4,485 direct and 37,899 indirect jobs, with a grand total for both combined of over 73,000 jobs (Rocamora, 1998). As Rocamora points out, in the city of Olongapo, home to 193,000 people and adjacent to Subic Naval Base, 85 percent of the city's income came directly or indirectly from Subic, and 43,488 workers (excluding those employed on-base) were displaced when Subic closed. In economic terms, in 1988 in the US, bases scheduled for closure contributed an estimated $540 million to the local economy in terms of firms supplying goods and services. Half of this amount came from construction and miscellaneous manufactured goods. Also significant were personal and repair services, fabricated metals, wholesale and retail, and educational services (Warf, 1997).

The financial inputs to local economies may be significant. Military contracts may be awarded to local firms for the supply of goods and services, generating local revenues. The presence and award of contracts contributes towards the stability of local economies. Complex webs of contracting and subcontracting will be woven through local economies, but will vary greatly with the type of military establishment. The USAF, for example, relies on outsourcing and subcontracting to a greater degree than the Army or Navy and across the US subcontracting varies markedly in terms of degrees of vertical integration or separation (Warf, 1997, after Hall and Markusen, 1992). Lack of data is a problem, however, in drawing firm conclusions about sub-contracting and its economic consequences for localities (Warf, 1997). Financial inputs can be further subdivided into those that are direct or indirect; the former is relatively self-explanatory, the latter includes subsequent spending or income received by intermediary firms and workers within a host community, which provide the goods and services purchased by base workers, as well as by contractors providing goods and services to the base (Parai et al., 1996). There may also be induced impacts, which is additional spending and incomes attributable or in response to direct and indirect impacts, including capital expenditures. In a study of 44 Canadian bases which looked at their demographic impact, labour force impact, expenditure impact and grants in lieu of tax impact, Parai et al. (1996) found the following. Bases located in large host communities tend to have a small impact on the local economy, because of the relative size of the host community. Examples include bases in Vancouver, Calgary, Edmonton, Winnipeg, Toronto, Montreal and St. John's, which in general accounted for less than 1 percent of the host community activity analyzed. Bases in small host communities have a large impact because the community is small. Examples included Masset, Cold Lake, Petawawa, Goose Bay and Gagetown which account for 25 percent or more of host community activity being considered (Parai et al., 1996, p.17). Data on provincial trade flows were used, along with family expenditure data, tax data and population statistics for Canada. In smaller communities, dependence on and dominance by the military can be fundamental to the economic and social make-up of a place. Like resource-based and company towns dependent on a single commodity or company, such places are highly vulnerable to wider political and economic trends and the effects of the interactions of global and local forces.

A survey of the UK experience of defence dependency cautions against assumptions of total dependency, however. In 1996, the Rural Development Commission commissioned a study of the effects on rural areas of defence dependency and the potential effects of defence conversion. Six English case studies examined the experiences of five areas with one or more military base, and one area heavily dependent on the defence industry, all of which were scheduled for closure. The was no employment crisis discernible in any of the areas. The regions affected were relatively prosperous. The economies affected were all in areas experiencing high population growth, so for example school rolls were not affected by the decline of military personnel and consequently their families. The loss of military bases was mitigated by military expansions or relocations elsewhere in the affected regions. Furthermore, because the run-down of military bases or industries had been predicted or expected over a number of years, the affected regions had had the opportunity to adjust. Estimates of annual net income included £30 million in the Dorchester and Weymouth Travel-to-Work area on the south coast, £9.3 million in the north Norfolk districts containing RAF bases at Swanton Morley and West Raynham, and £4.2 million in lost income for the locality surrounding RAF Swinderby in Lincolnshire. Indirect and induced effects of defence closures were understood to have been minimized by low levels of local procurement (for example, with the procurement of supplies from the United States in the cases of the USAF at Sculthorpe and Fairford), and high levels of integration of local economies into larger sub-regional economies, which make the most of linkages and minimize single-industry dependence (EAG/Ecotec, 1996). We should be cautious about assuming an automatic economic benefit to a locality from a military presence; as the section below on conversion illustrates, the actual benefits (rather than assumed benefits) may be far less than imagined. Indeed, the imagination of benefit of the presence of a military establishment may be the significant factor in its contribution to the local economy, rather than any direct financial input. In short, it appears that the value to a local economy of a military establishment varies with levels of local procurement and levels of local employment. Military establishments may exist as isolated islands in a wider locality, with little connection to local webs of economic relations. For example, Soviet bases in Eastern Europe closed with minimal impact on the local economies because of the self-sufficiency of these bases (IABG and BICC, 1997). USAF bases in the UK are very self-contained, with food, supplies and entertainments provided on-base, imported directly from the USA. This pattern is discernible for US military establishments in other countries, and for British establishments overseas; why make do with local goods if you can get favourite delicacies from the NAAFI or PX? Yet for those bases which provide employment opportunities for local people – as we have already seen at the former Clark and Subic bases in the Phillipines – that contribution can be significant.

Ultimately, we should also remember that the measurement of the economic impacts of military establishments is a tricky business. There are boundary problems, because 'unless the community is somewhat isolated, the geographical boundary of this community, much like the most outer ripple emanating from a pebble dropped into a body of water, is not always precisely discernible' (Parai et al., 1996, p.9). Input-output models are often used (Warf, 1997; Solomon, 1996); indeed the US Department of Defense has used job-loss multipliers based on input-output models of the regional economy in project the economic impacts of base closures. However, models don't capture the ability an economy to adjust to shocks, and may overstate the true economic impacts (Hooker and Knetter, 1999).

Nonmeasurable impacts

Another approach to the study of economic influence exerted on localities by military establishments is to examine nonquantifiable or nonmeasurable impacts. Some activities originating in military establishments create income and trade for individuals, but lie outside the scope of official statistics. Examples include trade in nonregulated markets (for example, unlicensed trade in commodities such as alcohol), and illegal economic activities such as the sale of drugs, gambling and prostitution. Economic data on these activities is scant because of their very nature. For example, at the height of the US military presence in the Philippines at the Clark and Subic bases, an estimated 55,000 – 60,000 women and girls worked in the 'entertainment' industry. Prostitution, and prostitution-related establishments became normalized as part of the social and economic landscapes of the cities and towns surrounding the bases (Santos, Hoffman and Bulawan, 1997, cited in Euler and Welzer-Lang, 2000; Rocamora, 1998, makes the same point).

The social consequences of the dependency on prostitution of large numbers of women (and consequently families) are stark. Sturdevant and Stoltzfus (1993) set out images and women's life stories in the Philippines and Japan, lives which rest economically on the sale of women's sexual labour to US military personnel. They also trace the link between the destruction of traditional employment patterns under colonial and post-colonial economic development policies, and the availability of prostituted labour (see also Enloe, 1990, 1993). The social consequences of the presence of a military base have, for some, been dire. In terms of crime and disorder in Okinawa, Japan, US troops committed 4,700 reported crimes in the period 1971–2000, including murder and rape (Kirk et al., 2000). Since 1988, the Naval and Marine Corps bases in Japan registered the highest number – 196 – of court martial cases for sexual assaults of all US bases (Shorrock, 2000). In 1995, the rape of a 12-year-old girl by US soldiers stationed on Okinawa prompted not only calls for action against military violence but also a much wider crisis about sovereignty and the foreign military presence in Japan (Isako-Angst, 2001). Kirk, Cornwell and Okazawa-Rey (2000) argue that much of the crime and disorder originating amongst US military personnel in Japan and Korea impacts directly upon women's lives. Women are vulnerable to violence and sexual abuse, to AIDS and other health problems, and to drug and alcohol dependency. Korean mothers of children fathered by US military personnel are likely to be abandoned by their transient partners and their children face prejudice and discrimination as children and adults (Okazawa-Rey, 1997). In assessing the unquantifiable or unmeasurable aspects of militarized economies, then, the prostitution economy is only one facet; the social consequences that follow (also unquantifiable in many respects) will also have their own impacts. There is evidence too that even where prostitution is not an issue, there may still be complex economic relationships around the exchange of sex for resources. A study of an un-named garrison in the north of England found networks of fleeting, unstable relationships between local women (some of whom were extremely young) and a transient population of trainee soldiers. Rent money, food and gifts were routinely exchanged for sexual favours, with wider social consequences for the women concerned in terms of their reputations and dependency (Euler and Welzer-Lang, 2000). In summary, whilst for a small minority there may be economic and social benefits which accrue from association with a military presence, for many many more people, the consequences are ultimately debilitating because of the limits on labour market and trade opportunities imposed on local people directly and indirectly by the military presence.

Also unquantifiable are the economic controls exerted across space through the block military uses place on other land uses. The establishment of a military base will bring with it the disestablishment of existing activities. In the UK, the villages of Imber in Wiltshire and Tyneham in Dorset were (famously) evacuated during the Second World War, and ultimately erased, because of demands for military training (see Wright, 1995). The establishment of a US base at Manta, Ecuador, was predicated on the displacement of 2,000 farmers who lost agricultural and fisheries-based livelihoods. Furthermore, the levels of local employment and wages, promised in return for the base, never materialized (Reichard, 2001).

Obviously, land used for military purposes (a runway, a rifle range) is not usually available for other purposes – although grazing and forestry often coexist on larger training areas in Britain. Less clear are the blocking effects put on other activities in buffer zones adjacent to military establishments. We can speculate on how these might operate (for example, through the housing market or the planning system), but this is not an established area for economic investigation. For example, in the UK, of 506 proposals put forward to local planning authorities for the erection of wind turbines between 1999–2002, the MoD objected to 238 of them, on the grounds that they would interfere with radar with safety consequences for pilots conducting low-flying training (Renew, 2002). Locations in central Wales, Northern Scotland and the English/Scottish borders, areas of rugged, elevated terrain, were ideal for the generation of wind power. Unfortunately, they also happened to be Tactical Training Areas for the Royal Air Force. National targets for environmentally sustainable energy have been affected by national military objectives.

There are two points to make in conclusion. The first concerns the evidence for the economic impacts of military establishments. Military establishments can make a valuable financial contribution to the economic health of a locality, but we should be cautious about assuming that this contribution is indispensable or entirely positive in terms of the social consequences which follow from defence dependency. There are no hard-and-fast rules either; at face value it may seem that domestic bases are more embedded locally because of domestic supply chains than overseas establishments. Yet the employment opportunities brought by an overseas base may generate significant economic returns. The presence of an overseas base may be promoted through discourses of security and freedom for the economies of host countries, but the costs for local residents (particularly the vulnerable) may be horrendous in terms of enforced reliance on illegal or sexual economies.

The second point concerns data. Reliable evidence for the economic contribution of military establishments to local or regional economies is scant. Impacts are less than visible. This invisibility means a lack of audit-ability or accountability, further emphasizing how military control rests, as a consequence, on secrecy. With secrecy comes control.

The Defence Industry

Of all the possible military economic geographies which we could map, those determined by the defence industry have received the most sustained schol-arly attention. For this reason, the discussion here of the defence industry will be brief – the original literature can be followed up through the refer-ences cited below. Nonetheless, the salient points deserve summary.

Militarism and military activities shape local, regional and national econ-omies in less direct ways than obvious presence, through the collective locational decisions and knock-on effects of the defence industry. Eco-nomic development is inherently geographically uneven, in its growth, impacts and decline. Furthermore, local and regional responses to uneven development emphasize the variability of economic geographies and eco-nomic activity. Accordingly, the defence industry has been studied within a scholarly geographical tradition emphasizing the political economy of uneven development.

The creation and maintenance of military economic geographies through the defence industry, and the political economy of this, has long been recognized. The term 'military-industrial complex' was coined by US President Eisenhower in 1961, as a means of describing the alliance be-tween military, government and corporate elites; indeed, the confluence of interests of these groups has been identified as foundational to the militar-ization of peace-time society (Calhoun, 2002, p.309). Some analysts take this further, arguing that military, industrial and state relations are not merely organizationally close, but form a socioeconomic system (Lovering, 1990). Defence industrial 'systems' fix the relationships between militaries, economies, social life and political relations in space, and have long pro-vided a research focus for those seeking to explain the geographical out-comes of militarization in terms of its political economy. Furthermore, it would appear that the availability of reliable national data on defence industrial output has facilitated the study of the defence industry's eco-nomic geographies (in contrast to the data available on, for example, land use). The defence industry is not a neutral player in the creation of geog-raphies of both security and economic development: 'How it is organised, the resources it absorbs and the vested interests it generates also shape both perceptions of security and the direction of economic development' (Kal-dor and Schméder, 1997, p.2; see also Figure 3.1)

Is it worth it?
A new winter coat and shoes for the wife
And a bicycle on the boy's birthday
It's just a rumour that was spread around town
By the women and children
Soon we'll be shipbuilding

Well I ask you
The boy said, 'Dad they're going to take me to task
But I'll be back by Christmas'
It's just a rumour that was spread around town
Somebody said that someone got filled in
For saying that people get killed in
The result of our shipbuilding

With all the will in the world
Diving for dear life
When we could be diving for pearls

It's just a rumour that was spread around town
A telegram or a picture postcard
Within weeks they'll be re-opening the shipyards
And notifying the next of kin
Once again

It's all we're skilled in
We will be shipbuilding

With all the will in the world
Diving for dear life
When we could be diving for pearls

Figure 3.1   *Shipbuilding*, Elvis Costello and Clive Langer, from *Punch the Clock*, August 1983, Columbia records, No. 38897. Copyright: BMG Music Publishing Ltd. and International Music Publications.

The defence industry has a basic geography in terms of its location. This has been eloquently traced in the US by Markusen, Hall, Campbell and Deitrick (1991) who chart the development of the 'gunbelt' across the southern USA and coastal west and the territorial redistribution of wealth from the older industrial heartlands of the north-east United States.[3] In the UK, of an estimated 81,000 whose employment is directly dependent on defence equipment expenditure, 31,000 work in South East England, 14,000 in the South West, 11,000 in the North West 6,000 in Scotland and 5,000 in the West Midlands (Hughes, 2001). (For a discussion of other

European defence industry distributions, see Kaldor and Schméder (1997) and Serfati (2000).)

At a global level, the defence industry is worth about $200 billion per year (Carson, 2002). The USA, Britain, Russia, France and Germany are net exporters of defence industrial products, with Taiwan, Saudi Arabia, Turkey and South Korea the major customers. Globally, however, the United States dominates the defence industry.

In all developed economies, economic changes over the past decade have prompted significant restructuring of the industry. In the UK, defence spending constitutes a decreasing proportion of both GDP and the UK labour market. A recent UK government policy document on the defence industry talks up the proportions employed through careful wording, with 345,000 people being ascribed directly or indirectly to the defence industry, and that industry constituting 3 percent of the UK's manufacturing output, earning £5 billion per year through exports (Ministry of Defence, 2002). Carson (2002) is more pessimistic, identifying around 90,000 as employed directly in the defence industry (compare with Hughes's figures above), and calculating that the defence industry contributes less than 0.5 percent to the UK's annual GDP. Features of the restructuring of the industry from the late 1980s onwards included the shedding of labour, moves by defence companies to become more market than government-orientated in their corporate strategies, the rationalization of capacity in the industry, reform of industrial relations and employment practices, and a pattern of company mergers leading to the dominance of one key player (BAe Systems) (Lovering, 1998).

In the USA, a restructuring in the 1990s was marked by company mergers (with government encouragement) and the emergence of three dominant firms (Boeing, Northrop Grumman and Lockheed Martin). The top seven US defence firms employ around one million workers between them (Carson, 2002). Boeing boasts over 250,000 employees, Lockheed Martin talks of its 'facilities in all 50 states', and Northrup Grumman, with annual sales of £26 billion claims 123,000 employees in 44 states (Ciarrocca, 2002).

The consolidation of the industry through the emergence of a handful of globally dominant companies has created some very powerful globally operating corporate entities (Lovering, 2000). These companies, whilst not transnational in the strictest sense, are international in their reach and effect because of their use of partnerships and subcontracting on specific projects. As Kaldor and Schméder (1997) have observed, there is a sense in which the 'market research' conducted by defence companies is highly influential in shaping government definitions of security needs. Viewed in this way, the defence industry shapes not only geographies of industrial production, through the facts of location and the interchanges between civilian and military technology sectors (see Der Derian, 1998), but also is contributory and proactive in the shaping of military engagements themselves.

Conceptualizing Conversion

The nature and extent of military controls, militarism and military activities over (particularly local) economic geographies become most obvious when that military control disappears. For this reason, some of the problems in assessing the economic controls asserted by military establishments and activities can be overcome, to an extent, by looking at conversion issues.

Conversion has been defined as the process by which military resources (establishments, associated infrastructure, industry) are transferred or transformed from the military to the civilian sector (Brzoska, 1999a, p.131). Conversion is best conceptualized and studied as a process, rather than a once-and-for-all change. The political discourse of the end of the Cold War[4] in the early 1990s presented the consequences of geopolitical and geomilitary change as a 'peace dividend', a unique shift in the distribution of resources. This term proved popular in media explanations and commentaries about geopolitical changes in the early 1990s, bringing as it did notions of the cessation of warfare, the economic benefits of disarmament and the wish for realization of the biblical prophet Isaiah's vision of swords beaten into ploughshares and spears transformed into pruning hooks. The notion of a peace dividend has provided some researchers with a conceptual hook onto which to hang studies of the economic impacts of military establishments (see for example EAG/Ecotec's *The Impact of the Peace Dividend on Rural England*). Alternatively, the 'peace dividend' has been conceptualized as a process entailing a resource dividend (through cuts in military expenditure and the savings that this produces), a product dividend (with savings used to promote more efficient types of production, a notion predicated on the greater cost-effectiveness of civilian resource uses relative to military ones), and a welfare dividend (with positive national welfare effects following reductions in military expenditure) (Brömmelhörster, 2000, following Chan, 1995). The 'peace dividend' is thus the effect of real spending cuts on the well-being of the global population. Rather, the experience of advanced economies has been of the restructuring of military and defence industry capabilities in response to changing military requirements; some conversion of capabilities and facilities has happened, but this might better be viewed as a consequence of restructuring and remilitarization than of national desires for a peace dividend. In this chapter, then, the discussion will focus on 'conversion' rather than a 'peace dividend'.

The study of the conversion process reveals much about how the military control of space operates. There are two points to make at the outset. The first concerns power. Conversion is a management task involving many actors, particularly the military (BICC, 1996). Military participants in the conversion process maintain power over space long after it may have passed from established military use. The second point concerns the linkages between economies at different scales which conversion studies reveal. Conversion is a global issue, determined nationally with regional effects and local repercussions. The study of the conversion process shows much about the political economy of military establishments and their roles in shaping (uneven) development.

The conversion of military facilities has received the least attention from social scientists of all military resource reuse issues (Brzoska, 1998). There are a number of reasons for this. Military base conversion is a slow-burning issue, with events unfolding over years and decades; consequences will not be immediately discernible. There is a basic lack of information available on the conversion of military holdings partly as a result of its invisibility in public policy. Defence industrial restructuring has had greater policy input because of more immediate consequences (e.g. mass unemployment), hence the fact that the majority of The European Union's KONVER initiative funding was targeted by national governments at industrial conversion.[5] The conversion of military establishments, in contrast, has been very difficult to analyze because of the absence of reliable data (Brömmel-hörster, 2000). The conversion of military establishments is also highly complex, involving diverse types of establishments, partners and objectives. Because of the slow pace of change, policy invisibility, the lack of data and the issue's complexity, military base conversion is something of a Cinderella issue, appearing and disappearing suddenly from view on the whims and requirements of those good fairies, politicians. In Europe, what political (and public) interest there was in the conversion of military establishments waned significantly at the end of the 1990s with the conclusion of the KONVER programme (BICC, 2000). In the US, the slippage of the Base Realignment and Closure commission coupled with political changes in the White House has also pushed conversion down the political agenda. Yet the conversion of military establishments is important to consider as part of a discussion of military economic geographies because of the transparency the conversion process brings to an otherwise seemingly opaque world of military economic impacts.[6]

The Scale of Military Base Conversion

If figures on the size and distribution of military lands in the UK and elsewhere are hard to come by, so is data on disposals. There is a dearth of reliable, publicly available information on the conversion of former military lands and property. A 1996 analysis of the rural development implications of defence disposals was vague, noting that from 31 December 1990 to 3 May 1995, 28 UK bases were sold by the MoD 'and many more were closed' (EAG/Ecotec, 1996, p.2). No source was given for this information despite the scale of land sales. According to MoD sources at that time 'no systematic record of closures exist' (EAG/Ecotec, 1996, p.2). A 1999 consultants' report to the Department of the Environment, Transport and the Regions on the policy framework for the disposal process ducked the issue almost entirely. It gave no figure for the scale of land disposals, noting only the fact that government reviews of defence requirements have had an impact on the defence estate 'leading to the closure or rationalization of many military sites across the UK' (Fuller Peiser, 1999, p.15). An inquiry to the Defence Estates Organisation (DEO)[7] about the availability of data on defence disposals was met with the response that such records are not maintained because 'such figures are of no particular value to us' (DEO, 1998). The UK is not alone. As BICC (1999) observe, 'It continues to remain a challenge to obtain systematic data concerning the status of base closures and their redevelopment around the globe' (p.93). This lack of information is another mechanism for exerting military control over space; public scrutiny is impossible with the absence of information over the scale of the issue. Furthermore, the conversion of military lands is a serious and difficult economic and social regeneration issue, and over or underestimating the problem makes the task no easier.

For the UK, the information which is available on disposals comes from three sources. The first is information produced for the annual *UK Defence Statistics* by the Defence Analytical Services Agency (DASA). These give figures on free-and leasehold lands for the four countries of the UK, at five-yearly intervals from 1975 to 1990, and at yearly intervals from 1993 onwards (see Figure 3.2). These statistics are limited in their utility for tracking changes to the scale and location of military lands, because purchases and sales are not enumerated, and because they don't go below country level.

As the figures show, there is no case for the existence of a post-Cold War peace dividend in terms of land sales. The DASA data shows an overall reduction in land holdings of 18,100 ha between 1975 and 2002. Most of this reduction is accounted for between 1975–85. As the House of Commons Defence Committee noted in 1994, disposals in the early 1990s had not been on a large scale, though there was much potential for the release of unwanted lands (HCDC, 1994a). The House of Commons Public Accounts Committee in 1998 questioned why budget reductions and personnel reductions had not been matched by estate reductions or greater efficiency in land management and disposals (PAC, 1999; see previous chapter on the size/needs debate).

	1975	1980	1985	1990	1993	1994	1995	1996	1997	1998	1999	2000	2001	2002
England	211.7	203.0	195.3	195.4	194.5	194.2	192.7	193.4	192.6	191.5	192.1	191.8	191.7	190.2
Freehold	195.1	190.4	183.1	182.9	181.9	181.9	180.3	180.9	179.8	176.7	176.6	176.2	173.9	172.8
leasehold	16.6	12.6	12.2	12.5	12.6	12.3	12.4	12.5	12.8	14.8	15.5	15.6	17.8	17.4
Wales	22.3	22.0	21.0	21.0	21.0	21.0	20.9	21.0	20.9	20.7	20.8	20.8	20.7	20.7
freehold	21.6	21.3	20.4	20.9	21.0	21.0	20.9	20.9	20.8	20.6	20.6	20.6	20.5	20.5
leasehold	0.7	0.7	0.6	0.1	0.1	0.1	0.1	0.1	0.1	0.1	0.2	0.2	0.2	0.2
Scotland	21.9	22.1	20.9	20.8	23.1	23.1	23.2	23.2	22.9	22.9	22.7	22.7	27.3	27.1
Freehold	19.1	19.4	18.2	18.3	20.5	20.5	20.6	20.7	20.4	20.4	20.2	20.2	24.8	24.6
leasehold	2.8	2.7	2.7	2.5	2.6	2.5	2.5	2.5	2.5	2.5	2.5	2.5	2.5	2.6
N.Ireland	3.2	3.6	3.3	3.4	3.9	3.6	3.6	3.5	3.2	3.2	3.2	3.2	3.2	3.1
Freehold	2.6	2.5	2.5	3.0	3.5	3.3	3.2	3.2	2.9	2.9	2.9	2.9	2.9	2.8
leasehold	0.6	1.1	0.8	0.4	0.3	0.4	0.3	0.3	0.3	0.3	0.3	0.3	0.3	0.3
Total	259.2	250.7	240.5	240.6	242.5	241.9	240.3	241.1	239.6	238.5	238.8	238.5	242.9	241.1
Freehold	238.4	233.6	224.2	225.1	227.0	226.7	225.0	225.6	223.9	220.7	220.3	219.9	222.1	220.7
leasehold	20.8	17.1	16.3	15.5	15.6	15.3	15.3	15.4	15.7	17.8	18.5	18.6	20.8	20.4

Figure 3.2 The hectarage of the UK defence estate, 1975–2002.

Source: Defence Analytical Services Agency, UK Defence Statistics.

These figures give broad indications, but no detail. What were these sites, and what did they contain? Where in the UK were they? Which regions lost most land, or retained most military presence? Was the military presence consolidated anywhere or established anew? In the absence of detail, speculation and guesswork creeps in: for example, in 1998 in a report on the identification and sale of surplus MoD property, the National Audit Office estimated that 13,000 ha sat in the pipeline for disposal (16 percent of the built estate in 1997) (NAO, 1998). Yet information on the source of this statistic (presumably it came from the Ministry of Defence) is absent. In short, official defence statistics are little help in assessing changes in the control of land by the UK Armed Forces.

The second source of information on the scale of disposals is data on the value of sales. UK government documentation on land disposals usually talks of disposals in terms of receipts generated rather than hectarage. This proxy measure is a relative one, because of fluctuations in the price of land over the years. However, it is often all that is available. For example, a 1999 DETR report on disposals policies glossed over the absence of data on hectarage or types of site disposed of, substituting instead a figure of over £100 million for receipts for disposals for the year 1996–1998 (Fuller Peiser, 1999). The National Audit Office gave a figure of £100 million in receipts for 1996–7, and of £328 million for the period 1995–98 (against an expected £379 million) (NAO, 1998). The Defence Estate Organisation in 1998 gave figures of £397 million for the period 1995–9; £74 million in 1995/6, £180 million for 1996/7 and £143.8 million for 1997/98 (DEO, 1998) 'while for the past 8 years receipts total about £900 million' (excluding the transfer of MoD housing). The Strategic Defence Review anticipated a figure of £700 million for 1998–2003 (MoD, 1998), expected £280 million in 1999–2001 (MoD, 2000b) and realized £209 million in 2000/01 (MoD, 2001a).

The use of the financial value of receipts as a statistical indicator of the scale of military base disposals is indicative of three things. First, it reflects the fact that MoD concerns about disposals are limited to the revenues generated. The 1998 strategic review of the UK's defence capabilities rested financially in part on assumptions about the revenue to the MoD (£700 million between 1998–2002) to be generated by land disposals (MoD, 1998). There is a financial imperative to the disposals programme. The House of Commons Defence Committee had recognized this point when, in its 1994 report on the Defence Estate, it advised against the setting of rigid targets for the generation of revenue from property sales on the grounds that this put undue emphasis on once-off capital gains, rather than longer-term savings (HCDC, 1994, p.ix). The then Secretary of State for Defence was adamant however that the figure of £700 million was not an ambitious target or dreamt-up figure, but was based on a very careful analysis of the estate

(HCDC, 1998). The Corporate Plan for Defence Estates for 2000–5 noted that the organization was well on its way to achieving the projected figure (Defence Estates, 2000), and for the period 2001/2 – 2005/6 projected a target of £550 million to be generated by sales (Defence Estates, 2002). This is good news for the MoD as it relies on these receipts.

Second, the use of receipts as an indicator reflects a set of assumptions about what constitutes the public interest in the case of military base conversion. In policy debates on conversion, the 'public interest' is defined as the sale of land at the highest possible market value. The equation of financial imperatives, financial acuity, the free market and the public good, I would argue, is indicative of the political power of the Armed Forces in the UK in their ability to define the discourse through which policy debates on disposals are conducted. Consideration of the wider social and economic consequences of disposals is kept out of the equation, silenced by the terms under which the discussions of disposals is framed. These wider consequences include social benefits through land disposals, and are discussed further below.

The third point about the use of receipts as a measure of disposals is that generating data on disposals through receipts keeps disposals from view. Broad figures are available but disaggregated data on receipts generated through the sale of individual properties or sites is not, on the grounds of commercial confidentiality. In 1999, the House of Commons Defence Committee berated the MoD for unnecessary secrecy in withholding information on the price of individual land sales. The MoD's claims of commercial confidentiality were dismissed by the Committee, but the latter were powerless to change this practice (HCDC, 1999). Because defence disposals are constructed through policy and discourse as a financial or business transaction, public information on sales is lacking. There is no way of evaluating the feasibility of targets for receipts generated by disposals, nor of establishing whether they have been met, because the individual sales and the income generated are classified as commercially private transactions. Again, one interpretation would be that this constitutes a sophisticated mechanism for maintaining military control over lands until the point of sale. It has also been argued that the absence of information on the disposal of a public asset is antidemocratic in that it provides no facility for public accountability (Clark, 2001).

Whilst bearing in mind the difficulties of putting together meaningful statistics on the scale of military base conversion, it is still useful to look at what figures do exist for other countries in terms of the disposals of military lands, not least because it puts the UK experience in a wider context. The following figures are indicative, rather than exhaustive.

In 1945, at the end of the Second World War, Germany was occupied by military forces from Britain, the USA, France and the Soviet Union. Whilst some of the foreign bases established at this time have remained in place ever since, a large proportion were relinquished following geopolitical changes in Eastern and Central Europe at the beginning of the 1990s and the downsizing of the UK and US military forces. At the end of the Cold War, 47 US military bases, comprising 37 military communities and ten airbases existed. By 1995, 21 of these had reduced in size and in numbers of personnel by more than 80 percent. Only nine were unaffected by changes. Around 32,400 German civilians lost their jobs between 1991–5 as a result of base closure, which resulted in a loss of around US$3 billion to the German economy. Some 37,260 ha of land had been returned by 1995 (Cunningham and Klemmer, 1995). The *Länder* most affected were Rheinland-Pfalz, Baden-Württemberg, Hesse and Bayern. Rheinland-Pfalz had been home to 67,200 allied soldiers, and military activities had generated around 132,000 civilian jobs, in turn generating purchasing power of DM3.3 billion, which was lost once the bases closed. However, two-thirds of the roughly 500 former military sites vacated now have civilian uses; for example, the former US Air Force Base at Zweibrücken is now a technical college (BICC, 2000).

In the Baltic states of Latvia, Lithuania and Estonia, the Soviet Union had established large numbers of personnel, again as part of the post-Second World War settlement. With the collapse of the Soviet Union, sites were returned. In Latvia, 263 sites were abandoned by the Soviet military, and since 1995, 159 sites or parts of sites had passed from defence uses, sites with a value of US$9.1 million. The removal of foreign military personnel was significant; at Kiepaja naval base in the city of Karosta, over 30,000 sailors and their families left (BICC, 2000). In Estonia, 160 Soviet military bases and 505 Soviet military areas, covering 85,175 ha, were relinquished following Soviet withdrawal. Sites include the large Paldiski base near Tallinn (Jauhiainen, 1997). In Hungary, 3–400 former military sites, valued at Ft18 billion, are now vacant (BICC, 2000).

Other significant conversion sites are the former military bases in Panama, where over 4,000 troops were withdrawn from the canal zone in 1999, and the former Clark Air Force Base and Subic Naval Base in the Philippines, decommissioned after much international negotiation between the Philippine and US governments in the early 1990s (see Rocamora, 1998).

Further details on the conversion of bases in places as diverse as central America, the United States, South Africa, central Europe and South-East Asia is collated regularly by the Bonn International Centre for Conversion (BICC – an independent German defence conversion research unit) in annual conversion surveys (see for example BICC, 1996, 1998, 1999, 2000). Rather than repeating the detail, I turn now to the practicalities of conversion through a discussion of the effects of military base closures, the benefits and the problems.

The Effects of Military Base Closures

The announcement of the closure of a domestic military base is usually greeted with dismay by those in the immediate locality. Collective dread, usually at the prospect of economic decline, is probably the natural reaction, given the (often unsubstantiated) assumptions about the contribution which military bases to economic activity in affected localities. For example, the announcement of the closure of RAF Scampton in Lincolnshire initiated the foundation of a 'Save Our Scampton' Campaign against closure by local residents concerned about the job losses which would follow. Collective dread may also be based on a sense (if not on evidence) of security through association with the Armed Forces. The identity of a locality may also be bound up with the military presence; in Scampton, a base from which the RAF's 617 Squadron had flown on the dam-busting raids on the Ruhr in 1943, the local pub ('The Dambusters') and church (with its cross-stitched kneelers in airforce blue) celebrate this association. Reactions to the closure of a foreign military base may be more ambivalent, may even be cause for celebration. It is not my intention to examine here perceptions of the military presence and their place in local social and political life, but rather to explore directly the economic geographies that these bases construct and affect by their closure. The costs and benefits will be concentrated on the immediate locality, but a number of factors influence the degree to which localities and their wider regions suffer or benefit from this form of demilitarization.

The benefits

The consensus which has emerged from the US, a country with long experience of the economic and political management of base closures, is that the economic and social advantages of base closure and redevelopment outweigh the initial costs, even though these costs might be initially high. For example, the Kincheloe US Air Force base, Michigan, closed in 1977. Unemployment rose from 18 percent to 22 percent initially, but fell to 7 percent with around 2,600 people employed on the site of the former base, compared with 700 people (civilians) at the time the base closed (Hartley and Hooper, 1991). The conversion of the site to an industrial park and medium-security prison generated three times more jobs than previously, and tax revenues from activities on the site rose by 330 percent. Initial diagnoses of gloom, doom and economic collapse are not necessarily borne out in reality. In Oscada, Michigan, the former Wurtsmith Air Force Base, was rented out to businesses, providing local income, and providing a number of existing buildings which were put to community use. Myrtle Beach, South Carolina, had a less smooth transition but still showed evidence for employment generation (Minton, 1994). The long-term prospects for the regeneration of such sites tend to be positive because new activities tend to be more labour intensive than military ones, with higher employment multiplier effects than military activities. They have fewer extra-regional leakages so economic benefits stay in the locality. A 1986 assessment by the US Department of Defense's Office of Economic Adjustment found that following 100 base closures after 1961, 93,000 military jobs were lost, and 138,000 civilian ones created. At England Air Force Base in southern Louisiana, which closed in 1990, the conversion of military facilities into facilities for a lorry driver training centre, an aeroplane equipment testing company and a local school led to a surge in homes, jobs and spending (*New York Times*, quoted in Warf, 1997).

Boosterist stories of community rebirth following the death of the military presence rely on the ability of local population to interpret positively a complex of economic forces. The detail is brought out in Bradshaw's (1999) study of Castle Air Force Base near Merced County, California, the closure of which was announced in 1991. The factors mitigating against economic decline and collapse are applicable across the base closure experience, certainly in the US where the disposals system actively facilitates the involvement of local people and organizations in the reuse planning system. Mitigating factors are as follows:

1. Retail sales remain more or less stable. Military personnel shop on base, so there is minimal benefit to local retailers from military personnel prior to base closure. Military retirees in the region shift spending to private shops in the locality after base facilities close, rather than using base shops. Wholesalers, retailers and warehouse stores take sales from small retailers near a base, regardless of base closure.
2. Base expenditures have a small impact on local businesses. Bases purchase few items from local suppliers in any case. Base construction expenditure is replaced by that for toxic cleanup after closure (which may be costly).
3. Housing markets rebound after an initial decline. New housing construction is not affected by base closure in growing regions. Base housing often needs rehabilitation, delaying its entry into the local housing market.
4. Health care becomes privatized off-base. Medical services to retired personnel shift to local doctors and hospitals. Base hospitals and clinics become available to serve community needs.
5. Employment remains stable. Many civilian employees from the closed base take advantage of government worker relocation opportunities.

Local jobs, held by military spouses who are relocated, become available to dislocated and unemployed workers, or to people not previously in the local labour force. Unemployment rates do not escalate because the overall economy does not decline and military base workers have left the area.

6. Civilian population remains stable. County in-migration patterns continue. Current residents do not relocate because the economy remains strong.

7. Multipliers are lower than feared. Income and employment multipliers for military bases are low because of few local purchases. Local income multipliers are low in small economies and regions.

8. Community organizations are strengthened. Department of Defense planning assists local base closure processes and strengthens community organizations. (Bradshaw, 1999, p.204).

In the US a coherent policy framework for strategic planning in base closure under the Base Realignment and Closure Commission, coupled with a set of assumptions about local involvement in the reuse planning process, can smooth the reuse process considerably. In the UK, where experience has been more problematic, there are of course still economic benefits to localities of base closure. These include the release of brownfield sites for housing and light industrial development (Gallent and Howe, 1998; Gallent, Howe and Bell 1998, 1999, 2000), a significant resource in a densely populated island like Britain. The former RAF Swinderby in Lincolnshire, closed and sold in the mid-1990s, brought about 150 houses onto the local housing market for rent and released housing land in an rural district within commuting distance of the city of Lincoln. The rupture of this new settlement with the past was completed with the christening of the new site as Wittham St Hughes. The availability of brownfield sites is particularly important in the south east of England, where development pressures in areas surrounding London are acute; the development of land for housing at the former gunpowder mills of Waltham Abbey is a good example. The release of sites can also improve infrastructure; the former RAF base at Manston became licensed as a civilian airport, making its own little contribution to the economic boom in East Kent in southern England at the end of the 1990s.

The experience of military base closure in the UK, however, has been more mixed in terms of the nature of the economic benefits, and in terms of who these have accrued to. The story of the conversion of the former Royal Dockyard Chatham, in Kent, illustrates this well. In terms of the productivity of the site to new owners, the Chatham conversion is a 'success'. In terms of the resource costs for environmental decontamination, and the costs to the social fabric and well-being of the area, the results are more mixed. Chatham's dockyards can be traced back to 1547 with the construction there of storehouses for Henry VIII's navy. By the late eighteenth century, Chatham had become a centre for the construction and repair of naval vessels and during this time a significant proportion of the built fabric of the surviving dockyard was constructed. During the mid-nineteenth century, with the development of technologies allowing for the manufacture of ships using iron and steel, many of the earlier buildings in the original Georgian dockyard became redundant. The dockyard expanded onto available land adjacent to the historic core, leaving most of the original Georgian dockyard structures intact (although building maintenance wasn't a priority). As the dockyard expanded, so did the population of Chatham and the surrounding towns of Gillingham and Strood, supplying a workforce for the dockyard. Until 1980, Chatham provided repair and maintenance services to the Royal Naval fleet.

Then in 1981, closure of the dockyard was announced as a part of a national review of defence capabilities. It shut in 1984, with the loss of 7,000 direct jobs and double that number from associated businesses. The closures hit the town of Chatham (and the neighbouring Medway towns) hard. On closure, the site was divided into three portions. The outer basin of the modern (in fact, Victorian) dockyard was sold as a commercial port. The central section of the modern dockyard was christened 'Chatham Maritime' and designated for economic regeneration and residential development. The Georgian dockyard was handed to an independent trust tasked with conserving the impressive historic fabric of the site and promoting compatible economic activity (for a summary, see Woodward, 2000a).

Three things have been crucial to the regeneration of this huge and complex site; establishing the site's utility, reinventing the place, and time. In terms of the utility of the site, it had to be physically altered in order to allow the space to be economically productive. This was no small matter, as it involved significant ground clearance; 1,200,000 cubic m of soil contaminated with heavy metals and petrochemicals, the pollution of years and years of ship repair, were removed to a depth of 5 m. Site preparation also involved the construction of transport infrastructure, including a fast link road between the site and the motorway network (which involved an under-river tunnel); the dockyard had, after all, been strategically located in the first place on a peninsular where military security and secrecy could be maintained. Only once this work was complete could construction work begin on retail, business and residential areas. The second factor, the reinvention of the place, has been as important as physical reconstruction in the conversion process. The site required marketing, changing public perceptions of it from an isolated peninsular on a grubby tributary of the River Thames, to a buzzing destination for living a lifestyle. For example, the Chatham Maritime web site screamed to the reader to 'Succeed, work, learn, live, relax, invest, locate here'; 'regenerate, revive, rebuild, reborn, rethink, reality is here. Invest here, work here, live, learn, relax'. 'As more people discover Chatham Maritime as a place to work, learn, live and relax, their perceptions are completely transformed and they want to move here.' (Chatham Maritime, 2002). The third element was time; an evaluation of the success or otherwise of regeneration ventures only really has meaning if made at the appropriate time-scale. Five-year or ten-year assessments are inadequate in evaluating a site like Chatham in terms of the 'success' of the regeneration scheme. At the time of writing, almost 20 years after the closure of the dockyard, the site is at last economically productive, in that it hosts business, educational, retail and residential facilities. Many of the problems experienced at Chatham are inherent to all conversion stories on former military sites, and to these I now turn.

The problems

But, as we would expect, the regeneration of former military sites can be problematic in different ways for governments, for local authorities, for local residents, for local businesses, for local environments. The conversion of military bases is not a novel contemporary experience. Witzmann (1994) argues that contemporary problems of base reuse echo those encountered after both 1918 and 1945, when the return of lands occupied by militaries, home and abroad, happened on huge scale. The obstacles to successful conversion, such as the need for high levels of initial investment and problems with contamination, are long-standing (Brzoska, 1999a). But I concentrate on contemporary conversion issues here because of the particular economic development and environmental problems this process raises, which I deal with in turn.

An issue at the heart of conversion debates is that over the extent of the economic impact of the closure of a military establishment. Boosterist statements after the event can present a healthy economic future, but these do little to assuage fears of economic decline and associated social problems on the announcement of closure, and in the short term. Talk of potential problems can be a political strategy in order to maximize chances of drawing down available funding to assist the regeneration process. For example, the Single Programme Documents drawn up by local authorities in Lincolnshire and East Anglia for the receipt of European Union Structural Funds under Objective 5b in the mid-1990s and Objective 2 in 1999 emphasized the vulnerability and dependency of local economies on local military bases for employment and the supply of goods and services. In the short term, economic problems may be real enough. In the UK, the Association of District Councils in a 1994 survey of 167 local authorities, found that 62 percent reported problems as a result of the reduction in Armed Forces personnel in their localities, problems including redundancies, business closures, and loss of employment, trade and services (Municipal Journal, 1995). There can be a social knock-on effect; in Lincolnshire, following the closure of RAF Swinderby, local primary school rolls halved due to the absence of children from the local base.

Bradshaw (1999) summarizes the conversion problems for localities in the following terms.

1. Small towns without a diversified economy recover much more slowly when a base in or near them closes.
2. People who lose jobs in a base closure are generally not the ones reemployed by redevelopment. Those most affected are unskilled and semi-skilled workers, blue collar workers, operators and labourers (see also Warf, 1997).
3. When laid-off workers do find other work, their incomes are well below what they received working on the base.
4. The biggest job and wage losses from base closures are felt by minority employees who were employed in greater numbers by the military than in the communities.
5. The potential reuse of military base facilities is limited because bases did not need to comply with civilian environmental regulations and the mandates for good planning.
6. Administrative rules governing the reuse of bases are complicated and complying with them takes time.

A key issue affecting the abilities of localities to adjust to the absence of a military base is the economic health and vitality of the wider regional economy in which the locality sits. As the EAG/Ecotec (1996) report noted, on some UK sites economic problems had not been so severe because of the buoyancy of local economies. In many East and Central European states, the closure of former Soviet bases has taken place in the context of severe economic decline following the collapse of the Soviet Union. The absence of investment opportunities has been a contributory factor in, for example, the regeneration plans for the Raadi airfield in south east Estonia near the city of Tartu (Jauhiainen, 1997). The thickness of networks (relationships) between a base locality and a regional economy is also critical; isolated sites which have historically been self-sufficient or resourced from elsewhere will have fewer linkages in place.

Conversion can also mean facing up to severe environmental problems, which are both an issue in their own right (see Chapter 4) and an issue with implications for economic development. The types of problems seen as 'environmental' vary enormously, from pollution, to the poor state of footpaths. There seems to be some consensus that former Soviet bases in eastern Europe have particularly bad environmental problems such as the poor condition of buildings, severe contamination of land, and delays and uncertainty in the development process (Lobeck, Pätz and Wiegandt, 1994). For example, in the former Soviet base at Klomino, north west Poland environmental problems include the presence of both landmines and pollution. But with a national budget of £25 million to undertake conversion and environmental clean-up across 70 bases, lack of investment has limited remediation efforts (Guardian, 2000b). Former Soviet bases in the Baltic states of Latvia, Estonia and Lithuania deal now with petroleum residues and unexploded ordnance from years of military occupation. In Saxony, in the former East Germany, 170 sites covering 16,233 ha, relinquished by the Soviet Army in 1994, have found to be contaminated with unexploded ordnance and chemical pollutants (BICC, 2000). More generally, the huge problems of environmental contamination revealed on former US military bases in the USA have been one factor leading to the faltering of the base closure programme under BRAC. An estimated US$9 billion – 36 percent of all closure costs – have been spent on environmental cleanup on bases closed since 1988. In 1997, the US Department of Defense identified 4,660 sites which required environmental remediation. This is a costly process. Some types of contamination have no cure; for example, no cost-effective decontamination strategies have yet been identified to remediate groundwater contamination from unexploded ordnance. Furthermore, land intended for residential purposes require higher standards of environmental remediation than industrial land.

Measuring the 'Success' of Conversion

The measurement of the 'success' or 'failure' of conversion, in terms of economic development and social gain, is important because conversion concerns the redistribution of public finance; there is a public interest in conversion projects succeeding, in the sense that former military establishments can have value. The measurement of conversion success is no straightforward matter; success in base conversion depends entirely on what is evaluated, and how. Is that value economic, social, environmental? Furthermore, the evaluation of success or failure is rarely a politically neutral exercise in the sense that it involves judgement.

In national terms, the most basic indicator of the scale of a conversion programme is the number of sites sold. This gives no information on the impacts of conversion, other than just an indication that the disposal process is taking place. Also, simple measures such as these fall into what the Bonn International Centre for Conversion calls 'the base closure gap' (BICC,

1998) where a reduction in military capabilities and capacity can occur without a corresponding reduction in the number or area of bases. Measuring the size of the sites sold potentially gives a cumulative indication of the overall proportion of military lands converted from military use. But measurements such as this reveal very little; in the UK the number of military sites is currently declining due to an on-going programme of sales reinvigorated by the 1998 Strategic Defence Review, but the overall hectarage of the defence estate has remained fairly constant since 1985 (see Figure 3.2). Measuring the value of sites sold just gives an idea of the defence estate as an asset. If the scale of military base conversion is hard to quantify, then how is a wider public interest in the disposal of a public asset served?

Indicators of conversion success are hard to define; accurate information and sound reasoning are required (Buss and Dwivedi, 1997). Measuring the number of jobs created or lost in a locality following base closure fails to capture the full reality of base closure, its economic impact, and whether local needs are taken into account (Glassberg, 1995; Hill, 1998; Matsuoka, 1997; Hansen, Skopek and Somma, 1997). There may be social consequences which follow from employment decline, and these may be profound, but these require methodologies which capture them adequately: is priority given to the homeless or those in housing stress in new housing schemes? Is environmental clean-up happening? Are facilities available for local community uses as well as for economic purposes? What are local social needs, in any case? These aspects of regeneration are significant elements of the success of a conversion project, but are hard to quantify. Furthermore, the timescale within which 'success' is evaluated is significant; evaluation of 'success' may only make sense decades afterwards. For Warf (1997), this timescale was around 5–10 years. For Isserman and Stenberg (1994, quoted in Markusen and Brzoska, 2000), a timescale of 7–10 years was more appropriate. Hill (1998) suggests an even longer timescale for the appreciation of the full effects of closure and success of recovering; investments in public infrastructure are recouped over a much longer time period.

Success also depends on factors do to with the specificity of military bases, and the specifics of national policy frameworks which determine how the conversion process succeeds. What is so special about former military sites? After all, there are many parallels between the conversion of military bases and other large-scale regeneration projects involving changes of land use, in terms of the resources required and social assumptions about the need for efficient reuse. In answer to that question, a question which goes to the heart of efforts to establish effective, successful conversion outcomes around the world, Network Demilitarised (a European Union-funded network of defence-dependent regions) in 1994 identified eleven factors which the group saw as contributory towards that specificity. These were:

1. The scale and site of buildings.
2. The specialist or diverse nature of the buildings and facilities; buildings with military uses often have highly idiosyncratic appearances and layouts. For example, the Royal Aircraft Establishment Farnborough's wind tunnel in Building Q121 contains a 9 m diameter mahogany propeller. The building and contents are unique. Sometimes, the only effective reuse for a building is a military one.
3. The condition of facilities; many may be very substandard, and in construction and maintenance may not accord with current standards for residential or office accommodation.
4. The location of the site; isolated, rural bases, whilst great for ensuring security for military activities, are less well-placed in terms of available regeneration options because of the structural characteristics of rural economies which make conversion more problematic.
5. Environmental factors such scenic or conservation value, which can often be high in military areas because of the block that military uses puts on other environmentally destructive activities.
6. Contamination of land; military sites have particular problems with TNT, arsenic and other heavy metals, and petrochemical pollutants.
7. Historic, architectural and heritage issues; military sites often have a valuable architectural inheritance (see Clark, 2001). Farnborough's Building Q121, mentioned above, is protected as a Grade II* listed building, in recognition of its historic and architectural value.
8. A continued need for military security on a site which no longer has a direct military function.
9. The timing of base closures, which may not come at a point when the local and regional economy is sufficiently buoyant to support closure.
10. Problems and issues which follow from military ownership and doubts about sale; in the UK, the MoD is notorious for delays and indecisions about base closures. Furthermore, unlike defence industrial units which are owned by the private sector or the state, bases are disposed of by the military themselves (Markusen and Brzoska, 2000).
11. The loss of specialist workers at specialist sites, leading to employment loss in very specific industrial niches.

The specifics of national policy frameworks for base conversion

The second set of factors in determining the 'success' of military base conversion is the specifics of policy frameworks which set out how conversion proceeds. As Warf (1997) points out in the US context, base closures reflect labyrinthine interrelations among Congress, the Pentagon and local political constituencies vehemently opposed to the loss of such facilities which they view as central to their local economic health. Base closures illuminate contradictions between different levels of the state; they reveal the points of contention among different sets of institutionalized interests. In the US, in order to depoliticize the issue, the government established the politically independent Base Realignment and Closure Commission to oversee the process by determining which bases where to be closed. The list of closures then had to be accepted by Congress as a whole; individual sites could not be saved from closure by the protests of a single member. Four rounds of closures were set in process (1988, 1991, 1993 and 1995). However, the pace of closures slowed after this time because of presidential interference over the closure of McClellan AFB in California, and Kelly AFB in Texas, over concerns over job losses (see Mayer, 1995; Warf, 1997; Kitfield, 1998). Ultimately, the BRAC process faltered because of miscalculations about the value of lands offered for disposal (many sites were valued too highly), because of the levels and costs of environmental remediation required, and because in the end some bases never closed due to changes in forward planning by the military. The US Department of Defense, between 1990–2001, spent US$23 billion on closures under the BRAC actions; only in 1996 did some savings (US$100 million) overtake costs, and cumulative savings only eventually overtook closure costs in 1998 (BICC, 2000). 'Success', in these terms, has been limited. However, what the US policy framework did involve was a set of assumptions about the need for localities themselves – local communities affected by closure – to share involvement in the process of planning regeneration. The need for success to be evaluated in social as well as economic and environmental terms is enshrined within the policy framework.

In contrast, in the UK, policy on defence land sales is determined by Treasury rules, which dictate a first principle of sale of lands to the highest bidder in order to maximize the returns on public investment. Sales are required within three years from the date of closure. The overriding incentive is for financial gain, rather than for social or environmental benefits. As Clark (2001) points out, UK policies on base closures reflect a four-way split between incompatible objectives; the need for maximum financial return, the need for economically sustainable development; the need for the conservation and protection of built and natural resources; and local community requirements for economic reconstruction. No independent commission has overseen the closure and regeneration process in the UK; the open market (for sales) and the planning system (determining reuse) have been held to be sufficient. We shouldn't necessarily be surprised by this; as Brzoska (1999b) notes, military base conversion, of all conversion issues, is the one which has the potential to be the most financially rewarding.

Network Demilitarised (1996) have led calls for the establishment of a more efficient closure and regeneration process. In the UK, the process has been viewed as inefficient because of lack of coordination and communication over closures between central government (via the MoD) with responsibility for determining closures, and local government (at county and district level) who have responsibility for land use planning and thus determining which new uses would be allowed on released sites. Network Demilitarised also emphasized the need for partnerships between public authorities, military planners and the private sector in preparing for and guiding through the closure and reuse practice. There is some evidence that where redevelopment has been steered by public-private partnerships (something increasingly important in urban and rural regeneration), local interests are better served. Funds drawn down to assist regeneration, whether from the European Union (such as KONVER or the Structural Funds) or from UK sources (Single Regeneration Budget, and the former Rural Challenge) are often conditional on such partnerships and the demonstration of local input. However, in the UK, the specificity of the problems associated with the regeneration of former military bases has not been recognized at policy level. Central government has never budgeted specifically for base regeneration, even when drawing down funds under KONVER, intended explicitly for military restructuring.[8] Regeneration funds can be used, but applicants for funding for base regeneration compete with all other regeneration applications. In contrast with the assistance available to deal with the aftermath of the decline of heavy industry or mining, localities affected by military base closure are left unattended by policy intervention. Furthermore, responsibility for regeneration falls into the gap between departmental responsibilities. The Ministry of Defence takes no responsibility for regeneration; clearly it is not a redevelopment agency, but there have been criticisms about that department's lack of concern with closures even at the preclosure stage (Clark, 2001). The government departments with responsibility for rural and urban regeneration (currently the Department for Environment, Food and Rural Affairs and the Office of the Deputy Prime Minister, respectively) have not recognized base conversion as an issue carrying its own specific difficulties.

In the UK, then, sites are identified by the owner as surplus and sold to the highest bidder (often for an undisclosed amount), with the sole imperative for the owner being the generation of maximum sale value, in order to maintain targets established for estate sales. The public interest is defined in terms of value-for-money; finance raised by sales contributes to defence budgets, and the public interest is deemed to lie in maximizing the cash return to the taxpayer from disposals. There are no policy mechanisms to enable local social or economic interests a voice in the sales process; although local authorities can and do influence the reuse process via the land use planning system, they are no policy mechanisms to endorse, encourage or guide intervention. The 'public interest' is not defined in terms of generating economically and socially sustainable development. The system is efficient, insofar as it generates finance, but far from equitable or sustainable in other respects (see also Fuller Peiser, 1999; Doak, 1999; Woodward, 1998a, 2001a; Clark, 2003). Calls by the Arms Conversion Project (a local authority defence conversion network) that the Defence Diversification Agency established by the MoD in 1999 should include within its remit oversight of the management of military land sales were dismissed by the MoD (ACP, 1998; MoD, 2001b).[9]

Why Military Economic Geographies Matter

This discussion of military economic geographies is partial in terms of its focus. Issues such as the prioritizing of the use of natural resources for military objectives, and the economic geographies which follow from military action in pursuit of economic objectives, for example, have not been discussed. I have been concerned primarily with the military geographies shaped by those activities which ultimately facilitate conflict. These may seem a rather mundane area for study. But military economic geographies matter.

Military economic geographies consolidate the military control of space. There are intricacies to the economics of a military presence which do this. Furthermore, getting the measure of these effects is often difficult. The issue gets black-boxed, removed from public gaze and thus removed from critical appraisal. The absence of information is significant here. In the absence of data on the economic effects of military establishments, speculation creeps in, wrapped up in discourses which legitimize the military presence in terms which go beyond simple domestic or strategic necessity, to include assurances of economic input and economic stability. These are hard to unpick from the material facts of economic impact, and hard to counter politically. For this reason, arguing against a military presence can be construed as arguing against a valued contributor to the local economy. Military economic geographies are significant in their tenacity. They are the outcome of material practices which are supported and explained to the world by discursive strategies which tie in economic well-being to the military presence.

Chapter Four

Militarized Environments

I have never been to Nevada. Its environment, though, is familiar with its yellow, ochre, golden, and beige desert colours, the sage bush and grey scrub, the mountains and flatlands, the blue skies and high clouds, empty and silent. The environment is familiar because this is the terrain of Westerns – cowboys pushing forward the final frontier of nineteenth-century America, defeating bandits and natives to exert authority. It is also familiar as a nuclear landscape, captured in Richard Misrach's photography of the legacy of the nuclear age (Misrach, 1990), the 'poisoned, terminal landscapes of Marlboro Country' (Davis, 1993, p.51):

> The desert flats of central Nevada offer an eerie landscape of twisted I-beams, bent towers and deformed bridges, farm buildings ripped apart, and stretches of land scarred by craters – one so vast it rivals depressions on the moon (Johnson and Beck, 1995, p.41)

The desert flats of Nevada, and other states in the southwest United States are militarized environments. This chapter is about those militarized environments, or how specifically the natural environment is militarized. It is structured around two basic questions. The first is: what does military activity actually do to the natural environment? This is addressed by looking at issues of pollution and environmental modification, drawing on examples from around the world, and examining examples from nonconflict situations. The second question is: how does militarism deal with both its impact and with criticisms of its impact, and what do these responses tell us about the military control of both space and nature? This is addressed by looking at military actions and undertakings, at military environmental policy, and at military responses to criticisms.

Examining Military Impacts on the Environment

The vast majority of military activities, whether conflict-related or not, have some sort of impact on the natural environment. Maintaining military forces is itself an act with environmental repercussions. Armed forces demand the use of natural resources, to keep them equipped, supplied and trained. For example, the US military consumes about 2–3 percent of all US energy demand, just to maintain a standing armed forces, and an estimated 25 percent of all jet fuel worldwide is used for military purposes. Minerals and land are important resources for the military (for further information, see Middleton, 1995). The use of environmental resources will have its impacts. The majority of those impacts will be harmful in some way, for some duration of time, to that natural environment. Military activities disturb ecosystems through noise, physical damage to habitats and pollution, with a consequent reduction in biodiversity and repercussions for people living in an affected locality.

Although I'm concerned in this book with the military geographies of nonconflict situations, for reasons which I shall explain, the environmental consequences of such 'peacetime' military activities, as material entity and as discursive strategy, are best understood with reference to all types of military engagement. Narratives about wars or specific military campaigns usually explain something of the environmental impacts of warfare, and that explanation is usually written into such narratives as an inevitable product of military action. The reduction of large areas of northern France and Belgium to quagmire by 1918 is an example; the entrenchment of troops and continued artillery shelling reduced the landscape to a muddy wasteland. It is common to joke about a muddy patch of grass resembling the battlefields of the Somme or the Yypres salient, but this joke is of course tasteless:

> The worst has gone, or at least sunk beneath the surface; turf has covered what a French survivor once described to me as 'a sort of human jam' of putrefaction and mud. But these places are not yet picturesque. Beside the country roads, farmers still stack the shells they plough up. The mouths of dug-outs, saps and communication tunnels still gape. Buttons, identity tags, nameless bones still slither from the earth into daylight. (Ascherson, 1998, p.24).

Following the 1991 Gulf War, Barnaby (1991) argued that the sanitized television coverage of the conflict masked the true environmental consequences of bombing, the effects of torching of Kuwaiti oilwells (over 600 set ablaze by the Iraqi army), oil spillage and bombing of Iraqi nuclear establishments (see also Baudrillard, 1995). The torching by the retreating Iraqi army of the Kuwaiti oilfield was explained as a desperate defensive manoeuvre. The use of depleted uranium-tipped ammunition, leaving an uncertain legacy, was explained as a military technological advance, a force multiplier in the fight against the Iraqi regime. A similar explanation supported the use of napalm and defoliants in the jungles of Vietnam, and over the border in Laos and Cambodia, in the 1960s Vietnam war. It was explained as a strategy for assisting US military objectives for clearing ground cover which could potentially conceal the enemy. Antipersonnel mines have been justified as a mechanism for rendering agricultural land uncultivable, and thus maintaining areas as uninhabitable to (potentially oppositional) people. Environmental impacts become woven into war stories.

The attitude towards (acknowledged) environmental destruction as a necessary by-product of war has in some ways hampered attempts to undertake critical, independent analysis of this topic. There is some literature on this available, making the case both for the environmental consequences of military activity, and also the levels of recovery and remediation that might be anticipated on affected lands. But it should be recognized at the outset that the examination of the environmental impacts of military activity is, with pun fully intended, a bit of a minefield. This is also an issue of its time; with the emergence of the post-War environmental movement in the 1960s and 1970s, a critique of the environmental impacts of war developed in its present form (Lowe, 1983). The environment is a political issue, in a way that it was not seventy years ago.

At the outset, the issue of relativism in environmental impact should also be recognized. Military activities are not alone in shaping the environment; intensive agriculture and heavy industry, for example, also have profound and often deleterious impacts on the natural environment. Most forms of economic activity across the globe shape ecosystems. Furthermore, distinguishing between the environmental consequences of economic activity on the one hand, and military activity on the other, may be hard (Weissflog et al., 1999). For example, the discharge of polychlorinated biphenyls (PCBs) into the River Clyde in Scotland comes from heavy industry, manufacturing and urban conurbations as well as from military sources (Edgar et al., 1999). Other activities can have just as much of a deleterious impact; the Fresno Kangaroo Rat found at the Naval Air Station Lemore, California, is endangered at federal and state levels by military activities and by land cultivation which both affect its habitat (Morrison et al., 1996). Bear two points in mind, though, when thinking through this issue of relativism. First, military pollution, from such contaminants as chemical and nuclear wastes, biological weapons and explosives, may be of a qualitatively different nature from that from other sources (Finger, 1991). Second, military activities may be regulated by different environmental pollution controls to civilian activities.

Perceptions of the nature of the relationship between the military and the nation state will also affect perception of the military environmental hazard. Joni Seager (1993), unstinting in her exploration of the links between military activities, militarism and environmental degradation and destruction, sees a 'chain of militarized environmental destruction that stretches around the world' (p.14). She is unequivocal: militaries are major environmental abusers. All militaries wreak environmental havoc, whether this is predetermined or unintentional. They are also privileged, hiding behind the protective blanket which discourses of 'national security' can provide. Matthias Finger (1991) is damning in his accusation that the military shrouds its polluting in secrecy and maintains considerable efforts in order to avoid environmental regulation and monitoring; the secrecy granted to the military by the nation state has its privileges. Kuletz (1998) talks of the nuclear contamination of sovereign foreign territory as 'nuclear imperialism'.

There is also the issue concerning the level of distinction drawn between environmentally deleterious impacts produced as a result of warfare, and those produced as a result of peace-time activities. The distinction between both states is increasingly tenuous with the increase since the early 1990s in 'Military Operations Other Than War' (MOOTW). As a rule, offensive and defensive military engagements have an impact of a greater order of magnitude than peacetime preparations and MOOTW. But the distinction can be a dangerous one to sustain. Environmental destruction can often be endorsed analytically and politically if wrapped up in justifications based on the state-sanctioned force; for example, during the build-up to the 1991 Gulf War, US Pentagon relaxed its requirement for environmental assessments of military projects (Finger, 1991). Low levels of environmental impact from military activities in peacetime are easier, relatively speaking, to discount if of lower magnitude than the impacts of war. There is also the omnipresent question about the suitability of established methodologies for the assessment of the degree of environmental impact from any single military-related activity. For example, McGowan (1991) has argued for prewar environmental assessments to be included in assessments of the environmental damage caused by the Gulf War, drawing on mechanisms applied to assessments of environmental damage by private corporations under the 'polluter pays' principle. Drawing a distinction between wartime and nonconflict environmental impacts is tricky; we might expect impacts during armed conflict to be higher during times of conflict, but this is not always the case. There is also an issue of the visibility that conflict-related impacts enjoy, relative to destruction caused in nonconflict situations.

In this chapter, examples are drawn primarily from nonconflict situations, but reference is made to the environmental effects of some military strategies in conflict where this will illuminate the wider issue of military environmental consequences. Within the examples chosen, I have been indicative rather than definitive, given the potential scope of this topic; again, further references should lead the reader to the wider literature, as required.

Environmental Pollution

Pollution is the single largest environmental impact of military activity. Pollution is defined here using Mary Douglas' phrase, as 'matter out of place' (Douglas, 1966). Military pollution comes in many guises, but levels of military contamination are often hard to assess with accuracy, either because of lack of access to sites or because of secrecy about contaminants. For example, in much of eastern Europe and the US, serious contamination problems have often not been visible until military bases have closed (see Fonnum et al., 1997).

The rubbish and detritus of military activity is often the most visible aspect of military pollution. Orford Ness in Suffolk, a former nuclear and explosives testing establishment on the North Sea coast, has been managed by the National Trust as a nature reserve since 1993. This shingle spit, the largest in England, is littered with twisted, rusted pieces of metal, the remains of 80 years of military use (see Figure 4.1). The bed of Holy Loch in Scotland, the site of a US Navy nuclear submarine base, is covered in rubbish from military sources to depths of 10 metres in places. Some of the physical artefacts discarded by the military can be highly dangerous. 'Moor guide drops explosive toilet tip' ran a news headline announcing the withdrawal from public circulation of a campers' guide for Dartmoor giving advice on latrine digging. A risk of hitting unexploded ordnance on a former live training area was discovered (Guardian, 2001a). At the Jefferson Proving Ground, Madison, Indiana, a decommissioned former major weapons testing facility for the US Army, 100 sq. mi.are thought to contain 1.5 million rounds of unexploded ordnance, 6.9 million bombs, plus mines and shells. Some have argued that the scale of the problem and the expense of the clean-up operation are so great that it would be more viable economically to create a 'national sacrifice zone' instead (Wegman and Bailey, 1994).

Chemical pollution is often invisible, but constitutes the biggest environmental problem caused by military activities on military bases. A 1994 US Department of Defense report to Congress listed more than 10,400 sites at 1,722 installations in the US as 'active' (i.e. potentially contaminated). Of

Figure 4.1 Twisted metal, Orford Ness, Suffolk, 2002. Copyright: Rachel Woodward.

these, 60 percent were polluted with fuel and solvents and 30 percent of contained toxic and hazardous wastes (Wegman and Bailey, 1994). Sometimes problems only become apparent on closure, when the gates of a base are opened and the environmental impacts appear for public scrutiny. For example, in the US the first two rounds of base closure under the Base Realignment and Closure Commission (BRAC) identified over 500 contaminated domestic sites. Twenty-five of these were so badly contaminated that they were included on the national Priorities List, a roster of the most hazardous waste sites in the US which pose the most serious threat. As well as contamination on military bases, pollution from the defence industry is also a problem; for example, the military industrial complex on the Trubia river in Spain produces wastes which have been identified as genotoxic to fish (Ayllon et al., 2000).

Some pollution problems take time to emerge. White phosphorus, used in explosives such as grenades, was thought to be innocuous after use until it was linked, in 1990, to thousands of waterfowls' deaths in the Eagle River Flats impact area at Fort Richardson, Alaska, USA where explosives had been used. White phosphorus contamination proved difficult to remediate. Dredging risked disturbing unexploded ordnance. In-situ remediation through draining and flooding affected areas was counter-productive to the maintenance of wetland habitats in the area. Measuring the problem accurately was also difficult (Walsh, Walsh and Collins, 1999). Evidence at

Vieques, Puerto Rico, is slowly emerging of contamination of the soil (and thus the food chain) from heavy metals such as cadmium, lead, mercury and uranium from the US Navy's activities on their bombing ranges on the island (Lindsay-Poland, 2001).

Fuels and fluids inevitably leak and cause contamination. Rocket fuel is a contaminant; its constituent parts include xylidine, which is nonbiodegradable and carcinogenic. Keila-Joa, a former Soviet military base in Estonia, has high levels of ground water pollution from these fuels (Preis, Krichevskaya and Kharchenko, 1997). Organophosphates, used as flame-retardants in hydraulic fluids for aircraft, are frequently lost through leakage. Organophosphates have a proven toxicity to fish, but their impacts on soils is less clear. Analysis of soil samples at former US Air Force bases (Mather AFB, California; Stead AFB, Nevada; and Beale AFB California) found them present there (David and Seiber, 1999). Polychlorinated biphenyls (PCBs), used in insulating and cooling liquids, are now no longer produced but were used widely from the 1920s in lubricants. PCB contamination is a big problem in former Soviet bases in Poland (Lulek, Szafran and Lasecka, 1999). PCBs stick in soils, which become the main source for atmospheric circulation. Polar regions have become an environmental sink for atmospheric PCBs. Remediation is difficult; contaminated soils can be excavated and disposed of elsewhere, but disposal has to guard against leaching of PCBs through drainage. In sites such as the early warning radar stations in at Iqaluit, Sarcpa Lake and Resolution Island in Canada, remediation on these tundra areas has proved problematic (Poland, Mitchell and Rutter, 2001).

Explosives such as 2,4,6-trinitrotoluene (TNT), hexahydro-1,3,5-trinitro-1,3,5-triazine (RDX), and dinitrotoluene (DNT) frequently contaminate soils and groundwater in testing areas (Charles et al., 2000). An estimated 0.82 million cubic metres of soil in former military installations in the USA is contaminated by TNT (Peterson et al, 1998). Explosives are problematic because of the unpredictable behaviour of their constituent molecules in soil. Concentrations or 'hot spots' in soil are often found many kilometres from source. Clean-up procedures employ a number of techniques including granular activated charcoal filtration systems, composting, phytoremediation through the use of grasses, and natural attenuation or biodegradation of the explosive with microbes to change the chemical structure of the explosive. This is a time-consuming and costly process (Bennett, 1994; Shriver-Lake, Donner and Ligler, 1997; Siciliano and Greer, 2000; Riefler and Smets, 2002). TNT contamination of groundwater has been identified, for example, at Umatilla Army Depot, Hermiston, Oregon, and the Naval Submarine Base Banger, Washington. Munitions storage depots are also prone to contamination. The clean-up of explosives-contaminated soil and water is essential prior to site disposal, because of the dangers posed by potentially live explosives, their potential toxicity as mutagens, and their mobility through soil and water. The US Federal Environmental Protection Agency (EPA) lists a number of Super-fund sites on former military munitions manufacturing, storage and testing sites (the Superfund being a programme established in the 1970s by the EPA to identify and clean up particularly polluted areas). Proving contam-ination and its consequences is difficult, however. Pollution of aquifers due to the use of explosives and heavy metals from the Massachusetts Military Reservation has been linked with above-average cancer rates in the Upper Cape, Cape Cod, Massachusetts. The US Department of Public Health disputes these claims (Shaw, 1999).

Nuclear, Chemical and Biological Risks

The legacy of chemical and biological weapons, controlled to a degree by the 1925 Geneva Protocol on the use of biological weapons and the 1972 Biological Weapons convention, leave their legacy through their nonuse as well as via their use in conflict. Organoarsenic-based chemical warfare agents have been a problem in former military bases where chemical weapons have been stored. Contamination has come to light, for example, at the former military bases at Heeresmunitionsanstalt I and II, (HMA) near Löckniz on German-Polish border. On this 300 ha site, underground tanks of around 3,000 tons capacity were used during the Second World War to store diphenylchloroarsine (CLARK I), diphenylcyanoarsine (CLARK II) and phenyldichloroarsine (PFIFFIKUS), which were later decanted into grenades and other missiles. The base was destroyed 1946, and one consequence was the leaking of organoarsenic compounds, pollut-ing the soil. Plant contamination (bioavailability) has been comparably low, but is still an issue. There have been fears of the contaminants entering the food chain (Pitten et al., 1999) There are also management and security issues involved in bioremediation (Kohler at al., 2001). Large quantities of chemical warfare agents were dumped in the Baltic sea after the end of the Second World War; 32,000 tons chemical munitions containing 11,000 tones of chemical weapons agents were dumped into the Bornhom Basin, and 2,000 tons of chemical munitions containing 1000 tons of agent were dumped in the Gotland Basin. The contaminants have been distributed throughout the Baltic sea because the containers were dumped in the sea in wooden crates, which have long since rotted. The long-term environmental consequences of this are unknown (Glasby, 1997). Anthrax spores, de-veloped during biological weapons testing by the UK during the Second World War, still contaminate Gruinard island off the western cost of Scot-land, where spores were released for military experiments in 1942. The island was declared uninhabitable by government decree until the late 1980s (Szasz, 1995).

Environmental warfare through use of herbicides sprayed to destroy forest cover and enemy food crops has been practiced by the US military. Although this is a conflict rather than a nonconflict use, and thus potentially out of place in this chapter, the use of herbicides requires mention because of the severity of their lingering effects, and the potential for these effects to be present, to a lesser degree, if these weapons have been tested, spilled or dumped in nonconflict scenarios. In Vietnam, 15,000 sq. km of jungle was defoliated leaving a legacy of pollution from dioxins present in the defoliants. Agent Orange, a herbicide effective against broad-leaved plants, was used widely in the US military actions in Vietnam. Agent Orange contains the dioxin TCDD (2,3,7,8-tetrachlorodibenzo-p-dioxin), and was used by aerial spraying to clear the jungle canopy and reveal enemy troop movements to invading US force. Some quantities were also spilled or dumped. Agent Orange has affected soils and consequently the food chain; high levels of dioxins have been found particularly in duck and fish fat, and breast milk (Dwernychuk et al., 2002). Other herbicides – such as Agents Purple, Green, Pink, White Blue – were also used. Fifteen different herbicides were sprayed in Vietnam between Jan 1962 and Sept 1971, 72 million litres of chemicals in total. 66 percent of this was Agent Orange. Claims were made by the US Government at the time that these herbicides were harmless, although there is also evidence the government was aware of the terrible and long-lasting effects of the dioxins this herbicide contained. An estimated 650,000 people are currently living with the after-effects, now spread over three generations, and an estimated 500,000 have already died. Agent Orange has caused a range of chronic medical conditions and birth defects, and has been called the 'largest chemical warfare campaign in history' (Scott-Clark and Levy, 2003).

Then there's depleted uranium, variously described as 'a post-war disaster for environment and health' (Laka Foundation, 1999) and an 'agent orange of the 90s' (Military Toxics Project, nd). Depleted uranium is produced after fissionable uranium, used for nuclear weapons and the nuclear power industry, is processed from natural uranium. Depleted uranium is not capable of atomic chain reaction and is not radioactive, but in particulate form as uranium oxide, is very hazardous if inhaled, as a chemical poison and carcinogen. Munitions are tipped with DU in order to enhance their armour-piercing properties. When weapons tipped with depleted uranium are used, and when they burn, particulate uranium oxide is released.

Contamination from depleted uranium has followed peace and wartime use. In peacetime, as part of training programmes for artillery, over 6,000 shells tipped with depleted uranium (with a total weight of 20 tons), have been fired into the Solway Firth in south-west Scotland from the Dun-drennan range. Environmentalists became concerned after traces of beryl-lium (a component of depleted uranium) were found 30 miles away, when there appeared to be inadequate monitoring of both pollution levels and dangers from unexploded ordnance. These fears were denied by the MoD, which maintained that there was no known threat from shells: 'You have to remember that there is uranium present in the sea naturally and that these shells have never been shown to alter that level' said Dr Lewis Mooney, Defence Minister. 'We are testing the accuracy of the shells by firing against soft targets; the alleged health risks occur when the shells are fired at hard targets, like tanks' said a spokesperson from the former Defence Evaluation and Research Agency (DERA) (both quoted in Scott, 2001).

The biggest scare to date, however, has concerned wartime use, and use during the 1991 Gulf War in particular. Concerns have been (and still are) expressed about the health of both civilians and military personnel, both receiving and delivering depleted uranium-tipped ammunition. During Operation Desert Storm, according to US Department of Defense sources, US planes and tanks fired 860,000 rounds of ammunition containing 290 tons of depleted uranium (Edwards, 1999). M1A1, M1 and M60 tanks used large calibre depleted uranium penetrators. American A10 and AV-8B aircraft shot depleted uranium rounds. Tanks were equipped with depleted uranium armour, releasing particles of depleted uranium on impact with incoming fire (Laka Foundation, 1999). British tanks fired 100 rounds of ammunition containing less than 1 ton of depleted uranium. An estimated 387 tons of spent uranium munitions were left by US military forces in Kuwait and Southern Iraq (Military Toxics Project, nd). A range of health problems contributing in part to 'Gulf War Syndrome',[1] plus a six-fold increase in birth defects in affected localities have been associated with the use of depleted uranium-enhanced weapons. In the 2003 war in Iraq, British and US forces again fired munitions tipped with depleted uranium. The long-term environmental and health consequences for Iraq, its people and for the forces themselves are unknown. In Kosovo, the US fired depleted uranium munitions against Serb forces, but little information exists on the extent of depleted uranium contamination in the Balkans following the wars in the 1990s. The irony for one commentator is that in using depleted uranium-tipped ammunition, NATO forces have poisoned the very land and people that they were ostensibly aiming to protect (Edwards, 1999).

Nuclear contamination as a result of military activities is a deadly issue. Nuclear contamination is the result of either testing nuclear weapons, the use in wartime of nuclear weapons, leakage during the manufacture of nuclear weapons, contamination during the preproduction stage for the fissionable materials, and contamination associated with that by-product of nuclear weapons, the nuclear power industry. Nuclear contamination is fundamentally serious because of its highly toxic nature, because of its invisibility to the naked eye, because of its tenacity and long life, and because of the reluctance of governments – such as the US government, for example – to admit liability for it. Test sites in the Nevada desert have been used since 1952 for over 900 nuclear detonations, releasing an estimated 12 billion curies of radioactivity into the atmosphere. Groundwater aquifers are contaminated by tritium to levels 3,000 times in excess of those accepted for safe drinking water standards:

> Here is the heart of the nuclear landscape – the epicentre of the geography of sacrifice where each atmospheric test contained as much radiation as the Chernobyl disaster, where underground tests leak radiation, and where purposeful 'vents' allowed radioactive emissions into the air. Moving outward from this now imploding atmosphere are the winds of death: death for the downwinders in Utah, Nevada, Arizona, and others farther afield including the Indians (the lowest 'low-use segment of the population') who were largely invisible to the technicians playing with power in the desert. (Kuletz, 1998, p.72).

Parts of Nevada, Utah, New Mexico, Arizona and Southern California have all been affected by nuclear contamination as a result of nuclear testing there since the 1950s (see Misrach, 1990; Loomis, 1993; Kirsch, 1997 and 2000; Vanderbilt, 2002; Beck, 2002; Johnson, 2002 for a wider discussion of the environmental and landscape legacies in the USA of the Cold War). Davis (1993) is highly critical of a western environmental imaginary which fails to recognize its existence or extent in the USA, but which sees nuclear contamination from the Cold War in the former Soviet Union.

A former Soviet Union nuclear test ground near Semipalatinsk in eastern Kazakhstan covers 2,000 sq km of contaminated land. A secret nuclear weapons processing plant in the Urals has left its nuclear legacy on the landscape. The Mayak site, 80 km northwest of Chelyabinsk was the site of an accident (the explosion of a nuclear waste tank) in 1957 which released 2 million curies of radioactive elements over a 90,000 ha area. Around 10,000 people had to be evacuated, and access to the area is still restricted (Middleton, 1995). Davis (1993) documents how 3.3 percent of the surface area of the former Soviet Union – across 45 different sites – is contaminated. Bikini atoll in the Marshall Islands of the Pacific bears the physical and nuclear scars of US atomic bomb testing; the islands cannot be inhabited permanently because of the levels of caesium 137 and strontium 90 in the food chain (Niedenthal, 2001). On Kiritimati (formerly Christmas Island) in the Pacific, atmospheric nuclear tests conducted by the British armed forces between 1956–8 and the US military in 1962 left detritus, radioactivity, and fears for the health of the local population from radiation-related illnesses for the estimated 12,000 British and Fijian troops stationed on the island, who witnessed the tests. Successive British governments have refused to pay compensation (Hugill, 1997).

The possibility of nuclear contamination is a fearful one. Speculation about contamination at, for example, Greenham Common air base in the UK in 1958 (Croudace et al., 2000) and Thule Airbase in Greenland in 1968 (McMahon et al., 2000) following accidents involving aircraft suspected of carrying nuclear weapons, has not been supported by evidence of soil and seawater pollution. Yet rumours will always persist.

Environmental Modification

Military activities, during the conduct of and preparations for war, cause environmental modification in more general terms. The use of live ordnance during military artillery training has an obvious physical effect. The Redesdale impact area on the Otterburn Training Area, Northumberland, UK, is pock-marked with the craters caused by exploding practice ammunition. Shell craters 1 m deep and 6 m wide mark Great Knesset Tor on Dartmoor, a legacy of Army howitzers (MacEwan and MacEwan, 1982). The activities of military training, as well as the noise and environmental pollution that they generate, have been causes of concern.

Environmental modification also involves modification of atmospheric and weather conditions, such as techniques for the generation and dispersal of fog and clouds, the generation of hailstones, alteration of the earth's electric fields in order to generate or direct destructive storms. Middleton (1999) lists a range of military modifications to the oceans, such as the generation of tsunami and the addition of radioactive materials, and to land including the generation of earthquakes and avalanches, and the diversion of rivers.

Military training areas may be home to specific species affected by the modification of their habitats; the Fresno Kangaroo rat (Morrison et al, 1996), the red-cockaded woodpeckers at Fort Bragg, North Carolina, and the mule deer of Pinon Canyon Maneuver Site in southeast Colorado (Stephenson, Vaughan and Andersen, 1996) have all suffered from peacetime training. Habitat destruction as a direct consequence of the construction of military facilities in Okinawa, Japan, has been a constant cause of complaint from those contesting the military presence (Itô, Miyago and Ota, 2000). Habitat destruction during wartime has often been a deliberate military strategy (see the story of Agent Orange in Vietnam, above). In Thailand, the military campaign against the Communist Party of Thailand involved deforestation in order to deny refuge to insurgents hiding out in forested areas. The Khor mountain, a 1970s (forested) communist stronghold is now a treeless area devoted to the monocultural production of cash crops and reliant on the widespread use of chemical fertilizers and pesticides because of the incompatibility of crop to location (Lohmann, 1991).

Criticisms of the military impact on natural environments, particularly during military training, have generated any number of studies aimed at establishing the precise nature of the impact and suggestions of remediation practices. Ground erosion by tracked vehicles is a case in point. Studies of the US Army's M113 tracked personnel carrier at the Gilbert C. Grafton South State Military Reservation in North Dakota measured increases in soil bulk density and decreases in vegetation cover (in this case, Kentucky bluegrass). Soil compaction was a problem because it impairs root and plant growth, and heavy use was proven to be more detrimental than moderate use of tracked vehicles over specific areas. There were, however, no changes in species composition or litter amounts (Prosser, Sedivec and Barker, 2000). Experiments at the Yakima Training Centre in central Washington judged soil wetness and the damage caused to wet soil from tank ruts (Halvorson et al., 2001). Foot traffic also adversely affects the bulk density of soils, infiltration rates for water, total above-ground biomass and litter, and soil erosion rates (Whitecotton et al., 2000). Levels of damage depend on the activity undertaken by troops and the time allowed for time recover; the effects of military training on arid areas was measured at the US Army's Yuma Proving Ground in Arizona. The site had been heavily used in the 1939–45 war, but the impact of vehicles on soil compaction was still discernible (Kade and Warren, 2002). On the Salisbury Plain Training Area in Wiltshire, UK, studies have attempted to discern the long-term effects of tracked vehicle training. About 40 percent of Britain's remaining unimproved chalk grassland is found on the training area, which covers about 38,000 ha and contains three Sites of Special Scientific Interest. Using analysis of aerial photography over randomly selected areas, rates of loss of about 25 ha per year were measured. Losses of unimproved chalk grassland were particularly rapid since the early 1990s because of intensification of use of the training area following the drawdown of troops from training areas in Germany. Changes in the later 1990s were 12 times the average rate for 1994–5. Disturbance was also influenced by the creation of training features, and the use of new mobile weapons such as the tracked AS90, a heavy artillery system. The loss of 25 ha per year only constitutes 0.07 percent of the training area's total, but was cause for concern, leading to the introduction of an Integrated Land Management Plan for the area (see Hirst, Pywel and Putawin, 2000a and Hirst, Pywel, Putawin and Marrs, 2000b).

Environmental modification and environmental pollution, then, combine a range of impacts originating in military activity and affecting the natural environment. This brief discussion of these impacts has skimmed the surface of a pool of scientific information aimed at ascertaining with precision the nature of impacts and their consequences. As with the discussion of the military control of economic space in the preceding chapter, a feature of the discussions of military environmental impacts is the absence or paucity of reliable information on environmental impacts. The pool of scientific information is a small one, but it is apparent that military activities have a range of environmental impacts ranging from the relatively minor, such as the creation of ruts from tank tracks, through to the major and catastrophic, such as the nuclear contamination of areas of the American southwest.

However, 'facts' about environmental pollution and destruction are never just that. The 'facts' about military environmental impacts are themselves contested terrain. Needless to say, military authorities (defence departments and armed forces) have been quick in recent years to respond to increasingly vocal criticisms of military activities and their impacts. These responses have a politics of their own, and in turn suggest strategies by which military control over space is exerted, through the construction of a military environmentalist politics. The next two sections deal with policy responses, and discursive responses, respectively.

Actions and Strategies: Policy Responses to Criticism

Environmental policies are one British and US military strategy for dealing with the environmental impacts of military activities. Policies – mechanisms established in legal and advisory frameworks – establish military responsibilities with regard to environmental protection, and set out the limits to those responsibilities. Military control is asserted by military definitions of what armed forces will and will not do with regard to environmental protection.

The development of policy mechanisms for establishing military environmental responsibilities is a recent one, attributable primarily to the growth of the environmentalist movement in the 1960s. This was a global phenomenon with local inflections. In the US, the emergence of stories from Vietnam about the environmental and social costs of military engagement contributed to a wider leftist and green critique of militarism and its manifestations. In the UK, the growth of an antinuclear movement following public marches on Aldermaston, the UK's nuclear weapons research facility in the 1950s, and the emergence of the Campaign for Nuclear Disarmament was again part of a wider green and leftist critique, seen with the growth of organized environmentalist politics and pressure groups such as Greenpeace, and Friends of the Earth. A green critique of militarism and industrialism, of the causes of environmental destruction as well as its consequences, had its own impacts on the ways in which military environmental impacts were dealt with by the armed forces concerned. Until this time, the environmental consequences of nonconflict-based military activities could basically be ignored, whilst the environmental impacts of active military engagement could be justified by the 'just cause' of the wars themselves. Military secrecy also allowed negative environmental impacts of war and peace to be obscured and denied. Paternalism in land management underpinned strategies of concealment. Sigmund (1980) points to the use of the Official Secrets Act to prevent knowledge about chemical and biological warfare emerging in Britain in late 1960s and early 1970s.

In the UK, the policy frameworks via which military environmental impacts are mediated have been built up incrementally since the early 1970s. In 1973, the Defence Lands Committee inquiry chaired by Lord Nugent responded to growing public and policy concerns about environmental impacts by recommending the establishment of Conservation Officers on major training areas, to coordinate conservation work. A simmering public debate about how appropriate it might be to conduct military training in national parks led in turn to an MoD 'Declaration of Commitment to the National Parks' in 1987 which stated that:

> In managing land which it owns or uses within the national parks, the MoD declares that it will endeavour to promote the objectives of the park authorities wherever these are compatible with the needs of national defence.

This Declaration obliges the MoD to release surplus land with proper advance notice, to consult the local planning authorities, and to have regard to access and conservation matters. The key thing to note here is the principle underpinning the Declaration that defence needs are paramount and that park objectives will be promoted where compatible with this overriding need. Environmental protection has its limits. Declarations of Intent signed with Scottish Natural Heritage in 1993, with the Countryside Council for Wales in 1995 and with English Nature in 1996 make the same point. These commit the MoD and armed forces to adhere to standards of environmental protection demanded by legislation and practices established by these statutory governmental advice bodies. Again, defence needs are prioritized. The MoD will:

> aim to ensure the integration of environmental considerations into all policy areas having regard to the desirability of promoting nature conservation wherever this is compatible with the needs of national defence. (Ministry of Defence and English Nature, 1996)

My point here is not to express surprise at the prioritizing of defence needs by the military; rather, the point is to stress the caveats surrounding military environmental policies, which clearly define their limits. As Chaffey comments, with reference to the management of the Lulworth tank firing ranges in Dorset on the English south coast:

> Issues where there is evidence of conflict between military and conservation interests are usually resolved by compromise, although where such compromise proves difficult or impossible, military interests take precedence. (Chaffey, 1998, p.32)

Sometimes, the 'needs of national defence' are themselves threatened by military impacts on the natural environment. On the Salisbury Plain Training Area, covering 32,000 ha of Wiltshire, damage from tracked vehicles in wet winter of 1993 rendered parts of the Plain unusable. This, and approval by NATO of an environmental policy statement committing armed forces of member states to build environmental considerations into military exercise planning, led to the development of a process (still ongoing) of producing what were termed Integrated Land Management Plans. This process was piloted on the SPTA, and rolled out across the Army's training estate. It involved establishing a baseline assessment for the strategy of monitoring impacts of military training, with remedial activities being taken as appropriate. The ILMP process was reliant on the establishment of Environmental Steering Groups, bringing together representatives from the MoD, Defence Estates, local authorities and statutory bodies (such as English Heritage and English Nature, and their Scottish and Welsh counterparts, via whom nongovernmental organizations with an environmental remit could make representations). Again, the establishment of evaluative methods for assessing whether an activity was causing environmental damage, and the establishment of mechanisms for remediating that damage, lay ultimately with the military. Nonmilitary authorities were co-opted into a process which essentially asserts military control.

The co-option of nonmilitary authorities was also established within policy mechanisms in the *Strategy for the Defence Estate* produced in 2000 (MoD, 2000a). This document was presented by the MoD as a blueprint for the future management of the defence estate, and was a direct result of the 1998 Strategic Defence Review (MoD, 1998). The *Strategy* includes a reiteration of military adherence to environmental protection. It is significant because of the emphasis put on managerial efficiency in the running of the defence estate (Woodward, 2001a). An environmental appraisal of the Strategic Defence Review was also conducted (MoD, 2000e), which stated that 'most of the SDR's decisions are unlikely to have major effects on the environment', and emphasized that the process of environmental appraisal demonstrated that 'the environment has been placed at the heart of MoD's decision-making' (MoD, 2000f). A new Memorandum of Understanding was signed in February 2003 between MoD and Government regional, environmental and agriculture departments, to take account of new rules under the EC Habitats and Birds Directives (Natura 2000 sites) and Ramsar Convention on Wetlands Sites. The *Strategy*, the environmental appraisal and the 2003 Memorandum of Understanding all stress incorporation of environmental considerations into MoD policymaking.

In the US, Canada, New Zealand and Australia, the evolution of military environmental policies has followed a similar trajectory, with the gradual incorporation of environmental concerns within a framework which ultimately prioritizes military requirements. As with the UK, the establishment of a framework for assessing and understanding military impacts is very much controlled by the military. Two common features stand out. The first of these is the construction of the environmental impact issue as very much a managerial problem, that is, a problem which in its nature and magnitude is amenable to resolution through managerial efficiencies. Sympathetic commentators on US military environmental policy have seen environmental legislation as a framework for assessing a balance between military and environmental issues, and for determining 'when environmental sacrifices are necessary to protect us from sovereign aggression or terrorism' (Dycus, 1996, p.xiv). Dycus takes an optimistic view, constructing the issue as one of mutually compatible options: 'National Defence vs. Environmental Protection: We Can Have It Both Ways' asserts the concluding chapter's title. Commentators from within the military establishment, in presentations of US military environmental policy, talk of the application of a 'regional ecosystems management approach' to environmental management, with the use of partnerships and stakeholder participation, and reliant on scientific knowledge to produce an ecological approach and ecosystem integrity (Boice, 1996, 1997). This is a specialist, technical, managerial problem.[2] Advances in military technologies have also been justified in environmental managerial terms, in, for example, the use of virtual reality simulation technology to substitute for some types of live training which may cause environmental damage (Doxford and Judd, 2002). I return to this administrative rationalism below.

A second feature of understandings of military impacts on the environment is the reluctance to consider the remedy of environmental damage, either during use or once military installations have closed down. Analyses from a variety of different national contexts illustrate the complexity of environmental clean-up operations on current and former military sites (Coulson, 1995; Fonnum et al., 1997; Stolpe, 1999). As I mentioned in the previous chapter, the environmental impacts on former military sites can be enormous. Examples from the US and UK indicate military reluctance to engage with the issue. For Wegman and Bailey (1994), discussing the US context, the US military appears slow in dealing with the problem because of lack of finance, lack of clarity over responsibilities, haphazard implementation of legislation, differences in environmental legislation standards between home and abroad, and the simple problem that the US military does not have an impressive record of cleaning up after itself (Wegman and Bailey, 1994). In the UK, the Parliamentary Environmental Audit Committee has been highly critical of what it has seen as minimal efforts by MoD to complete land quality assessments across the defence estate to ascertain the extent of contamination (Environmental Audit Committee, 1998, 1999). An unintended outcome of laxity in the application of standards for environmental protection is the imposition of greater restrictions. This is certainly McKee and Berrens' (2001) conclusions of the US Army's interventions at Fort Bragg, North Carolina, to protect the federally listed red-cockaded woodpecker.

Policy and managerial strategies, then, are one mechanism by which the impacts of military activities on the natural environment are managed, and through which military control is exerted. Another set of strategies is discursive in nature.

Discourses of Military Environmentalism

Military activities are environmentally destructive, in that virtually all military activities have an environmental impact. The difference is in the degree of damage and the possibilities of remediation. Given this, I want to turn now to consider what military authorities themselves say about the environmental impacts of their activities. The previous section outlined some of the mechanisms by which policy directives framed military interventions to prevent or minimize environmental damage. This section will consider some of the discursive strategies used to give meaning to these actions, strategies which I term, collectively, military environmentalist discourses.

The conceptualization of discourse used here follows Mills' definition of discourses as 'groups of utterances which seem to be regulated in some way and which seem to have a coherence and a force to them in common' (Mills, 1997, p.7). The central idea is that discourses act as linguistic frameworks in which things are made meaningful. Those frameworks are constructed linguistically, through 'groups of utterances' and thus an analysis of discourse entails the analysis of language for its meaning. It focuses on how language is used, the function of particular rhetorical strategies within a discourse and the interpretation made within a discourse of particular vocabularies. A discourse analytic approach problematizes the idea that meaning in language is automatically transparent or straightforward. It argues instead that a purpose of this approach is to deconstruct the seemingly commonplace and commonsensical in order to unpack the naturalizing function of discourses (Gregory, 1994; Mills, 1997). So, for example, an analysis of military environmentalist discourses rests upon an unpacking of apparently innocuous or neutral-sounding statements about military activities on the defence estate, with a view to understanding their wider meaning or intent.

A second key point about the conceptualization of discourse used here is that processes around the construction of meaning are part and parcel of processes of social reproduction. The purpose of discourse analysis is not just the interpretation of how material realities are discussed and interpreted, but how this is also a social practice. Discourses have a social context in which they operate. The analytic task is therefore also a consideration of this social context, a questioning of the political and social accomplishments of different discursive strategies, and an assessment of how such strategies can legitimate or challenge power relations. In short, an analysis of discourse entails consideration of the political functions of discursive formations (Fairclough, 1995; Pratt, 1996). Needless to say, the political functions of military environmentalist discourses all involve the assertion of control by the military over space.

For many armed forces, over long periods of time, a common discursive strategy was the use of silence; military activities were deemed secret and public debate was deemed unwanted and unnecessary. 'The state insists that it does not have to produce any evidence to support its judgements of military necessity' (MacEwan and MacEwan, 1987). As I discussed above, a leftist and green critique of militarism and its environmental consequences has to a degree filled that silence, although this still happens. In the UK, for example, it is still difficult to get definitive and accurate information on the consequences of military training activities, such as the toxicity of artillery rocket efflux.[3] Kuletz (1998), in her study of the consequences of the US nuclear testing programme for Native Americans living near uranium mining and milling areas in the USA, remarks on the legitimation given to official (i.e. military) evidence, relative to more anecdotal commentaries, yet how such 'scientific' evidence is notable by its absence.

However, it is with the emergence of environmental issues on public policy agendas that military environmentalist discourses have hit their stride. A key strategy is the marketing of military establishments as places of environmental protection. This is vital; potent public perceptions of what military action actually constitutes (guns, bombs, warfare) don't sit easily with views of environmental protection which see the object of stewardship as calm, quiet and beautiful. As Greenberg et al. (1997) note with reference to the US, the imagery of the mushroom cloud which follows a nuclear explosion can be a big hindrance to public involvement in the re-use planning process for former nuclear weapons testing facilities. Development plans for the UK's Atomic Weapons Establishment Aldermaston have faced similar problems. A local Greenpeace spokesperson was unconvinced by the plans:

> The main thing this [exercise] confirms is that they are looking at building a brand new bomb making factory in the heart of Berkshire, while telling the public its all about nice piazzas and pavilions. The site is dirty, dangerous and decrepit; no amount of MDF and planting is going to do anything to sort it out. (Kelso, 2002)

So if public perceptions need changing, because of the link between warfare and destruction in many peoples' minds, a useful strategy is often the celebration of biodiversity. For the US Department of Defense:

> DoD installations contain some of the finest remaining examples of such rare native vegetative communities as old-growth forest, tall-grass prairies, and vernal pool wetlands. Approximately 200 different federally listed species are known to occur on at least one DoD installation – the highest known density per acre of threatened and endangered species found on any federal lands. Many candidate species may be found on lands under DoD control. More than 200 installations provide habitat for at least one candidate or listed species. (Boice, 1996, p.1)

In the UK, successive publicity documents about the management of the Army's training estate celebrate this diversity:

> The 7,000 acres of Porton Down . . . are the jewel in the crown of the Ministry of Defence conservation. For example, at Porton Down there are more species of butterflies than anywhere else in the United Kingdom, the largest remaining tract of chalk grassland, one of the top stone curlew breeding sites and a major Neolithic industrial flint centre. Preservation of the natural environment of this gem is a valuable side product resulting from the ownership and care of the 7,000 acres by the Ministry of Defence Chemical and Biological Defence Establishment.' (Pearson, 1992, npn).

The annual UK Defence Statistics often includes listings of protected habitats. A high-profile MoD conservation magazine, *Sanctuary*, celebrates the work of the conservation groups with the flora, fauna and archaeology of defence lands in the UK and overseas. The 1998 editions, for example, included features on the RAF Ornithological Society, Magilligan Training Centre in Northern Ireland, and the strandline beetle at Frainslake Sands, Castlemartin, Wales. The 2000 edition discussed the flora and fauna of Belize, the fungi of Stanford Training Area in East Anglia, and Benson's Folly, 'a lost monument at Porton Down'.

Another discursive strategy is to connect the responsibilities of armed forces for national defence, with ideas about environmental protection. In India, for example, the military portrays itself as an environmental protection agency. Environmentally beneficial military activities include aforestation, the use of renewable energy sources, antipollution measures, and a public education role in the best use of resources (D'Souza, 1995). D'Souza cites other examples of military engagements in environmental protection, with the Venezuelan National Guard protecting Venezuela's national resources, the creation by the Bulgarian Army of a 'soldier's forest' where each soldier plants two trees during his two years of national service, and the role of the Nepalese army in monitoring pollution in the Himalayas. A sober Australian Defence Environment Statement makes this link explicit:

> In carrying out our mission to defend Australia and its national interest, we are supported by the Government and the Australian community. Our armed forces are not, however, simply a security service provided by the Government. The Australian Defence Force (ADF) reflects the kind of country we are, the role we seek to play in the world, and the way we see ourselves. Similarly, the community has a strong interest in the way we go about our mission, including how we manage the assets and resources placed at our disposal. In response to these expectations, Defence must be an integral part of and positive contributor to the community. We must embrace the issues of importance to the community, both at the local level and across Australia, wherever we are based. Defence is entrusted with the stewardship of more than three million hectares of land. We are also a significant use of the waters in and surrounding our country and the air space over it. We need to demonstrate to the Australian community that we are worthy of their trust in the contribution that we make to ensuring a positive legacy for future generations. (ADF, 2001, npn)

A further strategy is to connect the existence of environmental diversity on military lands, with that very military presence (a sort of military creationism). For example, on the Otterburn Training Area in Northumberland National Park, where the MoD and Army in 1995 presented plans to develop the army's ranges to facilitate heavy artillery training, one of the arguments supporting the developments rested on the presentation of the Otterburn landscape as a military creation. The Armed Forces Minister at the time argued that:

> Although military training may not conform to the general perception of quiet enjoyment, it is often forgotten that it is that very military presence which has helped to preserve and secure the exceptionally beautiful and varied landscape which attracts so many visitors to the National parks. (Hansard, 1995).

An opponent of the scheme, responding to this argument two years later, remarked tartly that surely 'the curlews have been there since the beginning of the Holocene?'. The claims of military creationism appear in a number of circumstances. The biodiversity of the boundary area separating North and South Korea is celebrated as a consequence of the 4 km-wide Demilitarized Zone. This strategy not only attributes environmental diversity to military activities; it draws a connection between military activity and environmental protection. The MoD celebrated the sale of the former Purfleet Rifle Ranges at Rainham Marshes, East London, to the Royal Society for the Protection of Birds. Much of the area was a Site of Special Scientific Interest: 'MoD use has preserved this environmentally significant landscape during a period when so much similar marshland has been lost.' (Defence Estates, nd). The environmental qualities of the many US Department of Defense installations are celebrated in a similar fashion:

> DoD lands are found in many different habitats across the country and contain rich and varied natural and cultural resources. Limited access due to security considerations and the need for safety buffer zones have protected these resources for decades from development and other potentially damaging uses. (Boice, 1996, p.1).

There is humour in this apparent contradiction, which makes for a good story. 'Shrimps thrive on battlefield', announced a *Guardian* headline (2000); 'Rare fairy shrimps are thriving in the water-filled ruts made by army tanks on Salisbury Plain, Wiltshire'. For Shields, the very name Porton Down, Britain's chemical and biological defence establishment, 'still causes a frisson in the civilian mind, to judge by the number of two-headed rabbit jokes I endured before my visit' (Shields, 1996, p.92). Press releases from the MoD play on the paradox between environmental protection and military destruction; ' "Operation Newt" a Great Success' announced one (MoD, 2000c) 'When a gathering of amphibians made their home in a tank at RAF Fairford, it was all hands on deck for 'Operation Newt'. Great Crested Newts, a protected species, were discovered in a concrete emergency storage tank at RAF Fairford in Gloucestershire a fortnight before the Fairford International Air Tattoo. English Nature licensed the 'newt relocation' and 28 newts moved to new site. The *Times* newspaper celebrated Britain's Armed Forces as 'ecowarriors' after publication of the Strategic Environmental Appraisal of SDR in 2000.

These stories make good copy. They also serve military interests, in that they encourage us to look down at close range to small, protected creatures rather than focusing on the bigger picture which tells a more critical story about military activities and their impacts on the natural environment. Such stories also naturalize the military presence. A discourse of 'crater-as-habitat' – the phrase is Patrick Wright's – puts the practice and detritus of military activity to environmental uses:

> Because much Army land lies untouched by development, the plants flourish, the invertebrates prosper and the birds and mammals find ideal homes. Wildlife show remarkable tolerance of the noise of exercise battle. Pied Wagtails nest with equanimity under tank bridges, Barn Owls watch troop action from homes made out of surplus ammunition boxes, while rare bats roost the darkness of pillboxes. (HQ Land Command, 1995, p.15)

Detritus and pollution becomes matter in place, rather than matter out of place. Places become militarized through the naturalization of military remains within the ecology of a place. Patrick Wright reports an encounter and slide show with an MoD conservation officer which celebrates precisely that:

> [The Conservation Officer] declares his theme to be 'the interaction of wildlife and the military artefact', and, as the slides clatter by, it becomes clear that he relishes this as a story of paradoxical co-existence. Such is the MoD's version of the pastoral tradition, that, as its leading exponent, Colonel Baker likes nothing better than a picture of an ammunition case that has been turned into a breeding box for owls, or of a moorhen pecking at the fins of a mortar bomb stuck in the mud of a pool. (Wright, 1995, pp.358–9)

Discourses naturalize things: they define what is natural and what is not. This naturalizing strategy is not unique to the military, of course. For example, the environmental discourses of other groups or institutions similarly draws on such strategies to legitimize their activities and claims to space, often in the face of opposition. One example would be the use of 'green marketing' strategies to legitimize the corporate activities of the business sector, particularly through the promotion of industrial infrastructure or food products (see for example Bansal and Howard, 1997, Beder, 1997). Another would be the discourses deployed within British agriculture to construct farm wastes as a 'natural' output of agricultural activity bearing few risks for the natural environment, rather than as an environmental pollutant (Lowe et al., 1997). What is unique about the military is not the fact of this naturalizing strategy, but rather the basic material entities or evidence used to construct this strategy.

This discourse of crater-as-habitat naturalizes the detritus of military activities by portraying it as part of the natural environment. Wright, in his encounter with the MoD conservation officer reports that:

while conceding that conservation may have started as an accidental 'spin-off' from training [the Conservation Officer] is not content to rest with this passive idea of benign neglect. The 'interface' between military training and conservation can be managed in a way that provides benefits on both sides. Fallen trees, if left to lie, provide good cover for riflemen as well as for beetles and fungi. Soldiers train for surveillance duties in Northern Ireland by guarding the nests of red kites in Mid-Wales and ospreys in the Scottish Highlands. (Wright, 1995, p.359).

Wright is told about remedial work; this is widespread. For example, the Army's regiment of Gurkhas are reported in their efforts to 'hug a tree' to help the environment (Army, 1997). The emphasis in much military environmental discourse is on the compatibility of military training with environmental protection:

> The B-2 Stealth Bomber is one of the aircraft tested at Edwards Air Force Base, California, in the western Mojave. The light-coloured area on the ground below the B-2 is Rogers playa, a dry lake bed with a uniform, flat clay surface. Conservation of this natural feature is vital to Edwards' flight and testing mission because the playa provides vital landing areas for aircraft. (DoD undated, a, p.29)

Balance metaphors support these military environmental discourses. They imply a moderate course or compromise between competing objectives. They also imply the possibility of balance; they bring together what many would regard as two fundamentally oppositional ideas – environmental protectionism and militarism – to argue that equivalence between these two interests is attainable. The Integrated Land Management Plan for the Salisbury Plain Training Area, discussed above, rests conceptually on the possibility of this balance of interests. The ILMP:

> provides a holistic approach to land management by ensuring that all land uses and interests are considered as part of one document. The process of integrated land management planning provides a means of fully integrating military activities with other land uses, such as nature conservation, cultural heritage, agriculture, forestry, landscape and recreational interests and provides a framework for resolving potentially conflicting objectives. It creates a mechanism for optimal planning of military activities and allows the long term sustainability of new training activities to be assessed. (Defence Estates, 2001c, p.3)

The Defence Minister's comments on the launch of the original ILMP stress this balance too, by the press release's headline – 'Conserving the Balance' – and by the ideas expressed therein:

> Farming, hill forts, stone curlews, butterflies, chalk downland – Salisbury Plain has them all and more. Above all, however, the training estate has to

meet the ever-increasing demands of training our forces for the difficult and
dangerous jobs we ask them to do, such as they are currently doing with
distinction in Sierra Leone. (MoD, 2000d, p.1)

The balance metaphor similarly underpins successive Army publications –
Striking a Balance – on the management of their training estate (HQ Land
Command, 1995, 1997, 1998). The emphasis in US Department of Defense commentaries is also very much on a balance between military and
environmental concerns:

> Today, DoD strives to apply wise conservation practices to ensure that natural
> resources are not degraded from overuse. Through co-ordinated planning
> among military trainers and installation operators, DoD is identifying ways to
> eliminate potential conflicts between different land uses. Where the principles
> of natural resources management are being integrated with the goals of the
> military mission, revenue-generating activities, public access, resource protec-
> tion, scientific studies, and intensive military training may all be occurring
> within the boundaries of a single installation.' (DoD, undated a, p.2)

Indeed, the balance metaphor is central to military environmental discourses. Military land management is presented as the pursuit of compromise between two sets of interests. The idea of balance also implies
possibility of balance, that such an equivalence is attainable, that finding
and equal weighting between two interests is feasible. Accordingly, the
balance metaphor understands and presents military training and environmental protection as conceptually equal; like is being balanced with like. An
implication of this is that weighing up military activity and conservation is
possible on the same set of scales; that the two originate from a unified set
of objectives. The possibility that environmental protection and preparation for war might reside in quite fundamentally opposed moral orders is
denied, removed from the debate through the use of the balance metaphor
(Woodward, 2001b). See, for example, the US Deputy Under-Secretary for
Defense (Environmental Security)'s comments in a forward to a *Commander's Guide to Biodiversity*:

> As a critical element of ecosystem management, biodiversity conservation
> contributes directly to military readiness. Biodiversity helps us achieve mili-
> tary readiness in harmony with nature. (DoD, undated b, npn)

Administrative Rationalism

The above discussion has illustrated through examples how discourses of
military environmentalism work, and has suggested outcomes of these

strategies. I now turn to look at what underpins these strategies.[4] Administrative rationalism is foundational, in that it defines what environmental protection and conservation are all about, what they are and are not, and sets the terms of debate about the environmental impact of military land uses. The discussion of administrative rationalism which follows draws on the case study of the Otterburn Training Area, where developments were proposed in 1995 to enable heavy artillery (AS90 and Multiple Launch Rocket Systems) to train on this upland area, which is located almost entirely within the Northumberland National Park. The Otterburn Public Inquiry (OPI), conducted in 1997 and 1999, provided a forum for the proponents of the scheme (the MoD) and the opponents (the local planning authority) to debate the issue. The OPI is a significant moment in British military land use history because of the extent to which military controls over land uses were challenged. The OPI provided in microcosm all the debates about the use and control of land in the UK by the armed forces for military purposes. Chapters 5 and 6 discuss the OPI in terms of what it revealed about strategies for the representation of landscape and the challenging of control of military lands. Here, it is used to illustrate how British military environmental discourses operate.

The concept of a discourse of administrative rationalism is taken from John Dryzek's typology of environmental discourses, their forms and their functions, of which administrative rationalism is one (Dryzek, 1997). Dryzek defines administrative rationalism in environmental protection as a discursive strategy primarily of governments. Such discourses define environmental debates and disputes in terms which emphasize conflicts as problems to be solved (rather than, for example, symptoms of irreconcilable differences), where the role of the state rather than the citizen in achieving a solution to a dispute is prioritized, in a social context imagined as hierarchical. For Dryzek, the essence of discourses of administrative rationalism in conservation can be captured by examining the actual practices in the development of policies, institutions and methodologies, rather than in the words of theorists and activists. The social practices where administrative rationalism in conservation is manifest include professional resource-management bureaucracies, pollution control agencies, regulatory policy instruments, environmental impact assessment, expert advisory commissions and rationalistic policy analysis techniques:

> The essence of administrative rationalism can be found in the discursive 'software' that unites these six items around a common purpose. As a problem-solving discourse, administrative rationalism takes the political-economic status-quo of liberal capitalism as given. It then puts scientific and technical expertise, organized into bureaucratic hierarchy, motivated by

the public interest, to use in solving environmental problems without changing the structural status quo. (Dryzek, 1997, p.76)

Military environmentalist discourses, I would argue, are essentially discourses bearing the hallmarks of administrative rationalism. Dryzek suggests that discourses of administrative rationalism can be assessed in terms of four aspects: basic entities recognized or constructed; assumptions about natural relationships; agents and their motives; and key metaphors and other rhetorical devices. In order to illustrate the close equation between military environmentalism and administrative rationalism, and examine some of the consequences of this, in the remainder of this section I examine these four aspects of administrative rationalism with reference to a range of examples taken from the public debate conducted at the Otterburn Public Inquiry (OPI). The point here is not to test the adequacy of the fit between Dryzek's schema and military environmentalist discourses, but rather to seek at a theoretical level some explanation for the military environmentalist discourses that are used by the Army and MoD to define what environmental protection and conservation are all about.

Basis entities recognized or constructed

For Dryzek (1997), administrative rationalism assumes a context of liberal capitalism. Environmental policies constitute an intervention within that status quo. There is a strong conception of government as the administrative state, with the function of government being the rational management of resources, in the public interest. My argument is that public statements produced by the MoD during the OPI reveal how a case (for the developments) was constructed with these basic entities in mind. Government is taken as the manager of a resource (the Otterburn Training Area), within a framework set down by government policy:

> The defence estate . . . is ultimately held in trust for the nation. MoD recognises the duty to conserve the environment of Ranges and Training Areas in accordance with Government policy. (Otterburn AFTC, 1993, p.84)

That rational management of resources was presented as a process which had determined a specified pattern of uses for existing military training areas; great weight was attached to an exposition of the process using language to suggest that this had been careful, rational and efficient. Furthermore, claims put by opponents to the MoD that an alternative pattern of land uses might be possible, which might suggest that the OTA could be used for activities other than military live firing, were dismissed on the grounds of the rationality of the MoD's planning process for the use of military training areas. In the MoD's case at the Otterburn Public Inquiry, we can also see how Government was taken as the arbiter of the public interest. A consistent line of argument presented by the MoD was that it was in the public interest to permit the developments to proceed. Policy statements such as Planning Policy Guidance Note 7 (on land use in England's rural areas) were interpreted as supportive of an argument that developments should be permitted in National Parks where there is a demonstrated need, an absence of alternatives and where it is in the public interest to allow such developments to proceed. That public interest was defined, repeatedly, as the need for a national defence capability, rather than a less significant public interest in the protection of designated landscapes. Furthermore, that definition was promoted by an organization (the MoD) which argued that, as an arm of government, weight should be attached to its definition of public interest.

Dryzek also argues that another basic entity recognized or constructed in discourses of administrative rationalism are experts and managers, which the state denotes as providing the best expertise within the administrative monolith to advise on environmental issues. During the Otterburn Public Inquiry, continual reference was made by the MoD to the weight to be attached to the opinions of experts (i.e. consultants employed by the MoD, and serving Army officers) in contrast to the opinions of those appearing at the inquiry in a voluntary or nonprofessional capacity (e.g. local residents, or representatives of voluntary organizations). Similarly, the absence of objections to the MoD's proposals for the Otterburn Training Area by 'experts' from statutory bodies such as English Nature and the Environment Agency were accorded great weight in the MoD's arguments.

Assumptions about natural relationships

Dryzek argues that although administrative rationalism is not explicitly concerned with the fundamental character of relationships between human and nonhuman worlds, one assumption within administrative rationalist discourses is that nature is subordinated to human problem-solving. The environment cannot be left itself, but has to be managed, ordered, and conflicts solved through human interference; humans are the appropriate stewards of the natural environment. A clear example of this assumption about natural relationships from within the MoD and Army comes from a strategic estate management plan for the Otterburn Training Area, which gives an indication of the conceptualization of human/environmental relationships in reference to which conservation is defined:

Environment includes not just the natural environment (which in any case is only at best semi-natural due to the influence of man) but also the man-made features of historic importance. Conservation should not be regarded as preservation i.e. protection from damage, but comprises pro-active management to enhance the value of the environment. (Otterburn AFTC, 1993, p.84)

The definition of conservation given here describes it as active engagement with the land. Protection of the natural environment, in this framework, is a dynamic human activity. The existence of diverse natural habitats is not the function of land left to its own devices, but rather a consequence of human engagement with the land. This definition of conservation, which prioritizes human engagement, allows nature to be given a helping hand as a matter of course. This discourse allows even quite extreme practices, such as the creation of shell craters, to be incorporated within the definition of conservation. The implication is that natural landscapes can't survive without any kind of human interference, be it intervention through Environmental Steering Groups, Integrated Land Management Plans, Conservation Management Plans and black grouse monitoring projects, or through a broader block on other land uses through the very presence of the Army in that space. Again, this is not a view unique to the Army; Grint (1997) identifies a similar portrayal of conservation within business, reflecting a traditional Western approach to nature where, without human control, nature cannot be exploited for human benefit and where nature itself is viewed as an anarchic formation with no rightful place in the properly ordered world. Ideas of what is 'right' and 'proper' are both translated into material practices and also reflect the construction of how the natural world is.

For Dryzek, another assumption of administrative rationalism in terms of natural relationships concerns two complementary hierarchies. In the first, people are subordinated to the state. At Otterburn, this was evident in discussions about the unassailable importance of military training, in contrast with the relative (and by implication lesser) importance accorded to the rights of the individual over the territory of that state for recreation and related purposes. The second hierarchy prioritizes experts and managers above the citizen (as we have already seen); for Dryzek, implicit within this hierarchy is the denial of the existence of politics, i.e. a denial of the basic contestability of these hierarchies and the views expressed therein. At the Otterburn Public Inquiry, for example, an attempt by a local resident to widen the debate on the value of Environmental Impact Assessments by submitting an academic paper on the topic, was dismissed as irrelevant to proceedings. The paper, an examination of the politics of Environmental Impact Assessment by Sharon Beder (1993), was itself dismissed as 'a rather unpleasant article' by the MoD's barrister during the OPI and discounted on account of its 'political' nature.

Agents and their motives

The significant agents in administrative rationalism are representatives of the state – again, the experts. For Dryzek (1997), in administrative rationalism, the discovery and application of the public interest is a technical procedure. For this reason, significant weight is attached to techniques such as cost-benefit analysis, landscape assessment procedures and environmental impact evaluations. At the Otterburn Public Inquiry, for example, evidence indicating that a type of rocket used in MLRS training could produce a toxic efflux of potential danger to the natural environment, was dismissed by the MoD on the grounds that expert opinion from both external consultants and from the Government's statutory advisers on environmental issues had concluded that the efflux was safe. A similar technique was used to counter objections on the noise effects of the Apache helicopter.

Key metaphors and other rhetorical devices

Dryzek notes that administrative rationalism, unlike other environmental discourses, has a muted rhetoric and little in the way of grandiose claims. Environmental problems are recognized as existing, but are there to be solved in isolation, not understood as sufficiently serious to warrant fundamental changes in the way in which society is organized. So, for example, MoD evidence to the Otterburn Public Inquiry placed great emphasis on allaying concerns about the environmental impacts of the use of heavy artillery live firing in a National Park by first offering recognition that those concerns existed, and by then putting forward a range of mitigating measures to be undertaken to ensure that those impacts would not then take place. The idea that the concerns about environmental impacts could be serious enough to warrant a rejection of the MoD's proposals was dismissed or sidelined with reassurances on the effectiveness of existing policy and legislation in countering any potentially harmful environmental effects.

Military Control and the Natural Environment

In conclusion, what are the features of military control over the natural environment? Where does power and control lie? What conceptual frameworks do we need to unravel the practices and politics of military environmentalism? Again, as with the preceding chapters, I would argue that there are four significant areas where we need to look. There is the fact of physical presence, the ability of military forces to shape, preserve, enhance or destroy natural environments merely by being there. The fact of environmental change, for better or worse, as a result of military engagement follows from this. This is a significant area for research in its own right. There is also, secondly the issue of information availability, what is known and not known about military impacts. Despite the growing number of case studies of military environmental impacts around the world in nonconflict situations, the paucity of accurate data from military sources remains an issue. Third, there are issues of governance and the policy frameworks put in place to manage military impacts on the natural environment, and issues about their efficacy. Fourth, there is control over the natural environment as a discursive or representational practice. These discourses are significant in how they contribute to military definitions of 'security' and 'defence'. The greening of military activities, which these discursive strategies represent, is problematic because this process obscures the idea that military activities themselves are environmentally damaging. There may be an issue of degree between the damage caused by warfare and the damage caused in preparation for military action, but my point is to assert that military activities in many different ways cause damage to the natural environment, an issue obscured through the military 'greenwash'. The consequences of this, articulated with passion by Ross, are worrying. He views the 'greening of the Pentagon' as part of a wider agenda establishing environmental security as a new doctrinal cornerstone for the US defence establishment, in compensation for the loss of the old Cold War enemies. For Ross:

> In its attempts to identify a new global enemy in the existence of environmental 'threats', the Defense establishment displays yet again its structural need for all forms of planetary life to mirror its own bellicose mentality. Risk assessment, among other things, is emerging as the new managerial language for preserving this mentality. If the Pentagon succeeds in its kinder, gentler mission, it may result not in the greening of the military but in the militarization of greening. (Ross, 1996, p.44)

According to this argument, the development of ideas of environmental security divert attention from the military's complicity in environmental destruction. Others have argued for a more nuanced interpretation and approach to the issue of environmental security, concerned with the implications for international security of environmental damage and resource scarcity, and with the military agendas developed in response to such threats (see Homer-Dixon 1991,1999; Käkönen, 1994; Parkin, 1997; Le Billon, 2001; Dalby, 2002). This literature suggests, as this chapter does, that military control is exerted not only through material practices which affect the natural environment, but also through discursive or representational practices through which those material practices are made meaningful. The study of militarized environments requires attention to both.

Chapter Five

Military Landscapes

The Power of Military Landscapes

The poet and author Robert Graves, recuperating at the end of the 1914–18 war from wounds received during active service in the trenches, reflected in his autobiography on how his military training in the tactical reading of terrain still influenced how he viewed landscapes:

> When strong enough to climb the hill behind Harlech and revisit my favourite country, I could not help seeing it as a prospective battlefield. I would find myself working out tactical problems, planning how best to hold the Upper Artro valley against an attack from the sea, or where to place a Lewis-gun if I were trying to rush Dolwreiddiog Farm from the brow of the hill, and what would be the best cover for my rifle-grenade section. (Graves, 1929, p.235)

This chapter is about this military imagination of landscape. It considers, first, how the soldier is trained to see the landscape, and how techniques for doing so are inculcated into the recruit during training. It then goes on to look at how armed forces imagine the landscape. I look at readings of military landscapes produced by the passive exercise of being there. I then look at how armed forces themselves image landscapes through the process of representation of landscape for military purposes. The chapter finishes by looking at the process of military landscape representation as constitutive of wider ideas, using the examples of gender and national identity in the construction of military landscapes.

Seeing it Like a Soldier

Robert Graves acquired a habit for viewing landscapes through the lens of fieldcraft. Fieldcraft is the art of survival in the battlefield; it is about reading the land in a specific way. That way of reading the land prompts a reaction in the soldier, trained to a degree that it becomes automatic. Fieldcraft is about military manoeuvres in the field, and these represent a military method for the construction and interpretation of landscapes, for practical purposes.

Fieldcraft involves the acquisition and deployment of low-level tactics and survival skills. Fieldcraft is about the activities which we immediately recognize as 'soldiering', through their representation in countless war films; the patrol moving silently through woodland is a classic movie image. Fieldcraft is about camouflage, concealment and moving without being detected, blending in to the landscape. Fieldcraft is about being able to read the landscape. The Common Military Syllabus (Recruits), the British Army's syllabus for all recruits undergoing Phase I Basic Training, sets out the skills that fieldcraft training develops: map reading, judging distance, static observation, mobile observation, camouflage, concealment, stalking. This, alongside complementary skills in terrain analysis and orienteering, requires the development of new skills to read a landscape:

> You'll learn camouflage techniques and have your first taste of night training. That means using your eyes and ears in a different way – exploring how to identify noises at night, and how to see more clearly using off-centre vision. On your first night exercise, you and your battle partner operate in a buddy/buddy team. You'll build a shelter which you'll sleep in, you'll cook your rations, and look out for each other. (ARG, undated, npn).

The recruit, depending on his or her chosen career group, will go on to develop these skills during special-to-arms training, with different careers requiring different levels of familiarity with fieldcraft techniques.

Those going on to join infantry regiments will hone these skills to a fine art, learning to read the landscape tactically, seeing instead of hills and hedges, dead ground and cover.[1] They are trained in what to look for, how to describe it to fellow patrol members, and how to neutralize the threat. A mnemonic device is used-'GRIT'-to communicate the identification of enemy features in the landscape, a template for descriptions passed between one patrol member and another of the terrain under evaluation. GRIT stands for Group (i.e. which group is to fire); Range (the distance in metres to the object or feature); Indication (a prominent object or feature identified as a reference point) and Type (i.e. of fire). This is a method of reading landscape, breaking it down into constituent parts, a necessary technique for exerting military control over space during military action.

Gillian Rose (1993) has argued that 'a landscape's meanings draw on the cultural codes of the society for which it was made' (p.89). The cultural codes of the military ascribe whole new meanings to the landscape. Adam Ballinger, in his account of the selection process for the SAS, describes how recruits are trained in new ways of reading the landscape. The soldier's perception of the countryside is changed by that experience:

> We were taught perspective, to train our eyes and search for a focal point. We had to scan the landscape and pick out the dominant features, just as an artist would peer ever deeper trying to unravel colours. Like the painter who is restricted by the size of his canvas, we were constrained by our arcs of reference. We were also instructed in interpretation: countryside became terrain, rolling hills became gradients that slow down one's progress across country, wild hedgerows became camouflage, mountain streams became obstacles and sources of water. (Ballinger, 1992, p.129)

They are taught to see the landscape in three dimensions, to understand its relationship to two-dimensional representations in map form, and to understand how the various elements of a specified area interlock (see Figure 5.1). Stephen Ambrose (1992) in his account of a US Airborne division's experiences during the 1939–45 war, describes their training experiences prior to the invasion of mainland Europe in 1944:

> Once a week or so they went out on a two- or three-day exercise. The problems were designed not only to give them a working knowledge of the mechanics of combat but to teach the most basic thing an infantryman has to know: how to love the ground, how to use it to advantage, how the terrain dictates tactics, above all how to live on it and in it for days at a time without impairment of physical efficiency. Their officers stressed the importance of such things, that it would make the difference between life and death, that the men must do it instinctively right the first time, as there would not be a second.
>
> So the men of Easy [Company] got to know the English countryside. They attacked towns, hills, and woods. They dug countless foxholes, and slept in them, learning how to do it despite rain and cold and hunger. (Ambrose, 1992, p.46).

This military reading of landscape is a rationalistic one, possibly even a masculinist one where seeing and knowing are conflated (WGSG, 1997). Once understood, the features are renamed; hills and streams become barriers, hedges turn into hideouts.

This way of seeing is trained into soldiers; as Robert Graves pointed out it becomes habitual. Mike Bell, in his study of 'Childerley', a village in

Figure 5.1   Reading the Landscape. Copyright: Army Training and Recruiting Agency.

southern England, describes how an ex-soldier with experience of active service in Cyprus, Northern Ireland and Algeria points out the landscape around the village in terms of military manoeuvres, strategy and tactics:

> Tom thinks about the land with this same military imagination. In our conversation where he described his photographic memory for 'the lay of the land', he went on to say, 'I quite often go down the back of the woods in our place. And I just have a walk around, and that. Quite often I stand there and think, well, this is a good tank position. Its all clicking in.' He pointed to his head. 'You know, I need to move that wood a bit or put a hedge in there, like [to make it perfect]. You can go from A to B there. I always look at it from a fighting position.' . . . As he said himself, 'Eighteen years in the bloody tanks, you get to look at these positions . . . Its bred into us. Bullied into us, you might want to call it. You still look at the land like that. (Bell, 1994, pp.216–17)

Terrain analysis – the study of land forms and landscapes for strategic and tactical military objectives – is also one of Military Geography's key areas of concern (see, for example, O'Sullivan, 1991).

Military readings of landscape are consolidated through the process of mapping. There is an existing literature on the politics of the representation of territory and landscape through maps, and I won't revisit it here (see

Monmonier, 1995 and Black, 1997, for an introduction). We should remember, though, that the very history of cartography is bound up with the history of military-led imperial expansion. Maps were prepared for and by armed forces to aid military campaigns in the service of global expansion. The tools and techniques of mapmaking and graphic description have long been developed to serve the military requirement for accurate maps. The British Ordnance Survey was founded for military purposes, as its name implies. This tradition continues through to the GIS techniques developed over the past 20 years to represent shifting conflict and contact zones to battlefield commanders. Indeed, one interpretation of the idea of a 'revolution in military affairs', a descriptor of contemporary techniques of warfighting, is of a revolution in technologies allowing commanding officers to 'see' the battlefield and its changes in real time through sophisticated graphical and mapping techniques. Whatever their form, maps are essential to military campaigns: 20 million maps were printed for use by British forces during Operation Granby, the British Army's engagement in the first Gulf War (Hodson and Gordon, 1997).

These military readings of landscape are about the domination of space. They are about the representation of physical three-dimensional space in order to serve tactical and strategic military purposes. The military readings discussed so far are about the tools of landscape reading and representation for use at the sharp end of soldiering. The military reading and interpretation of landscape is also a representational strategy for more general use in legitimizing a military presence, and I go on now to discuss domestic examples of this from nonconflict situations.

Reading the Iconography of Military Landscapes

Militaries and military activities construct landscapes to support claims to territory, to define places as legitimate locations for soldiering, to prioritize particular land uses over others. Military control is exerted through the representation of landscapes, the narratives developed in order to describe the view to others, and to assert the legitimacy of that view. Military landscapes in this sense refers to the ideas and politics behind military readings of physical features and their purposes.

Military activities will always scratch their marks on the surface of the earth, and these, it seems, are always of interest to us as a means of understanding military invasions and defences. Our interest is institutionalized in the statutory protection granted to castles as ancient monuments and other listed military structures, and expressed in our desires to visit these sites. I won't examine here the ways in which landscapes as physical forms have been changed by military intervention, and I will not be documenting the physical remains of landscapes of defence.[2] Be aware, though, of the sheer scale of historic military remains across the landscape of the British Isles. For example, the threat of German invasion of Britain in 1940 caused a rapid transformation of the English landscape, with 20 percent of the UK land surface controlled by the Armed Forces; 'there was not one square foot of land that was not subject to some detailed defence scheme' (Foot, 2001). Taken literally, this may be hyperbole, but the sentiment is indicative of the profound nature of changes brought by defensive actions:

> To meet this peril the country was being transformed – its fields stuck with stakes, its signposts disarmed, its milestones buried, its church bells silenced, its skies cleansed of racing pigeons, kites and fireworks, its key bridges and beaches mined, its piers cut in two, its ancient trees felled to clear firing arcs, its headlands capped with concrete pill-boxes, its vacant corners filled with static water tanks. (Turner, 2002, p.13).

The armed forces, the country's protector, shaped its countryside at a time of real invasion fears. The Armed Forces continue to do so in peacetime, moulding and imprinting itself across space, and providing explanations for these activities.

It is that process of explanation that is of primary interest here; the inscription of marks onto the earth's surface is taken as given. What I'm interested in in this next section is military landscapes as *iconic* in nature; 'there exist specific icons which symbolize for us (or symbolized for our forebears) military defence and which have a meaning which goes much further than their overt presence' (Tivers, 1999, p.303). Military landscapes are iconic, in that they have a symbolism or meaning beyond that which is indicated by just physical presence. They can be read or interpreted for their meanings. Military landscapes, Jacky Tivers argues, are texts to be read, and her analysis deserves repeating here not only for her observations but also as an indicator of a suitable methodology for reading military landscapes. She draws on an iconographical approach to landscapes, which aims to 'probe meaning by associating specific icons with their spatial contexts and analyzing ideas implicated in their imagery' (p.308).

The military landscape under Tivers' gaze is that of Aldershot, 'The Home of the British Army', a large military establishment on the shared border of the English counties of Hampshire and Surrey. It was established in the 1850s on infertile sandy heath and common land. It is currently the Aldershot Garrison of Fourth Division of the Army, with additional basic training located at Pirbright. Tivers' analysis homes in on the markers in the landscape which give it meaning, acting as identifiers of military status and encouraging the iconic construction of the landscape as one of military defence. Defensive features acquire iconic status and may have different representations at different times – medieval castles and World War Two pillboxes become heritage features, for example. Markers also can lose their iconic status by disappearing (by becoming overgrown with vegetation) or by being accepted and forgotten, not seen; there is a specificity in time to these readings of landscape.

An iconographic reading of the military landscape of Aldershot is possible in different ways, and will differ according to affiliation within or outside the military camp. Tivers explores these readings and meanings using David Ley's (1983) existential dimensions of meaning; places, for Ley, are experienced 'as a multidimensional topography of meaning' (p.145). Ley arranges these dimensions of meaning around three polarities: regions of security/regions of stress, regions of stimulus/regions of ennui, and regions of status/regions of stigma. These dimensions of meaning may refer to different locations, and also as different perceptions of places by different groups. To this Tivers adds perceptions of different (polarized) viewpoints held by various individuals and groups in military defence areas. For these are contested landscapes.

A landscape of military defence is (unsurprisingly) a 'region of security'. The armed forces are associated with the security of the nation state, and Aldershot's associations are of itself as the 'Home of the British Army'; home has both a national and an individual domestic context. Living on a patrolled, gated, fenced army base gives a dimension of safety. Yet this is polarized with the same landscape as a potential region of stress, which military defence landscapes can be, with the ceaseless movement of personnel and families, fear of attacks with the military as a target, and the stress of living in, and proximal to, soldier culture with its noise, rowdiness and drunkenness; national insecurity and local instability. A landscape of military defence also constructs meaning through regions of stimulus and its polar opposite, ennui. Stimulus comes from the constant movement of regiments, the excitement of army life (portrayed in recruitment posters throughout the twentieth century). Ennui appears through the isolation of soldiers and their families, the exclusion of outsiders, the uniformity of housing and environment, the lack of opportunities for wives and children, and restrictions inside and outside camps for personnel. A landscape of military defence is also a region of status. Whether a military presence adds status and benefit to an area is of course open to debate. It may bring social status and a social network. These may also be regions of stigma, associated with the means of violence and destruction, firing, pollution and contamination. Tivers concludes by reflecting on the representation of these landscapes: 'Military defence landscapes, like all landscapes, are representational; they may be used to reinforce ideology with little direct relationship to any actual threat. Even the word 'defence' itself is representational.'

(Tivers, 1999, p.317). It is to these representations and their politics that I'll now turn.

Military Representation as a Strategic Act

The military representation of landscape for 'external consumption', for the purposes of legitimizing the military control of space, is a strategy used to justify and explain military activities. The military representation of landscape is a political act. Examples abound; see, for instance, Baker's (1993) readings of the meanings of the Berlin Wall, the meanings bound up in 1914–18 war cemeteries (for example, Heffernan, 1995; Winter, 1995; Morris, 1997), or readings of the Nevada nuclear testing ranges (Johnson and Beck, 1995; Kirsch, 1997; Kuletz, 1998; Uzzell, 1998; Johnson, 2002). The meanings attached to military landscapes for the purposes of legitimizing the military presence were clearly discernible in the course of the public debate over the future of the Otterburn Training Area, and it is these representations which are my focus here.

The Otterburn Training Area covers 22,908 ha of open moorland in Northumberland, England's most northerly county. This place is many things. It is an area of upland moorland, rough pasture and wooded valley, coloured according to the seasons in muted browns, greens, golds and mauves and shades of white. It is a protected area, lying almost wholly within the boundaries of the Northumberland National Park, of which it makes up 22 percent. It is a place of extensive agriculture where 31 farms, scattered across the landscape, rent land under special tenancies mostly for 28,000 sheep and some cattle. It is a place where single-track metalled and stone roads weave off into the distance over the undulating moor. It is a place for bird watching, for ecologists interested in mires, for seekers of prehistoric and Roman remains in the landscape. It is a place for hill-walkers searching thigh-straining hikes up peaty hills.

The Otterburn Training Area is also a significant space for military training. It is one of the British Army's eight Army Field Training Centres and is an essential location for the British Army's preparations for war. It is a place where heavy artillery can train, firing live shells and rockets into the enormous impact areas without threat to human life. It is also a place for live firing training using small arms, training in the use of pyrotechnics, training in survival and orientation activities, low flying and parachute training. About 30,000 soldiers train there each year, troops from Britain and NATO allies. It is a place where public access is highly restricted in some areas, confined to specified rights of way and permissive footpaths and limited to the times when live firing is not taking place. Red flags snap in the breeze when the guns are out.

Figure 5.2   Otterburn Training Area, Northumberland, 1997. Copyright: Joe Painter.

The OTA is also, unsurprisingly, a place of conflict over military land uses. Reconciling the needs of a National Park with those of a military training area was never going to be easy. Military training in national parks has been contentious issue since the national parks were established in the 1940s and 1950s. The Northumberland National Park was established in 1956. The OTA had developed from a modest 7,600 hectares, bought by the War Office in 1911 allegedly after the landowner Lord Redesdale suffered a poor day's grouse shooting with Winston Churchill. The military training area was included in the National Park when the latter was designated. As with Dartmoor and the Pembrokeshire Coast National Parks, the co-existence of military training and environmental protection is an uneasy one at times, not least for the passions both military preparation and environmental protection stir in people (see MacEwan and MacEwan, 1982, 1987; Blacksell and Reynolds, 1987). Over this significant and symbolic site, there has long been a muted debate between those prioritizing preparations for war and those wanting protection of a valued landscape, but the park authorities have always accepted and worked with the Army.

The story of this particular debate starts in 1992 with an announcement in Parliament that the Otterburn Training Area would be developed for training using heavy tracked artillery systems (Hansard, 1992). The north German heathlands, where since 1945 a British military presence had lived and trained in expectation of attack from the East, were no longer required following the collapse of the Soviet Union and British forces were under pressure to return the Soltau Lüneburg training area to the German government. The heavy artillery units – the AS90 and Multiple Launch Rocket System (MLRS) would return home, to be based in the UK. The Artillery System 90 (AS90) is a 45 ton tracked self-propelled artillery system, and the Multiple Launch Rocket System (MLRS) is a 25 ton system for the launch of up to 12 rockets at a time, each with a range of up to 30 km. But where could they train?

By 1992, expanded to 22,908 ha, the OTA provided unparalleled facilities for artillery training using MLRS and AS90. Other Army Field Training Centres in the UK were either too small, or already used to maximum capacity by other uses. Otterburn seemed perfect. There was one problem, though. The AS90 and MLRS rely for their force on their firepower (not for nothing is MLRS advertised by its manufacturers as 'the force multiplier') and their ability to manoeuvre quickly out of harm's way to avoid incoming retaliatory fire. They shoot and scoot. The Otterburn Training Area consists of peat moorland. The AS90 and MLRS are very heavy. Despite being tracked, if driven on free manoeuvres across the peat, they would quickly become sitting targets, bogged down in the mire. The space of Otterburn was perfect for heavy artillery training, but the make-up of its ground surface was not. Infrastructure would be needed to enable the regiments to train in firing and quick manoeuvre, infrastructure such as better, wider, metalled and stone roads, and hardened gun spurs on which to park up and fire (Doxford and Savege, 1995). The National Park Authority started to get uneasy.

In 1995, the proposals were published (MoD, 1995a and b). The press couldn't resist the clichés. 'Army Fires Off First Salvo in the Battle of Otterburn', said The *Newcastle Journal* (11 April 1995). 'Retreating Army Targets National Park for Big-gun Training', said the *Independent on Sunday* (11 April 1995). Revised in the light of consultation, the final plans, contained in a Notice of Proposed Development were submitted to the local planning authority, Northumberland County Council (MoD, 1996a). Gun spurs would be built to accommodate the AS90s and MLRS rocket launchers whilst firing into the impact area. Of these, 5 existed at Otterburn already, 17 would be modifications of existing hardstandings and 24 would be new constructions. Those to be used by two guns (34 in all) would measure around 35 m by 25 m. A further 12 gun spurs would be larger (56.5 m by 25 m) to accommodate three guns simultaneously. Four of the existing gun spurs would be large enough to accommodate six or more guns without modification. Gun spurs would be constructed of dark coloured stone aggregate. The gun spurs were to be grouped into six Gun Deployment Areas (GDAs) – Alpha, Bravo-Charlie,

Delta, Echo, Foxtrot and Stewartshiels. Each GDA would also contain a Battery Echelon Area for ammunition resupply, maintenance and other support functions, with a circuit of track and a parking area concealed within woodland.

When manoeuvring between gun spurs, both artillery systems and their support vehicles would travel on the roads of the OTA. These are mostly single track and between 2.5 m and 3.5 m wide, and too narrow to accommodate some of the vehicles within an AS90 and MLRS regiment. Some 57.5 km of existing roads and tracks would be widened to either 4 m or 5 m, with an additional 1 m hardshoulder, and an additional 15.3 km of new stone track would be built. Of this, 3.1 km would form 18 Tactical Observation Post positions, consisting of a network of linked stone tracks along a ridge line overlooking the Redesdale South impact area. These would be used for target acquisition training. In order to train in the use of tactical observation, three Technical Observation Posts would be built in the northern part of the training area, again looking into the Redesdale impact area. These are effectively stone lay-bys measuring 40 m by 10 m. A 4.45 ha Central Maintenance Facility would be required next to Otterburn Camp for vehicle maintenance. Additional accommodation for 125 soldiers would be needed within the Otterburn Camp itself. The existing airfield would be used as a Regimental Replenishment Point for training in the resupply of stores under tactical conditions.

These, then, were the plans proposed by the MoD for the development of the Otterburn Training Area. They were contested by the local planning authority, by the National Park Authority, and by a number of amenity groups. I discuss the process of challenge to the MoD's proposals in the next chapter. Here, I focus on the military justifications for the use of Otterburn. A first public inquiry into the plans was held 1997, during which the Ministry of Defence, in support of the proposals, drew on a number of representations of landscape in order to support their case. Several strategies were used in order to do this (see Woodward, 1999 for a more detailed discussion of the following points).

The first strategy was to emphasize the importance of size. The preeminent quality of this upland landscape was held to be its sheer scale. This argument was developed by the MoD drawing on the observations of the late Brian Redhead, a journalist and broadcaster:

> The Northumberland National Park is a landscape of wide open spaces, where access is unrivalled and solitude easily found. Seventy per cent of it is open moorland. And yet it also contains the finest Roman monument in the land, the largest military training area in the north of England, and the biggest man-made lake and man-made forest in Europe. That is its majesty. It is rich in history and yet it feels as if its geography has not been tampered with. Every

inch of it has a story to tell, stories of Roman occupation, of Christian conversion, of border conflict. And every inch of it has been exploited, directly or indirectly. But it does not feel like that. It feels as it must have always felt with the clouds on the horizon and the wide sky. It is too large a landscape to be diminished by the activities upon it. (Redhead, 1995, quoted in MoD/R/3/1, 1997, p.7).

In the view of the MoD, presented by their landscape consultant, 'The quotation underlines the dominance and scale of the upland landscape which is such an important factor in assessing the effects of change.' (MoD/R/3/1, 1997, p.7).

The National Park, the military training area and the landscape are all, of course, large. My argument is that for the MoD, the sheer size of the area enabled them to develop an argument which denied that any infrastructure developments would have an adverse impact on the landscape, because of their relative sizes. 'What's a small gun spur when you've got 22,000 ha of moorland to play with?', quipped one MoD representative. The relative sizes of landscape and developments were used to construct a portrayal of landscape which facilitated military training. For example, two of the proposed gun spurs would not be intrusive

by virtue of their relatively small scale in the landscape.... Other factors which reduce their impact on views are the attractions of other more distant views away from the line of the road and the distractions of prominent features such as Henry's Wood which forms a conspicuous feature on the skyline. (MoD/R/3/1, 1997, pp.14–15).

The scale of the landscape would limit the impact of military training activities. Concerns that the flash and trace from artillery rockets would impact on walkers on footpaths near the training area were dismissed on the grounds of the 'breadth of the panorama from this elevation. The distraction would be short-lived and at a great distance.' (p.19). The landscape would be able to accommodate the changes brought by infrastructure developments.

A second strategy was the fragmentation of the landscape. The training area's landscape was portrayed as fragmented, a jigsaw of different types of areas combining into a unified whole. It was portrayed in terms which emphasized its variety 'ranging from wild open moorland in the northern uplands to wooded and enclosed farmland in south plateau slopes and valleys' (MoD/P/3, 1997, p.21). Criticisms of the infrastructure developments, that they would damage the integrity of the National Park, were countered with assertions that such generalizations overlooked '... the great variety of landscapes within the Parks and their different qualities and abilities to absorb development' (MoD/R/3/1, 1997, p.6). The north and south were different. For example:

The southern area is characterised by undulating topography where the plateau is incised by the river valleys, and a mixed land cover of moorland, woodland and farmland. It is also the main area of built development within OTA and incorporates the two military camps and the airfield. This type of landscape has the ability to absorb the scale of development which is proposed and plans for additional planting would increase this ability by reducing views of the infrastructure and enhancing the character of the landscape. (MoD/P/3, 1997, p.76)

A third strategy was the representation based on an understanding of landscape stressing its utility above its environmental and aesthetic values. Landscape was presented as something to be consumed by human visitors, preferably motor-borne. For example, the visual impact of two of the gun spurs would be reduced because:

> In views from the range roads the mobility of the viewer would also tend to reduce the impact of individual features and the lower eyeline sitting in a car would have the effect of reducing the vertical component of the infrastructure. (MoD/R/3/1, 1997, p.14)

In another example, the construction of Tactical Observation Posts would involve the construction of new tracks in open moorland in a National Park. The impact of this was played down. Topography would fragment views, only some of the road or track would be visible from any one point, and it 'would not be very visible' from lower elevations. 'However, the road/tracks would be relatively inconspicuous at this distance and military vehicles would appear as small (and camouflaged) features in the landscape' (MoD, 1995b, p.109). The impact of the developments was recognized only when there would be human observation of them. They would certainly have environmental impacts, but those on human visitors were represented as being more acute. In any case, the MoD argued, the affected area was already surrounded by evidence of military activity in the form of wire fences, red flags and road barriers. The developments would have an adverse impact on the character of the landscape, but the effect on views would be small, because of topography, ridge height and restrictions on public access.

The size, composition and utility of the Otterburn Training Area were all drawn on to develop the idea of the military as legitimate occupier of that space. Otterburn was also represented as a landscape with regional and national significance, a place unique to Britain because of the history of border warfare in the area between the English and Scots. This 'wild border landscape', the 'setting for Border raiders' and of 'the best-known of British narrative ballads' was represented by those opposing military infrastructure developments as an area of unique inheritance. A place of inhibited economic development due to feuds between Border farmer-thieves, so vividly described by Fraser (1971) had left a relict sixteenth-and seventeenth-century agricultural landscape surviving into the twentieth century, whilst the surrounding areas in northern England were now covered in forest plantations or intensive agriculture (NPC/P/1, 1997, p.7). The emphasis for both sides at the public inquiry was on very different cultural histories and the corresponding (and competing) interpretations of landscape which these histories supported. The Ministry of Defence laid emphasis on the history of the Otterburn area as the history of military land use:

> The War Office bought 19,000 acres [7,600 ha] of land in Redesdale in 1911 as an artillery range for the newly formed Territorial Army. Horse drawn artillery batteries came from all over Britain by train to West Woodburn and marched up Dere Street (now the A68) to camp in tents and huts near High Rochester (Bremenium), just as the Roman Legions had done in Hadrian's time.... The tramp of armed marching men has long been a familiar sound in these Border hills. For 300 years Roman soldiers controlled the country between Hadrian's Wall and the Antonine Wall in Scotland, using a network of roads, marching camps and forts begun in about AD80.(MoD and NNP, undated, npn)

In contrast, the Council for National Parks emphasized a much longer chronicle of human occupation and the inscriptions which successive generations had carved onto the land.

Ultimately, for the Ministry of Defence, Otterburn was a military place of national significance, essential for meeting national defence needs, for meeting readiness states required under NATO commitments, and essential for enhancing the operational capabilities of the Royal Artillery:

> We do not expect anyone to deny this nor do we expect it to become an issue, because failure to be properly trained in the use of these weapons means greater difficulties in succeeding in military conflict objectives and more causalities. The proposals now being put forward... are to enable those who use, and will use, these weapons to be fully and properly trained with the weapons and to be at required readiness states. So we say that the development proposals are of the highest national importance and self-evidently in the public interest. I say that this is beyond argument. (I/MoD/ 1, 1997, p.2)

The representations constructed by the Army and MoD of Otterburn were deliberate and strategic, developed with the explicit intent of consolidating their case for the construction of physical infrastructure to support military training in this protected area. The readings and representations of Otterburn were unique to that site but the strategic act of representation is not.

I shall discuss in greater detail in Chapter 6 the challenges to military readings of landscapes. The rest of this chapter moves the discussion of representation forward by considering in more detail the ideas bound up in specific representations of landscape. The ideas that are implicit within military representations consolidate those representations.

Military Landscapes and Identity

Implicit within military representations of landscape are ideas about identity. Here, I focus specifically on gender and nationhood as aspects of identity bound up in the act of landscape representation. In the case of gender, ideas about gendered identity are embodied in the process of representation through the development of the soldier. In the case of ideas about nationhood, ideas about national identity provide a driving force in the legitimization of military representations of landscape through the provision of wider cultural narratives about collective nationhood.

Gender identities

Military landscapes are places where the identities of soldiers are forged; these identities, what it means to be a soldier, as I have argue elsewhere, are not innate but rather are made. They are gendered, in that they incorporate ideas about what it means to be a man or a woman. And these gendered military identities are made with reference to military landscapes, physical spaces constructed and represented by armed forces as the location and context for the development of the soldier. (See Woodward, 1998c, 2000b, 2003 for a broader discussion of the following points).

The very process of becoming a soldier involves the construction, negotiation and reproduction of gendered identities. A key role of the military – the formation and mobilization of a body of individuals capable of engaging in military activities – requires the inculcation within that group of a set of values of sufficient potency and tenacity to enable that group to do the tasks required of it. These values rely extensively on specific ideas about the necessary attributes of those individuals. Those attributes are gendered, in that they are constructed with reference to the sexed subjectivity of the individual. Location consolidates the construction of forms of masculinity specifically associated with soldiering. Rural landscapes provide an important backdrop and context to the constitution of military masculinities within the British Army. They are not the only place where this happens, but these rural landscapes – the huge Army Field Training Centres, places such as Sennybridge in Wales, Salisbury Plain in the centre of Wiltshire and the Otterburn Training Area in Northumbeland – are significant for their role as the crucible in which gendered military identities are forged.

The vast majority of Army recruitment literature introduces Army life to the potential recruit with reference to the location of training in rural landscapes. The ruralities depicted are sometimes the tame bucolic rurality bound up in classic images of the idyllic English countryside, but more usually are the wild, open, windswept moorlands of upland Britain. These portrayals of cold, wet wilderness are used frequently as a backdrop, a challenging location against which the soldier-recruit is pitted, and in response to which the skills and identities of the soldier-to-be are constructed:

> The Army operates in all sorts of climates and terrains around the world and its men and women have to be ready to take up that challenge at a moment's notice. From steamy jungles to snowy mountains, you will be trained to carry out your specialist and military roles quickly and effectively. You will become fitter and stronger than you have ever been and you will learn to think on your feet and respond to rapidly changing circumstances. (Army Recruiting Group, undated, npn.)

Much of this training involves marches over rough terrain – tabbing (Tactical Advance to Battle), described as 'your bread and butter', and 'the staple of infantry soldiering' (BBC, 1999, 2000; Lukowiak, 2000). This is hard outdoors work. Soldiers have to transcend the seemingly overwhelming urge to go back to a warm barracks. Autobiographical accounts of soldiering almost always refer back to this point as part of the soldier's backstory. Ballinger's experience of training for the elite forces describes it in these terms:

> We walked, climbed and ran in our squadrons for nine hours without a break. We rarely used paths and never roads. We went from A to B, usually on a compass bearing. At the end, high up in the hills of North Wales, Scott [an officer] stopped us and each man sat on his bergen, grateful for the rest. We sat in a curve, two or three rows deep, around him. The wind whistled over the ridge, and our smocks, soaked with sweat, flapped against our skin. (Ballinger, 1992, p.57).

The outdoors is a place for inculcation of mental attitudes and attributes deemed essential for soldiering:

> Well with Guardsmen, you have to train them for an aggressive eventuality. At the end of the day they're the ones that's going to actually go in and kill the enemy, so they've got to have a little bit of physical robustness as well as a bit of aggression as well – once they hit the pain barrier then they start to get

annoyed, you hear all the grunts and groans and aggression coming out, and that's what they're basically looking for, in an Infantryman anyway. (Staff sergeant, ATR Pirbright, quoted in BBC, 1999).

I once watched this process happening. It was remarkable to civilian eyes. I went with a colleague to the Infantry Training Centre at Catterick to interview a senior Army officer about the process of infantry training conducted there. Our interview complete, we were then invited to go out onto the ranges to watch a company of soldiers in Phase II of their training – the special-to-arms training that teaches and tests their skills in their chosen career group. That day, the soldiers were training in close quarter battle and the use of the fixed bayonet. This is not only a necessary infantry skill; it is also an activity of immense symbolic significance because it is about learning the skill of attacking and killing the enemy at close quarter. It is significant symbolically in the popular imagination about soldiers and what they might be called upon to do. So we walked over the ranges, escorted up a shallow ravine as we watched the soldiers being taken individually with bayonets fixed to their rifles, to identify, scream at and stab a straw-stuffed dummy (the enemy) whilst being fired on (with blank ammunition), smoke from smoke grenades clouding their view, an over-powering smell of cordite lingering in the still spring air. All the while, the section commander egged them on as they sweated, grunted, puffed and groaned their way up the ravine. At the end of the exercise, we were invited to talk to some of the soldiers about their training. Their pride in their achievements that day was infectious, their confidence in their ability to do it for real unassailable. Their contrast to us, two middle-aged women academics, was striking.

National identity

Ideas about national identity are also implicit within military representa-tions of landscape, complicit in their construction. Readings of landscape are contributory to ideas about national identity. In this section, I want to focus explicitly on military landscapes and the role of national identity in their construction. My argument here is that ideas about what a landscape is, and what it represents, create spaces for the development of arguments about nationhood; we should be alert to the roles of military engagement and militarism to in contributing to arguments about national identity constructed via representations of landscape. The range of possible examples is very large; here I focus on two instances where ideas about landscape are used to forge connections between military activities and national identities. These examples are, first, the conflation of ideas of

England and rurality as a response to military engagements elsewhere, and second, the development and transposition of that rural England as a strategy for the legitimation of military engagement.

It is a truism that the use of rural imagery, and a specific construction of rurality, is implicit in the formation of ideas about English national identity. 'England is the country and the country is England', in Stanley Baldwin's famous phrase. The construction of rurality implicit in the formation of ideas about Englishness is geographically specific. A southern English arable rurality dominates, and speaks explicitly to England rather than Britain or the other constituent countries of the UK. It identifies rurality as comprising harmonious social relations resting on the paternalistic order of established agricultural practices, which themselves have developed a distinct landscape of rolling fertile fields, managed woodland, productive watercourses and small settlements in place in the countryside. This construction of rural England is a dominant image, influential in ideas about what the countryside is and should be, and in ideas about the country is (for further discussion, see Short, 1991; Daniels, 1993).

Many, many things have contributed to this idea and ideal of rural England, including industrialization, the fragmentation of social relations, the experience of imperialism and post-colonialism. Military engagements beyond the shores of rural England have made their own distinct contribution. Lowe, Murdoch and Cox (1995) point to the significance of the relationship between ideas of rurality in cultures of national identity and Britain's imperial past. They argue that the extension of the British empire across the globe entailed a reconsideration of the nature of England as 'homeland'. This imagined homeland was essentially a rural vision. As British domination receded, the rurality of images of 'home' was consolidated, producing an idea of the countryside as a repository of a way of life that required protection. The armed forces played a critical role in the shaping of this ideology of rural homeland in their position as dominant players in the colonizing process. The experience of soldiers during the First World War provides another example. Alun Howkins (1986) has argued for the 1914–18 war as a defining moment for this discourse, with three elements of particular importance. The first is the importance of the idea of rural England as a point of reference in much war poetry. Second, he notes the ways in which the shared experience of trench warfare echoes prewar metaphors of a united agricultural community working together under adverse conditions. Third, he argues that 'ordinary soldiers themselves could not but have had a romanticized vision of home'; the antithesis of Flanders to England could not have been greater (p.81) – Flanders as an anti-landscape (Daniels, 1993 p.213). Furthermore, an idealized vision of home was critical; for the sake of morale, a world outside the trenches had to be imagined, and this world had to be an idealized one, however little this reflected the reality of many soldiers' urban origins. The form of Great War cemeteries in the aftermath of this conflict similarly drew on distinct ideas about rurality. Gardens were mobilized as essential ingredients in the iconography of British war cemeteries, meant to represent the 'corner of the foreign field that is for ever England' a phrase enshrined in the language following Rupert Brooke's poem *1914* (Morris, 1997). The horticultural and architectural treatment of cemeteries 'represented an imperial national identity, continuity and rootedness, masking death and destruction, transfiguring the horrors of war which always threatened to surface. The war cemetery space is a matrix of tension, of complex and contradictory meanings, veneered by a verdant imperial turf.' (p.429).

A further example of the intertwining of discourses of rurality and national identity through military activity is that of the use of rural imagery in wartime propaganda. For example, a popular poster, still reproduced by the Imperial War Museum in postcard format, bears the slogan 'Your Britain: fight for it now' under a picture of the South Downs with shepherd, dog and flock heading home over rolling hills towards a small hamlet in a tree-lined valley. 'Your Britain' is equated with a specific, resolutely rural southern English ideal: the 'languid little England pastoral was a central ingredient of wartime patriotism' (Daniels, 1993, p.213). Even John Constable's skies were commandeered for the war effort (Gruffudd, 1990, 1991; Daniels, 1993). Rural images were not the only ones used, of course, but as Michael Bunce (1994) has argued, the rural imagery adopted was thought to have a particular resonance with ideas of nationhood and national identity. In short, discourses of national identity draw on ideas of rurality, and the activities of the armed forces have assisted in making this connection.

Ideas about the rurality of England have been developed and transposed as a strategy for the legitimation of military engagements beyond the English shore. Klaus Dodds (1998) has explored this in detail, looking at the role of representations of the Falklands landscape during the 1982 war for sovereignty over the Falklands / Malvinas between Britain and Argentina. Dodds argues that media and public support for the British military campaign was mobilized in part through government attempts to reimagine this remote colony in the South Atlantic as British sovereign territory. Part of this reimagination involved the use of rural imagery and the transformation of the Falklands into something like Britain through idealized geographical representations. In short, one element of government military strategy was to construct the Falklands as a place worthy of intervention and war. This was undertaken through the characterization of the Falklands as a quasi-Ambridge, the fictional setting for the long-running BBC radio soap opera *The Archers*. Frequent media references to 'Ambridge in the South Atlantic' reflected a myth of rural English idyll and its enduring importance within British culture, constructing the Falklands as a place worth fighting for.

As Dodds notes, in England, landscape representations – whether carto-graphic or photographic, pictorial or textual – have enjoyed a central role in the process of English nation-building:

> Moreover...these representations of English landscapes have been fre-quently accompanied by a fear that these geographical sites of national strength would be undermined either by invasion of hostile forces...or by the ambivalent forces of progress and technology. (Dodds, 1998, p.735.)

A strategy to promote the military campaign included strategies to equate the (remote) Falklands Islands as part of England. For example, television programmes shown in 1981 included implicit claims to the Britishness of these islands, confirmed with visual images and oral testimonies:

> Port Stanley was presented as a small village filled with tin-roofed houses, old-fashioned hostelries such as the Upland Goose Hotel, and the exclusive Colony Club. Pictures were shown of people drinking pints of beer, cultivat-ing small gardens, sheep rearing, playing bingo in a village hall, attending cocktail parties at the Governor's Official Residence, and shopping at the Falkland Islands Company shop. These television pictures, when combined together, created a potent mixture of environmental, social and cultural mythologies and symbols about Britain and these British people located in the Falklands. (Dodds, 1998, p.737).

However, the Falkland Islands were 8,000 miles from Britain. To bridge this gap, national mythologies and fantasies of the Second World War and Britain's history as an island were deployed. The distance of 8000 miles was collapsed as the Falklands was reimagined, encapsulated in images of rurality inherent in the idea of Ambridge. Furthermore, like Ambridge, this was a community which had to be imagined because there was so little geographical and pictorial information available.

The type of landscape imagined for the Falklands was significant, in that ultimately it undermined this strategy. The Ambridge image underesti-mated the social and cultural complexity of the Falklands and the diversity of rural imageries:

> The image of Ambridge is indicative of a southern Midlands Englishness rather than a hard Northern or Celtic rural place and as a consequence the Falklands could not easily be contained as an Ambridge. The rugged land-scapes and climate were more typical of a highland landscape rather than one found in Gloucestershire. The farming communities were scattered around the islands and preoccupied with sheep rather than dairy farming. (p.742).

Serving soldiers and media correspondents soon picked up the contrasts; for one Welsh Guardsman, later burned in an enemy attack:

> East Falkland looked green and pleasant – a ringer, I thought, for Pembroke-shire, with its little clusters of white washed, red-roofed houses beside the shore. [later his impressions changed] . . . there was nothing there. The Falk-lands were a god-forsaken place. The islands are empty, bleak, desolate, and inhospitable. I never saw a single tree. I never saw one of those famous sheep. (Weston, 1989, pp.128–31, quoted in Dodds, 1998, p.744).

Furthermore, the representations were shifted as a consequence of what actually happened on the Falkland Islands; a war was fought and serving personnel were killed. As a consequence:

> The mythology of military valour, almost by definition, had to be located in fearful and challenging places rather than a pleasant little southern hemi-spheric Ambridge. (Dodds, 1998, p.744).

Journalists were also disappointed; the rural imagery was shattered by first-hand experience.

Military Landscapes and Control

The idea of the 'construction' of landscape has been implicit throughout this chapter. In one sense it refers to the physical activities which shape the land and build structures, but in this chapter, I have used the term to refer to the representational activities which give meanings to landscapes. These have been discussed with reference to the ways in which soldiers see landscapes, the mechanisms they receive training in which help consolidate claims to space and control of space. I have also looked at the controls asserted by simply being there in the landscape, what a reading of these landscapes of presence can bring. I then went on to look at the process of representation or interpretation of landscape as a military strategy for the consolidation of control.

My concluding point for this chapter is to draw out, yet again, the features of military control which go towards shaping the militarized land-scapes. Military landscapes, as physical forms and representational strat-egies, are driven by agendas of domination and control. Military landscapes have a politics. The analysis of military landscapes is an interpretative act; military landscapes are texts to be read, not just physical collections of landforms. If we accept that they have a politics, then the task of landscape interpretation means a reading of these landscapes guided explicitly by questions about power, domination and control.

Two points about power follow from these observations about the politics and purposes of representation. The first is that there is never one single 'true' interpretation of landscape (be it an interpretation springing from military sources or from elsewhere). There are only ever multiple views about a single place or landscape. Many different representations will be in operation in one place. The second point, which follows from this, is that all representations are open to negotiation and challenge. Representations or interpretations of landscape have a politics; they are concerned, fundamentally, with power, with the assertion of one particular view over another. If we accept that multiple interpretations will always exist, then we also accept that interpretations or representations of landscape are always open to negotiation and challenge. Representations of any landscape, be it military in origin or not, will be contested. It is to these contests that I now turn.

Chapter Six

Challenging Military Geographies

Contesting Military Power

In 1946, Bikini went nuclear. The atoll, a coral speck in the Pacific Ocean, and one of the Marshall Islands, was identified by the US Government at the end of the 1939–49 war as an ideal site – for the US military, at least – for testing nuclear weapons. The atoll lies off main shipping routes, and the small, agriculturally-based population of the atoll was deemed removable. The islanders – all 167 of them – were taken to another island in 1946, and testing began. Many of our most powerful, iconic images of the nuclear age, images of fireballs and mushroom clouds, come from tests conducted on Bikini. Between 1946 and 1958, 67 nuclear devices were exploded there, including atomic and hydrogen bombs.

The islanders, having petitioned for years to be allowed to return home after suffering starvation, disease and the undermining of their economic, social and cultural systems on their temporary island homes, were allowed to return in the early 1970s, gradually resettling on the island. However, the effects of those 67 nuclear blasts had left their mark on Bikini. As well as physical scars on the landscape, the island was left with a legacy of radio-active contamination. High levels of caesium 137 and strontium 90 were found in the food-chain, and in the returning population, far in excess of 'safe' limits. The island was evacuated in 1978. The island is now a destination for an elite and wealthy group of travellers attracted to Bikini because of the quality of the diving. Old naval vessels, anchored in the lagoon and off-shore during the time of nuclear testing to enable US military planners to assess the impacts of nuclear explosions on ships, now lie on the ocean floor. The warm, clear waters (despite fears of radioactive contamination) provide ideal diving conditions. Only diving operators and a handful of US Department of Energy officials remain on the island. All food and water is imported, because of concerns about contamination in the food chain. The islanders – the descendants of those originally evacuated in 1946 – have campaigned for financial aid to assist a clean-up operation on the island, and for compensation for the disruption to their way of life. Progress is slow (Niedenthal, 2001, 2002).

Bikini is iconic. Here we have the ultimate expression of military power taking place on a hitherto pristine and self-sufficient island community – mushroom clouds blooming in a tropical paradise. Here, a whole society was shifted at the behest of military planners, who defined the place as remote and then set about testing nuclear devices there. Challenges to that military control and military power have been long-standing, tenacious and vigorous, yet it is an unequal challenge; the Bikini islanders and the government of the Marshall Islands on the one hand, the might of the US military and government on the other. Compensation and reparations for social and environmental remediation seem a long time coming, and seem meagre relative to what has been lost by the original population and the ecosystems of the island. The control and power of the US military is rendered starkly visible here.

Bikini is iconic, but not unusual. The previous chapters have examined the operation of military control over space in nonconflict situations, not by looking at the power expressed directly through the barrel of a gun, but by looking at economic control and the social and political consequences which follow from that, at the military control of the natural environment and of the agenda to interpret that control, and at the representation of military landscapes as a strategy for control of our understandings of military legitimacy. This chapter looks directly at challenges to that control, instances where the control of space and of militarized places has been countered by nonmilitary 'forces'. Looking at these challenges is useful, because the interactions between military and oppositional arguments over the use of space clarify how the mechanisms for control work, and show their extent and limits. In short, the study of conflicts over military land uses show how military power operates when challenged by civil society. That process of challenge, be it by intra-governmental negotiation, by direct opposition or by the production of alternative narratives about militarism and its imprint, always involves negotiation. Looking at those negotiations is helpful in making those mechanisms of military control visible.

The chapter examines challenges to military land uses originating both within and beyond the moral reference points of contemporary militarism. The chapter starts by examining challenges which have pitted the central state against the concerns of local governmental and nongovernmental organizations in debates over military training at the Otterburn Training Area in the UK. This challenge is revealing for what it indicates about the state of civil-military relations, and about the moral spread of contemporary militarism. The chapter goes on to assess direct challenges to militarism and militarism's geographies from beyond the state apparatus, looking at antimilitary protests where military land use practices are contested as part of a wider critique of militarism. The chapter concludes with a discussion of the reimagination of military spaces, places and landscapes implicit in the preservation of military sites, and the challenges (and endorsements) that this brings to military control.

Contesting Military Training in National Parks

The variety of nonmilitary conflicts over the use of land for military activities is impressive. Military low-flying is one example. The British Royal Air Force maintains that it needs to train pilots in high-speed, low-altitude flying. Those living in areas where much of the RAF's low-flying is practised maintain that the noise and risk of accident outweigh military requirements. The RAF counters these arguments with justifications of its own about the need to distribute low-flying fairly over underpopulated rural areas (which, because of their topography, offer challenging venues for pilot practice). Another example is conflict over military versus agricultural land use. In the UK, much military training land is used for agriculture, usually extensive livestock grazing. Farmers pay reduced rents in return for compromising farming for the benefit of military training. The system works well, most of the time, for both farmers and the Army, but problems can arise. For example, the MoD's moves to extinguish commoners' rights on the Warcop training area in Cumbria proved highly unpopular on neighbouring farms beyond the training area. A further example would be the conflicts that arise over access to military training lands by the public. Since the early 1990s, the MoD has been under mounting pressure from recreation and amenity groups to allow a greater degree of access to training lands when they are not in use. These groups argue that many training areas with high landscape and environmental value are underused by the Armed Forces, and that a greater degree of access could be allowed. The MoD and Defence Estates have countered that there are major safety and security issues raised by public access. The counter-argument emphasizes the need for better management and publicity of land uses in order to enable access to what many see as a public asset. There have also been long-running conflicts about the military appropriation of land during wartime, with no restitution in peace, as happened in Imber on Salisbury Plain, and Tyneham on the Lulworth Ranges, Dorset. The latter case has been chronicled by Patrick Wright (1995), who describes conflicts over land uses as representative of wider social debates over rurality and rural land use.

In this section, I focus on challenges made to the use by the British Army of the Otterburn Training Area in Northumberland, England, for heavy artillery training. The plans, and some of the military justification, were discussed in Chapters 4 and 5. Here, I focus on the ways in which this encounter challenged the practices of military land use. This was not a radical critique; the principle of military land use was unquestioned by those challenging the MoD and Army. At issue were the details of the scheme. The Otterburn Public Inquiry (OPI) provided a rare occasion for the MoD's land management practices to be scrutinized and questioned in public. Some questions were awkward, but as this case study shows, the scope of questioning was ultimately limited both by the format of the inquiry system, and by the fact that all parties shared a common set of values wrapped up in a discourse which emphasized their acceptance of the military and their acceptance of the need for a trained Army. As I shall argue, this shared framework for understanding limited the extent to which the Army's plans could be contested.

The MoD's case for the developments at Otterburn to facilitate MLRS and AS90 training rested on two sets of arguments. The first was that the proposals set before the local planning authority were the irreducible minimum necessary to meet the operational requirements of the artillery. The language used to make this argument drew on the idea of no compromise:

> The MoD has gone to great lengths to allay concerns about the proposals and take full account of the advice received from consultees. The detail would, of course, be a matter for negotiation with the National Park Authority, but the MoD cannot envisage a substantially different approach proving acceptable. The Army has a pressing need to train its highly sophisticated artillery regiments at Otterburn and a minimum level of infrastructure must be put in place if this training is to be effective. 46 gun spurs, the equivalent of 6 GDAs, Technical and Tactical OPs, a Central Maintenance Facility, a Regimental Replenishment Point and additional accommodation facilities are the minimum and this cannot (and has not been) compromised. (MoD, 1996a, p.27).

Within this argument, proof that the proposals did indeed constitute a 'minimum development necessary' was emphasized. *In Response to Consultation: Meeting the Minimum Requirement* talked of 'two years of careful study', of examining the issues 'in detail' and of comprehensive mitigation packages. The document stressed the integrity and reliability of the MoD's case for the use of Otterburn. *Striking A Balance*, a public relations document reinforcing the case for Otterburn as the place for heavy artillery training, emphasized the efforts made by those responsible for the most efficient use of the defence estate (HQ Land Command, 1997). As this document title suggests, the second argument on which the MoD's case rested was all about balance. The MoD's publicity documents about the scheme defined the issue of the developments as one of a balance between two sets of interests. These were the need for a trained army on the one hand, and the need for due concern for the conservation of the natural and cultural heritage of a National Park on the other. The MoD's case, defined within these terms, was presented as constituting an even balance between these two interests, a moderate course or compromise.

A moderate course or compromise? Not in the view of opponents of the scheme. Ranging from the local planning authorities, the Northumberland County Council and the Northumberland National Park Authority, via established amenity groups such as the Council for National Parks, to individuals on Tyneside with a love of Redesdale, opposition was deeply held and widely felt. 'Environment Groups Target Firing Range in National Park', said the *Daily Telegraph* (11 April 1995). 'Environmentalists Aim to Spike Army's Big Guns' ran the *Financial Times* headline (15 April 1995). The Northumberland County Council requested that the plans be called in by the Secretary of State for the Environment, and a local public inquiry held into the matter. It sat between April and October 1997, and then, following the publication of the Strategic Defence Review and the availability of some new evidence, again between March and May 1999.

Local public inquiries into planning issues are adversarial in nature, echoing the English legal system. A scheme is spoken for by its proposers, represented by Counsel, and against by its opponents, also represented by Counsel, via witness statements. Both parties have the right to cross-examine witnesses. Rebuttals can also be issued to challenge points made by opponents in cross examination. An Inspector sits and listens to it all, then writes a report making recommendations to the Secretary of State. The MoD were the scheme proposers with support from some local residents and farmers. There were two principal groups of objectors to the scheme; the Northumberland National Park Authority working together with Northumberland County Council to object to the impact of this development on a National Park; and a Consortium coordinated by the Council for National Parks objecting primarily about the environmental impacts of the proposed developments, and including the Council for the Protection of Rural England, the Northumberland Natural History Society, the Northumberland and Newcastle Society, the Association of Countryside Voluntary Wardens, the Ramblers Association and the Open Spaces Society. In addition, a large number of individuals, locally and nationally, protested either in person or in writing about issues such as noise, pollution, traffic increases, environmental damage and damage to the peace and tranquillity of this area.

The inquiry ranged far and wide across a huge variety of topics. The Inspector heard about the military need for artillery training, the value of the National Park, the environmental and conservation issues at stake, pollution and noise from big guns, traffic impacts from convoys travelling up to Otterburn to train, the impact on walkers, cyclists and riders of the proposed developments, the position regarding planning legislation, and the very fundamental question about wider military changes in land use and requirements and their impacts on the Otterburn proposals. This was a complex issue, requiring high levels of detail across a huge range of areas. As a consequence, there are many stories to tell about the Otterburn Inquiry (see Woodward, 1998b, 1999, 2001b, 2001c).

The core objection, put forward by both the Northumberland National Park Authority and the Council for National Parks consortium, was that the proposed developments would be fundamentally damaging to the character of the National Park, the quality of the natural environment, and public enjoyment of the area. The developments and the use of the infrastructure once it was built would cause noise, physical damage and pollution. The developments were presented by the opposition as conflicting with the spirit and philosophy behind the establishment of National Parks, which were intended for the protection of natural beauty and environmental quality and to provide opportunities for physical recreation and spiritual refreshment:

> The Northumberland National Park has a special character due to its wild, extensive, open moorland and forest; opportunities to appreciate wildlife and cultural heritage in a wild landscape; absence of intrusive activities and features; historical associations; a land form that provides opportunities for pleasant surprises; tranquillity; long views and spaciousness. (NPC/P/1 p.13)

The developments, the opposition argued, would have impacts that ran contrary to the purposes of the National Park. Government endorsement of the development plans, it was argued, would be damaging to the principle of National Parks, because endorsement would lead to an inference that National Parks could indeed be places where military training and live artillery firing could take precedence over environmental conservation and public enjoyment.

To match the military representations of landscape (discussed in Chapter 5), the opposition groups developed alternative narratives. The Council for National Parks emphasized a much longer chronicle of human occupation and the inscriptions successive generations had written onto the land than that imagined by the military. In this way, military occupation and use could be conceptualized as just another phase in a long a varied history. Regional distinction and specificity were important emphases in the opposition case; development would destroy these. The historian, G.M. Trevelyan, who had grown up at Wallington Hall a few miles from the training area, was quoted in support:

> In Northumberland alone, both heaven and earth are seen; we walk all day on
> long ridges, high enough to give far views of moor and valley, and the sense of
> solitude above the world below, yet so far distant from each other, and of such
> equal height, that we can watch the low skirting clouds as they 'post o'er land
> and ocean without rest'. It is the land of the far horizons. (Trevelyan, 1938,
> quoted in NPC/P/3, 1997, p.8)

This landscape, it was suggested, required a sensitive human response. The
preservation of this area for walking, with limits to military training, is:

> also a question of spiritual exercise and enjoyment. It is a question of spiritual
> values. Without vision the people perish and without sight of the beauty of
> nature the spiritual power of the British people will be atrophied. (Trevelyan
> to Standing Committee on National Parks 1938, quoted NPC/P/1/, 1997,
> p.9)

In short, the landscape of Otterburn could be valued for its innate qualities,
not understood as a resource for military use.

Furthermore, opposition groups argued that the developments ran contrary to the planning policies devised by national government, the local
planning authority and the National Park Authority to protect and maintain the landscape and environmental quality of the Park. The objectors
argued that national planning policy guidance tests for adjudicating over
development in National Parks had not been passed. These, set out in
Planning Policy Guidance Note 7 on the countryside, state that development in protected areas such as National parks will not be permitted 'save
in exceptional circumstances, where they are in the public interest, and
subject to rigorous examination about needs and alternatives'. The objectors argued that there was insufficient evidence that the MoD had conducted a thorough examination of its need to use Otterburn for heavy
artillery training and of the alternatives available to the Army elsewhere
on the defence estate. They argued that the decision to use Otterburn for
AS90 and MLRS training had been made in haste on the grounds of
expediency during a time of uncertainties following the return of artillery
units from Germany in the early 1990s. They argued that there was insufficient evidence that the Salisbury Plain Training Area, an alternative military venue for heavy artillery training, was used to capacity, and that the
training could be conducted there if the management of the training area
was improved. They also questioned the military argument that AS90 and
MLRS regiments had to train together. In short, the opponents argued that
Army and MoD had provided insufficient evidence to prove their claims
about the need to use Otterburn, and thus the military assessment of need,
required under planning policy guidance rules, was flawed. This was a
tough issue to prove; as I noted in Chapter 2, assessing military uses of

land involves a level of technical expertise not often available to civilians without the requisite knowledge of military training land management systems.

The MoD rebutted the objectors' case and arguments, through arguments and through tactics of their own. The arguments were dismissed. This was done through exacting and often pedantic adherence to the letter of the law, that is, planning legislation and guidance. The emotionalism of the objectors' case, with its appeals about the spirit of National Park legislation, for example, was countered with the rationalism of a tightly and expertly argued legal case. Dismissal of the objectors' arguments was also achieved through arguments which set out the military case with reference to military judgement, which was accorded weight and authority in the MoD's rebuttals and which was constructed as reasoned, logical and rigorous. The civilian origins of the objectors' case were highlighted, constructed as uninformed precisely because of their civilian origins, and dismissed. The arguments, in short, were rebutted through discourses which appealed to a higher authority – the need for national security:

> the development proposals are of the highest national importance and self-evidently in the public interest. I say that this is beyond argument. . . . We do not expect anyone to deny this not do we expect it to become an issue, because failure to be properly trained in the use of these weapons means greater difficulties in succeeding in military conflict objectives and more casualties. (I/MoD/1, 1997, p.2)

Throughout the inquiry, when similar statements were made emphasizing the weight that should be granted to the military case for the proposed developments, relativism was avoided. For example, on no occasion was an argument made that military requirements should be accorded greater weight than requirements for the protection of this nationally designated area. Rather, the arguments were all about the overwhelming dominance of the military arguments. One interpretation might be that this reflects the mind-set of military bodies themselves; that militarism and military activities operate in accordance with the contemporary military strategies of the world's dominant military powers, with their emphasis on offence, preemptive strike, and overwhelming dominance. The OTA was to be shaped in accordance with the military's views, which themselves were presented as beyond debate, naturalized and immutable.

At the heart of the inquiry, then, lay clues about the nature of contemporary British militarism and the operation of military influence in socio-political life. In its broadest sense, the inquiry was about the assertion of military control over a place (Otterburn), a space (the environmentally protected and socially valued national park), and a process (the public inquiry and planning systems). The MoD argued that the army's training needs were paramount; that it needed somewhere to train; that the OTA was the only suitable UK location for heavy artillery training; that the planning guidance on developments in national parks permitted such developments in exceptional circumstances if there was a national need and no alternatives existed; and that the developments in any case would not be damaging or detrimental to the qualities of the Park. This was not an argument that the MoD were prepared to lose. To have lost would have had repercussions for the Army's use of its training lands which would have been felt far beyond this remote and wind-swept northerly corner of England. Loss would be a loss for militarism.

The tactics that were used by the MoD to rebut the arguments of the objectors were also illuminating for what they revealed about the practices of domination. The meticulous production of proofs of evidence, the style of examination and cross-examination of witnesses and the attention to detail may have all been standard procedures for a defendant in a public inquiry. The point is that these practices rely on organizational capacity and the availability of resources (time, money) to employ those with high levels of competence and familiarity with the process. No point of criticism made by any objecting party, whether it was the National Park Authority itself or the views of a local resident exercising their right of representation, was left unanswered. Rebuttal proof after rebuttal proof issued forth from the MoD's offices, again indicative not only of the availability of resources to facilitate this, but also of sheer determination to argue away objections. Criticisms and opposition based on points of fact where rebutted with reference to supporting documentation. Criticisms and opposition based on differences of opinion, interpretation or understanding were shot down through arguments constructed as fact-based rather than subjective. In the inquiry venue, a modern hotel reception suite by Newcastle International airport, the authority of the MoD was established through the physical presence of an army of witnesses, consultants and military personnel (out of uniform, naturally); 'the junta', one witness suggested. On a day when the inquiry moved to a village just outside the training area to hear the views of local residents, the screech of low-flying fighter jets interrupted the proceedings on several occasions. An Army officer, part of the MoD team, told me that he'd requested the fly-past on purpose; was he joking? There were also allegations about underhand tactics whispered through the venue as the inquiry proceeded. One person alleged that a grievance case bought against an employee of one of the opposition groups had military origins and had been initiated in order to disrupt that organization's research and preparation for the inquiry. Another opposition member speculated, only half in jest, about the likelihood of listening devices being placed in rooms used during planning sessions by opponents of the scheme. The point about these allegations and speculations is not their veracity but their impact on the morale of opponents to the scheme.

The decision on whether to allow the developments to proceed was made by the Secretary of State for the Environment, on the basis of reports written by the inquiry's Inspector. The Inspector considered that: 'the proposed development would have harmful effects on the NNP which would not be outweighed by the suggested mitigating measures' (First Inspector's Report, nd). However, there was an overriding national need, with military requirements taking precedence:

> I consider that, being concerned with a matter of national defence, the circumstances of this application are exceptional and that the application has been most rigorously examined. (First Inspector's Report, nd, p.186)

The tests set out under government planning policy guidance had therefore been passed, on the grounds that the military developments served the public interest. Ultimately:

> In considering the issues at this inquiry I have weighed the undoubted importance for the nation of the Northumberland National Park, both in itself and as part of the family of National Parks, against the importance of army training with modern artillery to meet national and international defence needs. Taking account of the environmental assessment and the adverse effect which the proposed development would have, even when kept to a minimum and with mitigation, on the environment of the Northumberland National Park, and the lack of alternatives to training at Otterburn, I consider that the proposed development should be approved. (First Inspector's Report, nd, p.189)

The Secretary of State agreed:

> that the Government, having equipped the army with AS90 and MLRS artillery weapons, requires units at a particular level (regimental) to be at a specific state of readiness. [He also agrees with the Inspector's conclusions that] the opportunity for training to achieve this must be made available as a matter of national need. The Secretary of State attaches great weight to this factor. (p.10, decision letter, 4.10.01).

Military interests won in an unequal battle with conservation and environmental protection concerns.

Three points stand out in conclusion, in terms of the wider lessons of the OTA debate for the study of the contested use of military space. The first point is about power and (in)equalities in the exercise of that power. The general point here is that challenging the power of the state over its use of lands for military purposes is extremely difficult. The organizational capacity of the Ministry of Defence, backed by the Treasury Solicitors (providing legal representation), the Army and a range of consultants retained by the MoD, was immense, and backed by substantial financial resources. Against this were ranged a local planning authority and a collection of amenity groups funded by membership subscriptions and the occasional charitable grant. The disparity of resources between challenger and defendant was very great. Some groups opposed in the principle to the scheme did not even consider making representation to the public inquiry because of the financial and time resources that this would require. There are also issues about the power of influence; for example, it was suggested by some that the (former) Countryside Commission, the Government's statutory advisor on rural issues, did not make representations against the scheme at the inquiry despite its own declarations of unease about military intensification in Northumberland because of pressure brought to bear by MoD officers on senior Countryside Commission officers about the political expediency of allowing the developments to proceed. These allegations are hard to substantiate, of course; the point remains, however, that the contribution of the Government's statutory advisor on rural protection was notable by its absence.

The second point concerns inequalities in access to information. The general point here is that challenging military land uses effectively requires access to factual information which simply may not be available outwith military circles, making effective challenge extremely difficult. In the Otterburn case, the absence of information on military land use management practices and Army training management was a major reason for the length of the inquiry. Opposition groups seeking to undermine the MoD's case had to grasp every opportunity they could to cross-examine MoD witnesses at length in order to get precise information on the these land management practices. The MoD were not necessarily happy about this, but the public inquiry process obliged MoD representatives to comply. Ultimately, there appeared to have been a public interest argument in support of extensive cross-examination and information-gathering; much new information about military land management was placed in the public domain as a result of the inquiry. But the point remains that access to information revealed much about the abilities of the MoD to maintain tight control over decisions on the management of military training lands.

The third point concerns the supremacy of ideas about national security in wider land use planning debates. The MoD presented a case as a rational response to a set of objective facts; one way of the understanding the case would be as the deployment of administrative rationalism in the discourse of the MoD (see Chapter 4). This method of representation was itself bound up within parameters that defined the debate tightly as about a specific planning matter. The principles and practices behind that particular planning matter were defined as external to the inquiry. Furthermore, they were defined as being beyond question or debate. On face value, of course, this is obvious; public inquiries are defined purely by their terms of reference around specific issues. The point, however, is the visibility given to issues beyond the parameters of the inquiry by the MoD itself, in its own representations. These external issues – the need for national security – was held up as being beyond question. Discourses of national security have great power. To reiterate a point made in Chapter 2, as Martin Shaw (1991) notes, militarism in contemporary British culture is defined with reference to a 'national military myth', the central tenets of which are an ideology and imagery of totalitarian military threat, the belief that 'appeasing' such threats is wrong, and the notion that military strength is the foundation of security. Shaw argues that these ideas constitute a sustaining myth shaping the operation of military activity in relation to the state and civil society. At Otterburn, the discourse of national security proved powerful, resilient to challenge, and ultimately determined the outcome of the inquiry. This view on the national significance of Otterburn contrasts starkly with the view of a member of the public writing to the Inspector prior to the Inquiry:

> Father left the best years of his life in the Western Front, he was 31 years old when he got back home. His two sons my eldest brothers were killed in bomber command. Surely they didn't die to create death for some-one else and to deprive our people of some lovely landscape. (Letter to NPA June 1995).

Antimilitarist and Nonviolent Challenges to Military Land Uses

The debate over the use of the Otterburn Training Area for heavy artillery training looked at challenges to military control originating from beyond established structures of governance. Challenge here was about principles over the use of space, and these challenges questioned the necessity of established military training practices. The challenge, however, still came from groups broadly supportive of the idea that national security needs (however defined) had intrinsic weight. Despite the best efforts of the MoD to caricature the opposition as antimilitarist,[1] this was not the case. The local authorities and amenity groups protesting at Otterburn were not motivated by an explicit critique of militarism or a view on the immoralities implicit in military activities.

Antimilitarist challenges to the military control of space and its consequences sit in stark contrast to the protests at Otterburn, and it is to these that I now turn, to look at the causes of antimilitarist challenge, and the actions taken to counter military control.

The 1980s peace camps

Feminist antimilitarist challenges to militarism and its expression in the military use of space have a long and noble history, changing in form and method of protest with changes in the might and circumstances of military power. In this sense there is a direct connection through time between the establishment of the Women's International League of Peace and Freedom in 1915 and the women's peace camps of the 1980s (see Liddington, 1989). The UK's most famous example of this – both because of the long-lived nature of the protest, and because of the extensive media coverage of the protestors – is the women's peace camp at Greenham Common in Berkshire, England. Antimilitarist politics in the UK owes much to a feminist politics which has highlighted the connections between patriarchy and military aggression (although this aspect to antimilitarist protest is not unique to the UK). Antimilitarist politics also owes much to the long-established peace movement, manifest in organizational form by the Campaign for Nuclear Disarmament (CND), and other less high-profile organizations such as the Campaign for the Accountability of American Bases (CAAB) and Trident Ploughshares, campaigning against nuclear submarines. CND in particular has a long history of advocacy of nonviolent protest against the development, testing and deployment of nuclear weapons, an approach shared across the peace movement.

There is potentially much to say about the UK peace movement and its challenges to militarism and military activities; here I discuss just one facet, the establishment of peace camps. Peace camps are a physical manifestations of protest at the gates of military bases where nuclear weapons are located. Peace camps in the UK have been established both with and outwith the organized peace movement; notable examples include those at Faslane in Scotland, Molesworth in Cambridgeshire, Lakenheath in Gloucestershire, Greenham Common in Berkshire and Menwith Hill in North Yorkshire. These are all places where the geographies of militarism and military activities have faced challenge from an alternative politics critical of the military appropriation of space. It is the latter two examples which this section will focus on.

In 1941, Greenham Common, near Newbury in the county of Berkshire was requisitioned by the War Office for military use as an airfield. Following the end of the 1939–45 conflict, the US Air Force maintained a presence at Greenham, not least because the long runway was ideal for certain types of military aircraft. In 1979, NATO took the decision to base nuclear Ground Launched Cruise Missiles there, under the control of the USAF's 501st tactical missile unit. About 2,000 military personnel were stationed there. Facilities at RAF Greenham Common included runways for bomber aircraft, central administrative areas and a high security GAMA (Ground Launched Cruise Missile Alert and Maintenance Area) facility.

The decision to base US cruise missiles in the UK unleashed a wave of protest from the antinuclear movement. A feminist critique of the nuclear age was also finding voice. A 1981 peace march from Cardiff in Wales to Greenham culminated in the establishment of a women's peace camp at the gates of the US base. A high-profile 'embrace the base' event in December 1982 attracted over 30,000 women to the base. In November 1983, the first cruise missiles arrived. Women peace campaigners initiated a lengthy campaign of nonviolent direct action against the base and its contents, involving activities such as physical blockading of the base, incursions onto the base (particularly the GAMA facility), and a more general public campaign to raise public awareness about the facility. Government and media opinion towards the camp was largely hostile. (See Harford and Hopkins, 1984; Junor and Howse, 1995; Roseneil, 1995 and 1999 for authoritative accounts of the women's peace camp).

In March 1987, the Intermediate Nuclear Forces (INF) treaty was signed by USA and USSR. Its ratification in 1988 signalled for many the commentators the end of 'cold war'. In March 1991 the missiles were removed from the base, and in 1992 the redundant base was handed back to the RAF, and then on to the Defence Land Agent for sale. The site was sold to the local authority and at the time of writing is being reclaimed. The former base now includes areas of common land, some of which is managed for its ecology, and a business park. The women's peace camp remained until September 2000. A memorial to the camp has been established, the only trace of 19 years of antimilitarist protest.

Media coverage of the women's peace camp caricatured the protestors as a monolithic group of hostile, disruptive women. As Roseneil (1995) points out, a diversity of feminist thought inspired the political actions of the protestors, including ideas drawn from theories of maternalism, radical feminism and lesbian separatism. What united the protestors was a critique of the use of common land to support the means of enabling military aggression. This was an antimilitarist protest targeted at what many saw as the ultimate expression of uncontrolled military power – the use of nuclear weapons.

A key strategy for the protestors was the use of nonviolent direct action as a form of challenge:

> There were so many different ways, I suppose, that you could sort of outwit and startle the authorities, rather than this kind of brutish, unintelligent head on clash between completely unequal forces, in which you would inevitably be the loser. It never seemed to me to make a lot of sense. I mean nonviolent protest, as a form of protest, is much more intelligent, isn't it? (Pettitt, nd)

The essence of nonviolent direct action for these women was:

> that you shouldn't have any violent thing going on between you and the
> people that are moving you – and that's very very difficult. (Hipperson, nd)

This strategy was carried out by a group identified (by themselves and by outside observers) as explicitly 'other' to the military. This was an anarchic (i.e. nonhierarchical) group challenging military power through its presence, its appearance and its carnivalesque tactics (Cresswell, 1996). Challenge was not necessarily through established legislative procedures (although this did also happen) but through activities such as weaving webs of wool over protestors as they lay across muddy tracks, refusing to move in accordance to police requests that they stand aside, and confounding the constabulary when the latter was forced to intervene by their persistence in nonviolent resistance. This was a strategy which included not only the appropriation of space, but also the renaming of space; the reimagination of the geography of the base included, for example, renaming the gates of the camp after the colours of the rainbow. The strategy of protest involved tenacity, with the protestors living in benders – makeshift shelters constructed out of branches and plastic sheeting, with a minimal environmental and archaeological footprint (see Schofield and Anderton, 2000). Wet, cold and mud, and local and national media hostility were endured. Arrests, convictions and imprisonment were frequent and disruption of the camps and the scattering of belongings in the mud were commonplace. A persistent message linked a critique of militarism, and the US military's nuclear capabilities, with the responsibilities of civil society to resist the military activities; 'carry Greenham home' was a motto (a 1984 film title from independent film-makers Beeban Kidron and Amanda Richardson) which emerged to summarize this message. Greenham women were everywhere.

The peace camp at Greenham Common is not the only example from the 1980s of antimilitary nonviolent protest. Greenham stands out in the popular imagination because of the publicity it generated, stirred both by the tenacity of the process and its women-only make-up. In 1982, anti-nuclear protestors had established camps outside 16 military bases in the UK, primarily US bases with nuclear weapons or nuclear control facilities. For example, RAF Molesworth in Cambridgeshire, a redundant Second World War airfield, was chosen as a location for nuclear cruise missiles, which were scheduled for arrival in 1985. The camp was home to men and women. Specific activities here included the largely symbolic activity of cultivating land outside the base for planting wheat, destined for famine-stricken Eritrea in Africa, an activity planned to make visible the links between the expenditure of financial resources for military purposes and the lack of resources elsewhere leading to poverty, famine, disease and death. Another example is the establishment of a peace camp at Faslane Naval Base on Gareloch, 30 miles from Glasgow in Scotland, where nuclear-armed submarines are based. This camp was unusual in that it had the tacit support of the local planning authority, which had declared its institutional opposition to nuclear power and weapons. Although this was an entirely symbolic gesture, it had practical effect in the support the local authority gave to the camp through, for example, the renting of local authority land to the campaigners for a nominal fee, and the granting of planning permission to caravans parked permanently on-site. At the time of writing, the Faslane camp is still in place.

Menwith Hill Station

Nonviolent direct action, informed by a critique of militarism, informed protest (on-going at the time of writing) against the Menwith Hill Station on the moors outside Harrogate, in North Yorkshire. Again, the critique of militarism links a number of protesting groups with an 'interest' in the base:

> I am very concerned about the arms race and the proliferation of nuclear weapons. My involvement in the women's peace camp is... also because of the amount of money and time focused into warfare and weapons means that much of the world's population live in deepest poverty. Most of the victims of this lack of resources are women and children. (Helen John, Statement to the High Court, 3 February 1998).

Menwith Hill Station is an intelligence facility, run by the US National Security Agency. It contains no military arsenal as such (although it is heavily protected from incursion by armed personnel). The base is bounded on four sides by public roads, and it is possible to walk its perimeter. This is not necessarily a pleasant activity: there is no footpath and cars speed past on the straight road (Roman in origin) between Harrogate and Skipton. A police landcruiser drives round and round the perimeter roads. I once walked around the base, anticlockwise, to get a feel for the place, accompanying David Wood who was researching this place's military geographies (see Wood, 2001). Eventually, after several drive-bys, the police vehicle stopped, an officer got out, donned cap and lurid yellow reflective jacket, and stopped us. 'Go on', he said, 'I'm dying to know – what are you doing?'. We told him. He was completely nonplussed. Military geographies were not on his radar.

Why were we stopped? Because Menwith Hill is the most significant UK location for the US's intelligence and communications infrastructure, providing both military and commercial customers with mechanisms to eavesdrop on the telecommunications traffic of western Europe via ECH-ELON, the communications and interception facilities for SBIRS (Space Based Infra-Red System) for the interception of ballistic missiles, and other signals intelligence functions (for an authoritative and detailed account, see Wood, 2001). It provides a control facility for the US's National Missile Defense System, and SBIRS. It is a key node in a communications network stretching around the globe. The military facility appeared during the 1950s as a US 'intercept station' for monitoring Soviet military communications, and has expanded in function (though not in footprint; the 230 ha site is clearly bounded by public roads) since that time with the continual addition of radio masts and antennae, and radomes, structures which perch like giant mystic golfballs on the hill (see Figure 6.1). About 1,800 personnel are deployed at the base, consisting of 400 US military personnel, around 1,000 US civilian personnel (including defence contractors from companies such as Lockheed Martin), 5 UK military personnel and 400 UK civilians (Wood, 2001).

Control over this 230 ha site is absolute – almost. At one corner the fence detours away from the road, leaving a small triangular patch of grass and bushes. Notices indicating this to be a space governed by bylaws, limiting access to this spot, have been pasted over with counter-notices put there by protesters, asserting the illegality of the military control of this small patch of land. This alternative view sees Menwith Hill as functionally and symbolically crucial to US economic, political, military and even imperial dominance around the world. Conflict between this view and that of the site's users have made Menwith Hill a place of secrecy and security, and a target for a sustained campaign of challenge to the militarization of this space. Protest against the site and the activities carried out there has been on-going since the 1970s, with the establishment and activities of the Otley Peace Action Group (OPAG: Otley is a market town about 10 km from the base). A first antinuclear demonstration was held there in May 1981. A first weekend peace camp was held there in April 1983, and following the closure of the Greenham peace camp, protestors from the latter turned their attention to the militarization of North Yorkshire. The protestors have been diverse, constituting not one organized group, but several groups and individuals with a personal commitment to nonviolent direct protest against militarism and military activity. There have been differences in the detail of protest articulated and conducted by these various groups and individuals challenging the military presence at Menwith Hill, but two points stand out.

The first concerns the very use to which this locality is put. Menwith Hill, they argue, provides the means for the control of the US's nuclear capability. It also provides the means to respond to a perceived or actual nuclear or

Figure 6.1   Menwith Hill, North Yorkshire, 2002. Copyright: Rachel Woodward.

nonnuclear strike against the UK. Menwith Hill is thus a link in a chain of military nuclear capability, and also a potential target for military actions against that capability. It promotes an idea of 'security' predicated on the use of weapons of mass destruction in general and nuclear weapons in particular, which in itself is immoral. Furthermore, its presence and its use has promoted the use of resources for military purposes within a world perceived by the protestors as riven by struggles over the unequal distribution of those resources (Dean, 1986). In addition, the militarization of atmospheric space is resisted.

The second protest articulated by campaigners is that the US military presence, and the use of this space for US military purposes, runs counter to the principles of national sovereignty. The Campaign for the Account-ability of American Bases (CAAB) presents a critique, not only of Menwith Hill, which argues that not only does the military presence run counter to the interests of the UK as a nation state (by implicating it in the nuclear and nonnuclear arms race), but also that UK parliamentary and government scrutiny over the issue of the base's establishment has never been rigorous and thorough, given the significance of the site and its functions. The US National Security Agency, the argument goes, controls the site and its functions, yet is unanswerable to the UK government with ultimate juris-diction over the place. The NSA is unaccountable for its activities, there-fore, to the British people.

The forms of protest maintained against Menwith Hill have varied between the groups and individuals undertaking these actions. Again, there are differences between approaches, but again key points stand out. The first is that the protests have been essentially nonviolent, informed by a philosophy which emphasizes the need to provide an alternative to power, and not simply mirror it. This nonviolent tradition, for some protestors, has direct roots in a Quaker tradition of personal responsibility, of bearing witness to immoral acts, and of acting in opposition in ways which indicate alternatives. The metaphor of the open hand enclosing the clenched fist springs to mind. What is striking is the courage, commitment, determination and tenacity of many of the protestors, tolerating repeated arrests, convictions and imprisonment, not to mention bail conditions, orders to remain away from the base and surveillance and monitoring of their personal lives. Guiding the resistance of the CAAB is the anthropologist Margaret Mead's dictum, 'Never doubt that a small group of thoughtful, committed citizens can change the world: indeed its the only thing that ever does'.

A second point about the forms of protest, one which follows from the first, is that this is protest by subversion. Cat-and-mouse or David-and-Goliath metaphors are tempting here, to highlight the extent to which these are protests by the powerless against the powerful. In such circumstances, the most appropriate means of contest is by the subversion of military might. Examples include OPAG's strategies of digging through the rubbish and refuse of the base in order to find (shredded) documents, which have them been painstakingly pieced together, persistent efforts rewarded by incremental shreds of information. Another strategy has to been continually to highlight the insecurity of this top security installation by simply entering the base.

A third point about the forms of protest taken concerns strategies by which knowledge is obtained. Over the years, groups such as the WoMenwith Hill peace camp, the OPAG and the CAAB have in effect pieced together vast amounts of otherwise secret information, from a variety of sources, to construct a bigger picture of the purpose and functions of Menwith Hill. In part, this strategy rests on a willingness to use the parliamentary, legislative and planning systems against the military presence by using these systems as a source of information. Examples include not only information gleaned from rubbish bins but also papers in the Public Record Office, answers to Parliamentary Questions placed by sympathetic MPs, and information taken from planning applications submitted to the local authority. The control of space embodied by Menwith Hill rests to a great degree on secrecy and unaccountability, and the piecing together of snippets of information to make public the activities of the base, and the expenditure of energy and resources on publicizing that information, in turn renders the protestors more powerful. A final point here is that the critique against the use of this part of North Yorkshire for military purposes is connected explicitly, by the protestors, with other UK campaigns – against bases at Fylingdales in North Yorkshire, Digby in Lincolnshire, for example – and with campaigns with similar objectives on other continents – in Okinawa, Japan, for example, or Pine Gap in the centre of Australia.

Conclusions about the 'effectiveness' or otherwise of antimilitarist protests at places like Menwith Hill or Greenham Common critique such activities for their apparent inability ultimately to shift the object of their complaint. The WoMenwith Hill peace camp and caravan has been evicted; Menwith Hill station is still there. Legal sanction has been placed on a number of individuals persistent in their protest. Wood's interpretation of this, and of the lessons of the CAAB campaign and WoMenwith Hill camp, is positive, however. For him:

> both demonstrate that the state's use of legal remedies against ordinary citizens challenging state activities can be limited if those people simply ignore the sanctions placed on them. It seems that empowerment can truly counter conventional power, that indeed power may be an outcome of the creation of effective networks rather than a possession of large actors. (Wood, 2001, p.293)

Disarming Landscapes

I want to conclude this chapter by looking at some rather more indirect and ambiguous reactions to military control than those expressed by the protestors at Otterburn, Greenham or Menwith Hill. These are the practices of interpretation and reimagination which surround the preservation of military landscapes and historic military structures. These interpretative practices are vastly disparate – I'm hesitant about grouping them together at all – but are significant here for the questions they raise about the form and function of contemporary militarism. Some counter, directly or indirectly, the militarized landscapes discussed in the previous chapter and are about finding alternative interpretations which capture the significance of violence, loss and horror, without necessarily glorifying the ideologies which lead to and endorse armed conflict. Others are uninterested in (or claim distance from) the politics of representation. This section is brief, relative to the potential examples available and these issues they throw up, but aims to give at the very least a flavour of some of the issues at stake.

The preservation of historic military structures involves an array of choices predicted on a first simple act of designation for conservation. The UK's national programme for the protection of historic buildings and sites offers two categories for protection. Scheduled Ancient Monuments are designated by central government. Alternatively, local authorities can list buildings as either Grade I or Grade II. The scheduling or listing of historic military sites has granted protection to a wide variety of structures, varying from the Tower of London to the former prisoner of war camp at Harperley in County Durham. The significance of the listing of this camp may have been overstated – one newspaper argued that this 'declared [Harperley] to be as important a monument as Stonehenge and Blenheim Palace' (Carter, 2002) – but its listing makes the point that it is not just the fantastic or magnificent military structures which have been deemed worthy of protection, but also the mundane, and those which have less happy stories to tell about life during wartime.

That choice of sites to designate for preservation is increasingly wide. In a narrow sense, it is purely a managerial issue (see Barnes, 1998; Huck, 1997). However, the preservation of military landscapes and structures has become a topic for legitimate and necessary public debate, with multiple opinions on what should and should not be preserved (Dobinson, Lake and Schofield, 1997). The passage of 50 years, the 'arbitrary age at which the material present becomes the archaeological past', means that many Second World War monuments are now classified as 'archaeology', increasing the potential number of sites for preservation and examination (Chippindale, 1994). In addition, the restructuring of the British Armed Forces throughout the 1990s, with its associated disposals of lands and buildings, means that the quantity and quality of many structures and groups of buildings is only now becoming apparent. Popular interest in the physical heritage of war has also been prompted by anniversaries and the publicity which they bring. This, then, is an issue not just for conservators, managers and commentators, but one with a much broader currency.

The listing and surveying of war remains under English Heritage's Monument Protection Programme involves considering for statutory protection sites on the basis of rarity value and degree of integrity as a whole (Schofield, 2001). This framework doesn't allow for the preservation of every little pillbox, observation post and gun emplacement; these are too numerous. Accounting for a representative sample of structures has in itself been an enormous task. Documenting the Royal Observer Corps sites under the Monuments Protection Programme entailed a huge UK documentary survey of the distribution and dating of sites in nine major categories (Dobinson, Lake and Schofield, 1997). The Council of British Archaeology's 'Defence of Britain' project established a database and archive of 25,000 defence sites from the twentieth century, using information from the Public Record Office, local archives, and the contribution of text, plans and photographs from over 700 volunteers. All contributions were analyzed, interpreted, mapped and put into local and national Monuments

Records. In the course of recent massive recording exercises such as these, historical understanding has been deepened with the revelation of hitherto secret information. For example, the location of Eisenhower's HQ for overseeing the Normandy landings in 1944 has now been revealed as Sawyer's Wood, north of Portsmouth (Chippindale, 1994). Also uncovered were the formerly secret locations of stop lines – trenches – all 2,000 miles, 9ft deep dug across southern England in 1940 to halt the tanks of the anticipated German invasion (Wainwright, 1998). The documentation and preservation of the military past can also bring new insights about technological and industrial development; see, for example, the stories uncovered at the former gunpowder mills at Waltham Abbey (Cocroft, 2000). The range of historic military sites in the UK is vast, and the UK is of course not unique in its military heritage.

Given the wide choice of historic military sites available for designation, then, there is a basic issue as to what to protect. There follows from this a further question about how military sites are preserved and to what uses they are put. Military landscapes, through preservation and protection, can be reused and reimagined through the mobilization of ideas far removed from those which informed their construction. The process entails the inscription of different, nonmilitary meanings onto sites. The fate of these 'deserted bastions' and 'vintage ports' is culturally important; as Celia Clark (2000, 2001) notes, the task of finding a sustainable and appropriate new use for former military sites is symbolic of the national search for a postindustrial, postimperial future. One strategy has been the construction of former military sites as 'heritage' venues. In the UK, sites which can be packaged or marketed, which offer enough of an experience to warrant their use for the heritage industry, have particular appeal.

Eden Camp in East Yorkshire is a good example of this. This former Prisoner of War camp is now established as award-winning museum, the former prison huts converted into displays, providing a background for an impressive collection of military paraphernalia. The former exercise compound has been turned into a children's playground. Although artificial smells are piped into the huts to authenticate the experience, this marketing gimmick of course does no such thing. The horrors of war are absent in this venue, popular with families and school parties (see Figure 6.2).

The marketing of military sites as tourist destinations can be a deliberate strategy for wider place marketing. See, for example, an East of England Tourist Board 'Official Souvenir Map' of United States Air Force airfields, marketed to ex-US services personnel, providing the basis for a heritage trail. The map is a standard one of the road network in the East of England, overlain with red dots and triangles denoting 1939–45 war airfields and headquarters from the famous (Greenham Common, Alconbury) to the obscure (Headcorn in Kent). Many of these (indeed, these three examples)

Figure 6.2   Eden PoW Camp, East Yorkshire, 2002. Copyright: Rachel Woodward.

have now been disposed of and returned to other uses, leaving vague signs etched on the ground. Their vestiges, though, are celebrated in this touring map as seemingly innocent signs of previous military occupancy, notable only for the nostalgic memories these places might hold in the minds who flew from there, rather than for their original deadly purpose.

Most military sites, however, defy such easy packaging. Cold War sites, for example, are significant in their representation of what might have been rather than in their commemoration of actual conflict (Uzzell, 1998). These sites are 'collected' by enthusiasts: Subterranea Britannica's Cold War Study Group has tried to map structures relating to the Cold War period (see also Cruikshank, 1998; Cocroft and Thomas, 2003). They defy easy marketing. Orford Ness, now under National Trust management, was an establishment used for testing explosive devices as part of the national nuclear weapons programme. Access to the Ness was denied to the public during military use due to the secrecy of the work undertaken there. The testing grounds closed in the early 1990s, and Orford Ness, the largest shingle spit in England, cut off from land by the river Ore, sits on the Suffolk Coast with its ghostly remains gradually recolonized by nature. It is a place of strange contrasts. For the National Trust, its 'elemental nature' contrasts with the 'inherent dangers' of this place, a 'hostile and potentially dangerous site'. Military structures – the Bomb Ballistics Building, the

Figure 6.3   Deserted Structures, Orford Ness, Suffolk, 2002. Copyright: Rachel Woodward.

Black Beacon, the 'pagodas' used for explosives design – have been converted into viewing spots. This is not a celebratory site, however; there is ambivalence and doubt here, with regard to what is being physically and ideologically conserved.

Some sites leave little physical presence in the landscape, relative to their symbolic importance. As Schofield and Anderton (2000) remind us, in their discussion of the remains of the Greenham Common women's peace camp, 'heritage' rarely recognizes popular protest, particularly where that protest has been against government, and where a minimal footprint and legacy on the landscape is an intended objective. Some sites defy easy memorial and reinterpretation. Chippindale (1994), writing about the memorializing of nuclear testing in Nevada, asks '. . . what memorial, short of a whole scorched and exploded city, can stand for the scale of atomic war? Even in a test in the Nevada desert, the monster will vaporize whatever spindly towers might have supported it and its instruments' (p.478). Some sites may simultaneously defy reimagination whilst crying out for it for reasons of education, sense of place, commemoration and remembrance; former Nazi concentration camps are an example (see Azaryahu, 2003). The preservation or conservation of the military past, like any act of heritage construction, is not a politically innocent act. In the preservation of the 'materiél culture'[2] of war, conservation is intrinsically bound up with memorial. Those memorials may in turn bring challenges to the military ideologies responsible for the physical remnants in the first place.

The inscription of new meanings onto military landscapes is also an intensely personal act. We all do it. The Defence of Britain archaeological project, mentioned above, relied on individual contributors each bringing their memories and records for public collation. This popular interest was attributed to remains being more 'immediate, local and accessible than the machinations of politicians and higher command.' (Dobinson et al., 1997, p.289), a mechanism by which war could be remembered and made personal. This personal reimagination of military landscapes, this process of making connections to acts of violence through the emotions and meanings stirred by militarism's physical manifestations and remains, is significant to us all. The analyses of Dobinson et al. (1997), Virilio (1994) and Clark (2001) are all prefaced with admissions about the deep and enduring emotions these sites stirred in them as children. I'm no exception. I'm sitting here writing this book because as a nine year-old I gazed up in wonder and horror at the orange, red and brown-rusted hulks of the mulberry harbour remains, silhouetted against the grey sky at Arromanches in Normandy.

Challenging Military Control

Vieques is a small island to the east of Puerto Rico, a US colony. Vieques is the home of the US Navy's Atlantic Fleet Weapons Training Facility, where bombing ranges at land and sea are used for naval training. Land on Vieques has been acquired since 1938 by the US Navy, who currently occupy around 10,530 ha of the island's 13,360 ha – about 75 percent of the available land. The remainder of the island, a central strip, is home to a civilian population of just over 9,000 ha. Vieques is a small and little-known place, representative of a wider process and litany of complaints where military power (particularly, at the present time, US military might) is ultimately unmoved by local challenge.

Protest at the control of the land for military purposes has been directed by two basic complaints; de facto military control of resources, and pollution. Military occupation of the best agricultural land on the island has removed it from cultivation, with economic consequences for the island's farming population. In addition, the use of fishing grounds in the waters around the island for naval training purposes, including bombing training, has disrupted the fishing industry. Military purposes have disrupted the economic health and social vitality of the island. Levels of unemployment on the island are around 50 percent. The second complaint concerns the environmental impacts of military land uses. Islanders complain of eco-logical damage through bombing on the military target practice ranges, the release of chemicals in the payloads of missiles on impact, the generation of particulate matter from bombing, and the littering of the island with metal-lic residues and scrap metals as a by-product of bombing exercises. There are also concerns about the contamination of groundwater by TNT and RDX – a litany of complaints familiar from Chapter 4. There are also assertions that rates of illness from cancer on the island are at least 25 percent higher than on neighbouring Puerto Rico. Protesters from the island have demanded removal of the US Navy from the island, environ-mental clean-up, financial restitution, and support for sustainable eco-nomic development on the island.

Challenges to the military presence initially involved civil disobedience activities – the blockade of the off-shore bombing ranges by the fishing fleet, for example, was a tactic used during the 1970s. Protests became more vocal and more regular with the accidental death of a security guard in a practice bombing run in 1999. The political activism that ensued has challenged directly the US Navy's control of the island. In 2000, the Puerto Rican governor signed an agreement with the then US President Clinton, to the effect that the Vieques people would be able to vote in a referendum on whether the US Navy should remain on the island or should leave. However, in 2001, the new US President, George W. Bush, requested that the US Congress cancel the referendum, with the latter deciding that the US Navy would be obliged to leave the island only when training areas of equal or better utility for military purposes were found. Given that the appropriation of lands for military purposes has been increasingly difficult since the 1990s, because of the wide publicity over potential impacts, and given the observation made in Chapter 2, concerning the reluctance of most military forces to relinquish control over land, the US Navy looks set to remain on Vieques for the foreseeable future. (For authoritative accounts of the challenges to the US Navy by the people of Vieques, see Barreto, 2002; McCaffrey, 2002).

My point in concluding this discussion at Vieques is not to provide yet another example of a strategy of challenge but to emphasize that in the majority of places, challenges to military control, even in nonconflict situ-ations, involve unequal struggles and often invoke often violent responses. Challenges in the UK, with the exception of peace camps like Greenham, have largely been met by nonviolent reaction by the state. We should remember that the UK experiences of challenges to military control and militarism, in this respect, are unusual.

Chapter Seven

The Study of Military Geographies

Understanding Military Control

I walked out onto the runway once the rain had stopped, to look at the view. I was the only person there. It was early autumn, late afternoon, the light was fading, and the place was utterly silent. RAF Binbrook, now reinvented as a civilian settlement and renamed Brookenby, sits on top of a flat hill in the Lincolnshire Wolds, away from any major through-routes. Far off in the distance, I could see the green and grey hulks of the old aircraft hangars and behind these the top of the former control tower. Aircraft have now given way to animal carcasses in the hangars, the control tower houses a small R&D business, and the housing beyond has been sold and rented to a whole new community of people. The runway was distinguishable but battered, a two-mile long strip of concrete fringed with unmown grass verges, crossed with trenches and mounds of earth, scattered here and there with orange traffic cones and bits of domestic rubbish. Fly-tippers had left an armchair, and its foam and springs had split through its filthy, wet, pink, fabric. The old grey runway surface was still smooth in places, and shiny with water. I stood there. I circled round, shaking the raindrops off my coat, getting a feel of the place. I felt like an ant on a mirror. The place felt redundant and scruffy. It also still felt military; the use of the place had changed in 1993 but the imprint of that previous use was still absolute. It is hard turning an RAF base into a business park. The control was there, visibly and palpably. Militarism, as a capability of the state, had been scratched across this place. At military bases, you can see exactly how a moral order creates its own geography. These places are emblematic of domination, power and control. Even after they've closed.

So what about military control? The geographies which this book discusses, military geographies of space and place, environment and landscape, have all been identified as the outcome of military control, and I want to conclude by clarifying where I think control lies. Military control emanates from four distinct sources: physical presence; the control of information; governance and state/citizen relations; and the rhetoric of defence and national security. The future of military geography, for me, lies in unpicking and laying bare the mechanics and politics of military control.

The Controls of Physical Presence

Land used by the military is land controlled by the military, and physical occupancy is the primary sign of that. Most obvious are the controls exerted by military occupancy in conflict situations, control exerted down the barrel of a gun. Often less immediately visible are the controls exerted by what I have termed for simplicity's sake the base of the pyramid, those activities surrounding the constant preparations for war or other conflict-related engagements. The visible effects of a physical military presence accompany effects less tangible or immediate. Military geographies, the shaping of spaces, places, environments and their landscapes, rest on this fact of presence.

This fact of presence explains some of the features of military control, depending on what is being examined (which military geography) and its location. The examples chosen to explore these questions are indicative rather than definitive, but highlight some key points. In the UK, dominance is an issue. In my experience, the overall size of the defence estate often shocks people when they discover that it covers 1 percent of the UK, but they will often then recall the barracks or a radar station or a training area they know nearby. Domination of space in the UK context is subtle, but a feature of the estate nonetheless. But the crucial point about this domin-ance is its changeability. The defence estate may not have reduced in overall size since the 1980s, but the activities upon it shift constantly as a direct consequence of changing global power relations. Furthermore, mili-tary control in this sense ties localities directly to the global practices of international relations. Political requirements dictate the need for deploy-able military forces, which in turn require spaces to be. Military will is exerted over space ultimately for political ends.

We've seen the resilience of that will in the UK's size/needs debate and the resistance to challenges questioning the military's fact of presence. We've seen the knock-on effects of that will in the impact on jobs and livelihoods of localities hosting military facilities. The military requirement for spaces to be (for whatever reason) locks such areas, and the people who live there, into distant military engagements. The military's physical presence shapes the trajectories of economic development in host areas, squews social relations in host communities. Military presence is never benign, it produces its own political economies. This has long been recognized at a macro level. But these political economies of militarism are also a finer-grained, smaller-scaled thing, lived and breathed and controlled at the level of the locality. The fact of presence also has other effects, other controls. Chapter 4 looked at some environmental effects such as pollution and habitat damage, and at military efforts to legitimize such effects by naming them as an inevitable by-product of the military presence. Strategies which naturalize – greenwash – a physical military presence are used to justify its effects. Chapter 5 looked at the use of interpretations of landscapes as militarized in order to legitimize the fact of presence. Chapter 6 highlighted the obstacles posed to those challengers of the military presence faced with the material facts of secure occupancy.

In these ways, and in many others which I have not described, the military presence in nonconflict situations exerts controls over space. One of the tasks of military geography, as I see it, is to take the basic fact of physical military presence and question its consequences, in terms of the political economies it produces and imprints on people and the land. A related task is to think through more stringently the militarization of the connections between global economic networks and the consequences of this at local and regional levels. What military geography has to do is problematize the issue of presence and ask questions about the consequences of this seemingly obvious and taken-for-granted thing.

Information and Control

A second locus for control which I want to highlight is military control over information. If we want to subject the physical presence and consequences of military power to critical examination, we need to have information on what that presence constitutes and affects. A constant theme underpinning much of this book, however, is the difficulty in obtaining and verifying information in order to do that. Data inadequacies confound at every turn. The very facts about the location and extent of military lands, what is owned and where, are hard to find. Talking of the control of information is in some ways a delicate task, finding a way through an issue whilst avoiding either paranoid assumptions about the totality of secrecy or unquestioning acceptance of a military or state rationale. My argument here is to urge rigour in the use of data derived from military sources and in the application of data or information to the analysis of military geographies, and to argue for awareness of the ways in which our knowledge about military geographies rely on imperfect, constructed sources. The data problem bedevils investigation at every turn. As I argue in Chapter 2, the lack of information on land holdings and their purposes is not just an absence of data. Whether deliberate and strategic or whether a by-product of incompetence, the control of space by military establishments is easier to sustain when little information is placed in the public domain about those establishments and that use of space. A lack of information conceals things. Public interest in the defence estate is low not least because of the lack of public information about the extent of the defence estate. Material entities are brought into being by statistical information; public and political discourse on military lands relies on statistical information to describe those entities. In the absence of coherent information, that description falters. Power and control are exerted through the availability of information.

In reviewing the economic geographies of military settlements in Chapter 3, I made the point that not only is getting information on inputs and impact hard, but that there are also things that cannot be quantified thorough standard economic techniques. Data is control, because the absence of impartial information about impacts (i.e. from reliable nonmilitary sources) creates space for competing explanations based on conjecture. In this way, military contributions to local economies can be constructed as beneficial, even if the block that military occupancy puts on other, more socially or environmentally sustainable land uses is not. The lack of data about military bases equates with a lack of public accountability about the functions and impacts of those bases. Data is also a problem when looking at conversion, because the rhetoric of conversion masks fact that there is little information on this process. Furthermore, the use of financial data to measure conversion in the UK defines the public interest in terms of financial benefit to the MoD, rather than in terms of wider benefits of economic development to a locality.

The lack of data on environmental impacts was discussed in Chapter 4. There are issues to do with a basic absence of information; the environmental impacts of military occupancy are very hard to assess in the absence of reliable information. Where information is available, we need to be alert to its source, given what we know about the pressures on military forces to down-play to the public the significance of environmental impacts, and given what we know about the dismissal of nonspecialist or nonmilitary sources of information. There are also issues about what constitutes 'acceptable' data for the purposes of assessing impacts, with the valorization of quantitative information and the dismissal of 'nonscientific' or anecdotal information. The lack of information is also an issue in the construction and representation of military landscapes. What exactly are we looking at? For example, the un-named, unknown, redundant structures of the Cold War shape readings of the Nevada desert. Control over data is control over interpretation; the availability of information determines what questions can be asked. As I discussed in Chapter 6, challenges to the lack of data is one of the key issues for those seeking to contest military land uses, be it through protests against the moral authority of militarism, or challenges to the practices of military activities. One strategy of challenge by opponents has been the seemingly prosaic but highly necessary task of getting information in order to try to build up a picture of what goes on military sites.

The military control over data and information facilitates the military use of space, and in turn, our readings of military geographies are shaped by the information available. One reason for the lack of much contemporary geographical scholarship into military power, militarism and its effects is the lack of readily available, reliable information in order to understand the operation of control, despite differences between states in terms of freedom of information. A second task for military geography, then, is to develop creative ways of obtaining information, and more sophisticated ways of using available data to understand military impacts.

Governance and Control

Militarism is a capability of the state. Militarism isn't 'just there'. It is the active incorporation into governance of military influence. Military control flows from the state and the practices of government. Armed forces have the monopoly of legitimate (legitimized) violence in contemporary advanced economies; they are the state institutions holding the state-sanctioned, legally defined right to bear arms. This capacity for legitimized violence is most obvious when manifested by the state during armed conflicts. In nonconflict situations, the focus of this book, the militarism of the state may be less visibly obvious, but critical in the constitution and expression of military geographies. The state ensures and consolidates military control in myriad ways; military control lies with governance.

The role of the state in establishing military control was seen in Chapter 2 in discussions of the domestic control of the defence estate. Despite the occasional parliamentary challenge, the institutions of the state support not only occupancy but also information about that occupancy. The manner of that governance may change over time, but that control remains. State support for the defence industry shows not only the extent and thickness of the links between government and the corporate sector, but also the influence of the state in determining the economic geographies of military production. The moral order of militarism defines the geographies of production, reproduction and consumption around military bases, and these are sanctioned by the state. Legislative control consolidates military control through the mechanisms by which military lands are managed, and the mechanisms for their disposal. State controls sanction noncompliance with environmental legislation, whereby environmental protection is over-ridden by clauses establishing the preeminent needs of the military. State controls sanction the public interest as defence-based, endorsing the militarization of greening. Military readings of landscape are enshrined by the state, which sanctions accepted readings of landscapes, and accepted stories of how landscapes came to be. Challenges to the state which attempt to subvert the moral order of militarized governance are difficult to maintain.

I noted in the introductory chapter that this book was not concerned directly with describing the many geographies of militarism as they exist around the world. This is not to suggest that the task of mapping the contours of contemporary militarism is unimportant. A third task for military geography, I would suggest, is to explore the nature of contemporary militarism across states, with a view to understanding how the incorporation of military influence into the practices of governance shapes the control and use of space and place.

National Security Discourses and Control

Military control, then, is consolidated through the fact of physical presence, through the availability of information about that presence, and through the legislative support given to militarism by practices of governance. A fourth area where military control lies is the discursive realm where military actions are interpreted and legitimized. We should be alert to the contingency of this in different national contexts. In the context of the UK, I have argued that this legitimation is undertaken with reference to ideas about defence and resistance to invasion. These ideas are mobilized to explain and justify much about the military presence, the control over information, and the role of government in directing military power. My argument is not that we should be surprised by this strategy, but rather that we be alert to the power relations shaped by it.

Discourses of national security are used to justify the extent of the defence estate and the reasons for this. In the UK, ideas about threat of foreign invasion have promoted a powerful discourse around national security, although this is shifting with the loss of old Cold War enemies and the perception of new enemies identified by the United States' 'War on Terror'. Discourses of national security legitimize the military presence, at home and elsewhere. They open up space for the justification of military presence, consolidate support by providing justifications for the use of economic resources (land, materials, labour) for military purposes. The power of such discourses is seen in their abilities to shape nonmilitary activities in proximal space, through representation and through controlling the terms of reference through which impacts of military origin are understood. Legitimation discourses incorporate ideas about the economic contribution of military forces, often despite the lack of evidence for this. Discourses of national security legitimize military impacts on the natural environment, opening up the environment as a space for national defence. Even if those military activities are environmentally destructive, their impacts can be explained away with reference to a higher moral imperative, national defence. The creation of national sacrifice zones in the US in places where military and related activities have wreaked havoc is an extreme example of this. Less extreme, but existing on the same continuum, is the defence of military impacts through arguments which define them as part of the defence of nature in the cause of the defence of nation. The interpretation of landscapes, and of the impact of the military presence on landscapes, is similarly justified as a necessary by-product of a wider national requirement for national security. The point I am making is, again, not that we should be surprised by the use of this discursive strategy, but that we should be alert to the power and politics that are mobilized by it. Strategies of opposition and challenge have dealt in various ways with this, by, for example, questioning the ubiquity of ideas of 'national security' and challenging the definition of the national interest as a military one. What these oppositional strategies teach us is that we should be alert to the power of discourses of national security and defence in controlling practices and debates around those practices which have less to do with defence and security than is implied.

In terms of the study of military geography, this observation about the location of control as discursive as well as material supports the argument that the strategies of control and legitimation constitute a necessary focus for study. Strategies used by military forces and the state to justify the ways in which military geographies are constituted and expressed are critical in understanding those geographies in full, and this is a fourth task for military geography.

Why Military Geographies Matter

I want to conclude by reiterating why I believe military geographies matter so much. I argued in the introduction that in terms of the academic study and practice of contemporary geography in the Anglophone world, the study of military geographies currently constitutes a minor element of the discipline. To be sure, the militarization of space, materially and discursively, has its place in contemporary scholarship – see, for example, the development of studies of the geographies of violence and the growth of critical geopolitics. Geography as a discipline is not ignorant of the significance of militarism in shaping space. But it seems to me that this significance is less understood by the discipline as a whole. As to why this is, I am not sure. As a social science, Geography is a small discipline. The issue of data and information may be a factor. Lack of awareness may be another. But this muted appreciation of the power of militarism and military activities in shaping the world is regrettable. Military geographies matter.

They matter specifically for many of the reasons expanded upon in this book. But overall they matter simply because of the dominance of military conflict and military engagements in shaping the contemporary world. Militarism and its effects define the lives of the majority of the world's population, whether it be through living and dying in war, or through the dominance of military objectives and requirements in shaping agendas for public expenditure and development, whether it be through the use of resources, the shaping of spaces of production and consumption, or through the teaching of politics and the conduct of public life. We cannot be ignorant of militarism and military activities in shaping the geographies of the contemporary world. We need to look at militarism in its varied guises, examine its influence, pay attention to the conditions which make war and state-sanctioned violence possible. Militarism and military activities shape the earth, and Geography as a discipline should be more alert than at present it appears to be to the ways in which these geographies are constituted, and the ways in which militarism's geographies are expressed.

My plea for the recognition of the significance of military geographies extends to the tertiary curriculum. On the day US and British military force was (officially) unleashed upon Iraq in March 2003, a very senior administrative officer at my university sent an email to all teaching staff, asking them not to abandon the planned teaching syllabus in favour of discussions of the rights and wrongs of military engagement in the Gulf. Many ignored this instruction because they felt a need from their students for access to information and debate that would enable them to draw their own conclusions about the rights and wrongs of preemptive military action against the Iraqi regime, not least because of the lack of clarity in public and media debates about the logic of war. But in addition, many of us ignored the email and used class time to discuss the war and the things that made this war possible because we felt the need as teachers to make clear the links and disjunctures between the subject-matter of the curriculum and the impending conflict. Academic tertiary education, after all, is about making connections and developing explanation through critical scholarship. Military geographies matter, because they help us make sense of the world.

Notes

Notes to Chapter 1

1   For the French writer and urban theorist Paul Virilio, all human geographies are military geographies. Whether one sees such statements as paranoiac or realistic, his point, like mine, is to be emphatic about the pervasive influence of militarism and military activities on all our geographies. For an accessible introduction to Virilio's work, see Luke and Ó Tuathail (2000).
2   See for example Pepper and Jenkins, 1985; O'Loughlin and van der Wusten, 1986; O'Loughlin, 1986; Ó Tuathail, 1996; Shapiro, 1997; Dalby and Ó Tuathail, 1998; Flint, 2004.
3   I use upper case throughout to distinguish Military Geography from the military geographies discussed in this undisciplined book.
4   Much of the best current work in contemporary cultural geography and critical geopolitics is similarly based on an analytic approach which emphasises the significance of representation as a political strategy and the centrality of analyses of those representational strategies in academic analysis.
5   See, for example, Wood, 2001; Graham, 2002.

Notes to Chapter 2

1   For example, see Blake's comprehensive collation of information on airfields past and present in the UK (Blake, 1969, 1981, 1986, 1989).
2   My own application for public funding to collate information about the contemporary defence estate was rejected by referees who ultimately couldn't quite believe that such information wasn't already available.
3   I am not suggesting that those without a military background would be unable to make sense of military training needs and planning, but would highlight the demands on those outside the military in doing so. These complexities are explored in Doxford (2000).

NOTES TO PAGES 31–71   161

4   For a broader discussion of paternalism, land management, and social and political consequences of the paternalistic countryside, see Murdoch, Lowe, Ward and Marsden, 2003, Ch. 6.

5   The Armed Forces Minister announced to the House of Commons on 16 January 2003 that Landmarc Support Services had been selected by the Ministry of Defence to manage the Army Training Estates. Landmarc Support Services is owned by Interserve Defence Ltd and DynCorp International. The contracting-out of land management functions by the MoD to a private company has raised angry comment from MPs, concerned about both the principle, and by the specific criticisms of the companies concerned; DynCorp has been associated with drugs trafficking scandals in Colombia and the trafficking of young women in Bosnia (*Guardian*, 29 November 2002).

Notes to Chapter 3

1   My thanks to Catherine Ogden for this point; she has also warned that the date of the Gododdin, and the precise location of Catraeth, are matters of contemporary scholarly dispute.

2   In the UK, one notable exception is the work of the Centre for Defence Economics at the University of Hull.

3   See also papers by Atkinson, Campbell, Ellis et al., Markusen and Park, Scott, Warf, and Warf and Glasmeier, all 1993, in a special issue of *Economic Geography*, and Law et al., 1993.

4   The idea of the Cold War itself can be seen as a discursive construction; see Lovering, 1994.

5   KONVER and KONVER II were European Union Community Initiatives to provide financial support to restructuring in defence-dependent regions of the EU.

6   The issues associated with the conversion and restructuring of the defence industry are not considered here; see Kaldor and Schméder (1997), BICC's annual conversion surveys, Markusen and Brzoska (2000) for a discussion of key points, and papers by Oden, Accordino and Elsner, de Penaros and Serfati, Hassink, Perani, Gonchar and Opitz, and Kiss (all 2000) in the special issue of *International Regional Science Review* (2000) .

7   The Defence Estate Organisation was the MoD organisation charged with the management of the defence estate. It was relaunched as an Agency, Defence Estates, in 1999.

8   The KONVER initiative finished in 1999. Its nonrenewal following the restructuring of EU structural funds under Agenda 2000 reflects the declining importance of conversion issues on the EU's political agenda.

9   When questioned directly about this, the Defence Diversification Agency claimed that 'lack of resources' explained the lack of interest in taking on board military land sales; COST A10 Seminar, Glasgow, 19 November 1999.

Notes to Chapter 4

1 'Gulf War Syndrome' is the name used for a set of physical illnesses affecting Gulf war veterans to a greater degree than control populations. There has been some limited recognition of the fact of illness amongst military personnel who saw active service in the Gulf War, but the existence of a 'Gulf War Syndrome' has been contested by the Government in the absence of sufficient evidence to characterize the range of health problems experience by Gulf War veterans as a syndrome. Around 2,000 notices of intention to claim compensation from the Government are pending, from Gulf War veterans and their families, at the time of writing (see Hansard, 2003). The syndrome of connected illnesses is thought to have been caused either by the use of DU-tipped munitions, or by the combination of vaccinations against disease and chemical and biological agents given to military personnel prior to the war (Guardian, 2002a).
2 Training in the technical skills required for military land management is available, for example, from the Masters degree in Military Lands Management delivered at the Centre for Environmental Management of Military Lands at Colorado State University, USA.
3 See, for example, the Otterburn Public Inquiry, where information on the efflux from practice rockets used during MLRS firing was only reluctantly and partially given.
4 The argument which follows is also made in Woodward, 2001b.

Notes to Chapter 5

1 The landscapes that infantry recruits learn to read are rural agricultural ones; the majority of British Army infantry training for recruits who have completed their basic training is conducted at ITC Catterick in North Yorkshire, with further specialist training given at the Infantry Battle School at Sennybridge Training Area in Mid Wales. Fighting in Built Up Areas (FIBUA) training is still conducted in a rural setting.
2 See, for example, Watson-Smyth, 1993; Cocroft, 2000; Cocroft and Thomas, 2003.

Notes to Chapter 6

1 I once overhead a group of MoD representatives giggling wildly. 'What are they called again?', asked one wag, talking about a group opposing the proposed developments at Otterburn, 'Gay Badgers Against the Bomb?'.
2 The term is from Schofield, Jonhson and Beck, 2002.

Bibliography

Accordino, J. and Elsner, W. (2000) Conversion planning in two military shipbuilding regions: Hampton Roads, Virginia and Bremen, Germany. *International Regional Science Review*, 23 (1), 48–65.

Ambrose, S.E. (1992) *Band of Brothers: E Company, 506 Regiment, 101st Airborne from Normandy to Hitler's Eagle's Nest*. Simon and Schuster, London.

ARG: Army Recruiting Group (undated, c.1996) *Experience Life as a Solider*. Recruitment brochure. CP (A) 96.

Arms Conversion Project (1998) *Defence Diversification: Getting the Most Out of Defence Technology*, ACP, Glasgow.

Army (1997) *Gurkhas 'Hug a Tree' to Help the Environment*. British Army press release, 9 June 1997, Serial Number 111.

Army (2003) www.army.mod.uk/2div/Organisation. Visited 6 March 2003.

Ascherson, N. (1998) In this rich earth. *Observer*, 25 October 1998.

Atkinson, R. (1993) Defense spending cuts and regional economic impact: an overview. *Economic Geography*, 69, 107–22.

Australian Anti-Bases Campaign (2003) www.anti-bases.org/campaigns. Visited 27 February 2003.

Australian Defence Force (2001) *Defence Environmental Statement*, September 2001, ADF.

Ayllon, F., Suciu, R., Gephard, S., Jaunes, F. and Garcia-Vazquez, E. (2000) Conventional armament wastes induce micronuclei in wild brown trout Salmo trutta. *Mutation Research – Genetic Toxicology and Environmental Mutagenesis*, 470 (20), 169–76.

Azaryahu, M. (2003) RePlacing memory: the reorientation of Buchenwald. *Cultural Geographies*, 10, 1–20.

Baker, F. (1993) The Berlin Wall: production, preservation and consumption of a twentieth-century monument. *Antiquity*, 67, 709–33.

Ballinger, A. (1992) *The Quiet Soldier*. Orion, London.

Bansal, P. and Howard, E. (1997) (eds) *Business and the Natural Environment*. Butterworth-Heineman, Oxford.

Barnaby, F. (1991) The environmental impact of the Gulf War. *The Ecologist*, 21 (4) 166–72.

Barnes, I. (1998) The management of an archaeological landscape on the Army's training area on Salisbury Plain, Wiltshire. In Grenville, J. (ed.) *Managing the Historic Rural Landscape*. Routledge, London, 85–99.

Barreto, A.A. (2002) *Vieques, the Navy and Puerto Rican Politics*. University Press of Florida, Gainesville, Florida.

Baudrillard, J. (1995) *The Gulf War Did Not Take Place*. Indiana University Press, Bloomington.

BBC: British Broadcasting Corporation (1999) *Soldiers to Be*, Series 1. BBC, London.

BBC: British Broadcasting Corporation (2000) *Soldiers to Be*, Series 2. BBC, London.

Beck, C. (2002) 'The archaeology of scientific experiments at a nuclear testing ground.' In Schofield, J., Johnson, W.G. and Beck, D.M. (2002) (eds) *Matériel Culture: The Archaeology of Twentieth Century Conflict*. Routledge, London, 65–79.

Beder, S. (1993) Bias and credibility in environmental impact assessment. *Chain Reaction*, 68, 28–30.

Beder, S. (1997) *Global Spin: The Corporate Assault on Environmentalism*. Green Books, Totnes.

Bell, M.M. (1994) *Childerley: Nature and Morality in a Country Village*. University of Chicago Press, Chicago.

Bennett, J.A. (2001) War, emergency and the environment in Fiji, 1939–1946. *Environment and History*, 7, 255–87.

Bennett, J.W. (1994) Prospects for fungal bioremediation of TNT munition waste. *International Biodeterioration & Biodegradation*. 34 (1) 21–34.

BICC: Bonn International Centre for Conversion (1996) *Conversion Survey 1996: Global Disarmament, Demilitarisation and Demobilization*. Oxford University Press, Oxford.

BICC: Bonn International Centre for Conversion (1998) *Conversion Survey 1998: Global Disarmament, Defence Industry Consolidation and Conversion*. Oxford University Press, Oxford.

BICC: Bonn International Centre for Conversion (1999) *Conversion Survey 1999: Global Disarmament, Demilitarization and Demobilization*. Nomos Verlagsgesellschaft, Baden Baden.

BICC: Bonn International Centre for Conversion (2000) *Conversion Survey 2000: Global Disarmament, Demilitarization and Demobilization*. Nomos Verlagsgesellschaft, Baden Baden.

Black, J. (1997) *Maps and Politics*. Reaktion Books, London.

Blackout (1999) [photography exhibition and catalogue]

Blacksell, M. and Reynolds, F. (1987) Military training in National Parks: A question of land use conflict and national priorities. In Bateman, M. and Riley, R. (eds) *The Geography of Defence*. Croom Helm, London.

Blake, R.N.E. (1969) The impact of airfields on the British landscape. *Geographical Journal*, 135, 508–528.

Blake, R.N.E. (1981) The changing distribution of military airfields in the East Midlands, 1914–1980. *The East Midland Geographer*, 7 (8), 286–302.

Blake, R.N.E. (1986) Old airfields take off. *The Geographical Magazine*, 58 (6), 272–4.

Blake, R.N.E. (1989) *The Development of Military and Civil Airfields in the United Kingdom since 1909, with Special Reference to Land Use*. University of London PhD thesis.

Boice, L.P. (1996) Managing endangered species on military lands. *Endangered Species Update*, 13 (7and 8), 1—6.

Boice, L.P. (1996) *Managing Endangered Species on Military Lands*. US Department of Defense briefing paper.

Boice, L.P. (1997) Meeting current challenges to DoD's conservation program. *Federal Facilities Environmental Journal*, Spring 1997, 29–37.

Bracewell, M. (1997) *England is Mine: Pop Life in Albion from Wilde to Goldie*, Harper Collins, London.

Bradshaw, T. (1999) Communities not fazed: why military base closures may not be catastropic. *Journal of the American Planning Association*, 65 (2), 193–206.

Brömmelhörster, J. (2000) Military expenditures and the search for peace dividends: An introduction. In Brömmelhörster, J. (ed) *Demystifying the Peace Dividend*. Nomos Verlagsgesellschaft, Baden-Baden.

Bryson, J., Henry, N., Keeble, D. and Martin, R. (1999) (eds) *The Economic Geography Reader*. Wiley, London.

Brzoska, M. (1999a) Military conversion: the balance sheet. *Journal of Peace Research*, 36 (2), 131–40.

Brzoska, M. (1999b) Conversion in a Resource-Reuse Perspective'. In Jelušic, L. and Selby, J. (eds) *Defence Restructuring and Conversion: Socio-cultural aspects*. COST A10, European Commission, DG Research, Brussels,14–31.

Bunce, M. (1994) *The Countryside Ideal: Anglo-American Images of Landscape*. Routledge, London.

Buss, T. and Dwivedi, S. (1997) Military base closings and economic development. *Commentary*, 2 (1), 19–26.

Calhoun, C. (ed) (2002) *Dictionary of the Social Sciences*. Oxford University Press, Oxford.

Campbell, D. (1984) *The Unsinkable Aircraft Carrier: American Military Power in Britain*. Michael Joseph, London.

Campbell, S. (1993) Interregional migration of defense scientists and engineers to the gunbelt during the 1980s. *Economic Geography*, 69, 204–23.

Canadian National Defence (2000) *Environmentally Sustainable Defence Activities: A Sustainable Strategy for National Defence*. Available at www.forces.gc.ca/admin/dge/SDS.

Carson, I. (2002) Transformed? A Survey of the Defence Industry. *Economist*, 20 July, 2002.

Carter, H. (2002) Wartime capsule: PoW camp on par with Stonehenge *Guardian*, 19 July, 2002.

Carter, N. and Lowe, P. (1998) Britain: coming to terms with sustainable development? In Hanf, K. and Jansen, A-I. (eds) *Governance and Environment in Western Europe: Politics, Policy and Administration*. Addison Wesley Longman, Harlow.

Castle, T. (2002) Courage, mon ami. *London Review of Books*, 24 (7), 4 April, 2002.

Cawley, R.M. and Lawrence, R.M. (1995) National security policy and federal lands policy, or, the greening of the Pentagon. In Crotty, W. (ed.), *Post-Cold War Policy: The Social and Domestic Context*, Nelson Hall, Chicago, 274–92.

Chaffey, J. (1998) Managing the Wessex coast: the Lulworth Ranges. *Geography Review*, 11 (3), 30–2.

Charles, P.T., Gauger, P.R., Patterson, C.H. and Kusterbeck, A.W. (2000) On-site immunoanalysis of nitrate and nitroaromatic compounds in groundwater. *Environmental Science and Technology*, 34 (21) 4641–50.

Chan, S. (1995) 'Grasping the Peace Dividend: Some propositions on the conversion of swords into ploughshares.' *Mershon International Studies Review*, 39, 53—95.

Chatham Maritime, 2002 http://www.seeda.co.uk/chathammaritime/ web site

Childs, J. (1998) *The Military Use of Land: A History of the Defence Estate*, Peter Lang AG, Bern.

Chippindale, C. (1994) Editorial. *Antiquity*, 68, 477–88.

Ciarrocca, M. (2002) Northrup Grumann and TRW merger: sealing the deal. *Foreign Policy in Focus*, 29 July, 2002.

Clark, C. (2000) *Vintage Ports or Deserted Dockyards: Differing Futures for Naval Heritage Across Europe*. Working Paper 57, Centre for Environment and Planning, University of the West of England.

Clark, C. (2001) *'White Holes': Decision-making in the Disposal of Ministry of Defence Heritage Sites*. Unpublished PhD thesis, University of Portsmouth.

Clark, C. (2003) Are we wasting the 'peace dividend'? *Town and Country Planning*, 72 (5), 150–4.

Clout, H. and Gosme, C. (2003) The Naval Intelligence Handbooks: a monument in geographical writing. *Progress in Human Geography*, 27 (2), 153–73.

Cocroft, W. (2000) *Dangerous Energy: The Archaeology of Gunpowder and Military Explosives Manufacture*. English Heritage, London.

Cocroft, W. and Thomas, R. (2003) *Cold War: Building for Nuclear Confrontation 1946–1989*. English Heritage, London.

Coulson M (1995) (ed) *Pilot Study on Defence Environmental Expections: Proceedings of the International Symposium on the Environment and Defence*. CCMS Report No. 211, NATO. Department of Geography, University of Swansea.

Countryside Commission (1994) *Military Training in the Northumberland National Park*. CCP 471, Countryside Commission, Cheltenham.

Cresswell, T. (1996) *In Place/Out of Place: Geography, Ideology and Transgression*. University of Minnesota Press, Minneapolis.

Croudace I.W., Warwick P.E., Taylor R.N. and Cundy, A.B. (2000) Investigation of an alleged nuclear incident at Greenham Common Airbas using T1-mass spectrometric measurements of uranium isotopes. *Environmental Science & Technology*, 34 (21), 4496–503.

Cruickshank, D. (1998) Cold War sites. *One Foot in the Past*, programme notes for broadcast of 16 June 1998.

Cunningham, K. and Klemmer, A. (1995) *Restructuring the US Military Bases in Germany: Scope, Impacts and Opportunities*. Report 4, Bonn International Centre for Conversion, Bonn.

D'Souza, E. (1995) The potential of the military in environmental protection: India. *Unasylva* 183, vol 46, 57–62.

Dalby, S. (2002) *Environmental Security.* University of Minnesota Press, Minneapolis.

Dalby, S. and Ó Tuathail, G. (1998) (eds) *Rethinking Geopolitics,* Routledge, London.

Daniels, S. (1993) *Fields of Vision: Landscape Imagery and National Identity in England and the United States.* Polity Press, Cambridge.

Dardia, M., McCarthy, K., Malkin, J. and Vernez, G. (1996) *The Effects of Military Base Closures on Local Communities: A Short-Term Perspective.* RAND Corporation, Santa Monica, CA.

DASA: Defence Analytical Services Agency (2002) *UK Defence Statistics 2002.* The Stationery Office, London. Also web site.

David, M.D. and Seiber, J.N. (1999) Analysis of organophosphate Hydraulic fluids in US Air Force Base soils. *Archives of Environmental Contamination and Toxicology,* 36 (3), 235–41.

Davis, M. (1993) Dead West: Ecocide in Marlboro Country. *New Left Review,* 200, 49–73.

De Penaros, R. and Serfati, C. (2000) Regional conversion under conditions of defense industry centralization: the French case. *International Regional Science Review,* 23 (1), 66–80.

Dean, C. (1986) *Arguments Against the Continued Use of Yorkshire Moorland as a Spy Base.* Unpublished OPAG briefing paper.

Defence Estates (1999) *Corporate Plan 1999–2004.* Defence Estates, Sutton Coldfield.

Defence Estates (2000) *Corporate Plan 2000–05.* Defence Estates, Sutton Coldfield.

Defence Estates (2001a) Personal Communication on Ministry of Defence sites in Germany. 24 January, 2001.

Defence Estates (2001b) Personal communication on the size and location of USAF bases in the UK. 11 January, 2001.

Defence Estates (2001c) *Integrated Land Management Plan: Salisbury Plain Training Area. 2001 Review.*

Defence Estates (2002) *Corporate Plan 2002–07.* Defence Estates, Sutton Coldfield.

Defence Estates (nd) *Wading into EastEnd Deal with RSPB.* Defence Estates Press Release, undated (c.2000)

Defence Lands Committee (1973) *Report of the Defence Lands Committee.* The Nugent Inquiry. Cm 5714. HMSO, London.

DEO: Defence Estates Organisation (1998) Personal communication on defence lands sales, 2 November, 1998.

Department of Defense (undated a) *Defending Our Natural Heritage: Natural Resources in the Department of Defense.* DoD, Washington.

Department of Defense (undated b) *DoD Commander's Guide to Biodiversity.* DoD, Washington.

Department of the Environment (1974) *Statement on the Report of the Defence Lands Committee, 1971–73.* Cmnd 5714, HMSO, London.

Der Derian (1998) 'All but war is simulation' in Ó Tuathail, G. and Dalby, S. (eds) *Rethinking Geopolitics.* Routledge, London, 261–74.

Doak, J. (1999) Planning for the reuse of redundant defence estates: disposal processes, policy frameworks and development impacts. *Planning Practice and Research,* 14 (2), 211–24.

Dobinson, C.S., Lake, J. and Schofield, A.J. (1997) Monuments of war: defining Engalnd's twentieth-century defence heritage. *Antiquity*, 71, 288–99.

Dodds, K. (1998) Enframing the Falklands: identity, landscape, and the 1982 South Atlantic War. *Environment and Planning D: Society and Space*, 16, 733–56.

Douglas, M. (1966) *Purity and Danger: An Analysis of Concepts and Pollution and Taboo*. Routledge and Kegan Paul, London.

Doxford, D. (2000) *The Allocation and Management of Land Used for Army Training in the UK*. PhD thesis, University of Sunderland.

Doxford, D. and Hill, A. (1998) Land use for military training in the UK: the current situation, likely developments and possible alternatives. *Journal of Environmental Planning and Management*, 41 (3), 279–97.

Doxford, D. and Judd, A. (2002) Army training: the environmental gains resulting from the adoption of alternatives to traditional training methods. *Journal of Environmental Planning and Management*, 45 (2), 245–65.

Doxford, D. and Savege, J. (1995) 'The proposed development of Otterburn military training area in Northumberland National Park: A national perspective.' *Journal of Environmental Planning and Management*, 38,4: 551–60.

Dryzek, J. (1997) *The Politics of the Earth: Environmental Discourses*. Oxford University Press, Oxford.

Dwernychuk, L.W., Cau, H.D., Hatfield, C.T., Boivin, T.G., Hung, T.M., Dung, P.T. and Thai, N.D. (2002) Dioxin reservoirs in southern Viet Nam: a legacy of Agent Orange. *Chemosphere*, 47 (2), 117–37.

Dycus, S. (1996) *National Defense and the Environment*. University Press of New England, Hanover.

EAG/Ecotec, (1996) *The Impact of the Peace Dividend on Rural England*. Rural Development Commission, Salisbury.

Edgar, P.J., Davies, I.M., Hursthouse, A.S. and Matthews, J.E. (1999) The biogeochemistry of polychlorinated biphenyls (PCBs) in the Clyde: distribution and source evaluation. *Marine Pollution Bulletin*, 38 (6), 486–96.

Edwards, R. (1999) Too hot to handle. *New Scientist*, 5 June, 1999.

Ellis, M., Barff, R. and Markusen, A. (1993) Defense spending and interregional labor migration. *Economic Geography*, 69, 182–203.

Enloe, C. (1990) *Bananas, Beaches and Bases: Making Feminist Sense of International Politics*. University of California Press, Berkeley.

Enloe, C. (1993) *The Morning After: Sexual Politics at the End of the Cold War*. University of California Press, Berkeley.

Environmental Audit Committee (1999) *Sixth Report: The Greening Government Initiative*, HC426, TSO, London.

Environmental Audit Committee (1998) *The Greening Government Initiative*, HC517, TSO, London.

Euler, C. and Welzer-Lang, D. (2000) *Developing Best Professional Practice for Reducing Sexual Abuse, Domestic Violence and Trafficking in Militarised Areas of Peacetime Europe*. Research Centre for Violence, Abuse and Gender Relations, Leeds Metropolitan University, UK.

Evinger, W.R. (1998) *Directory of US Military Bases Worldwide*. Third Edition. Oxryx Press.

Fairclough, N. (1995) *Critical Discourse Analysis: The Critical Study of Language.* Longman, London.

Ferlie, E., Ashburner, L., Fitzgerald, L. and Pettigrew, A. (1996) *The New Public Management in Action.* Oxford University Press, Oxford.

Finger, M. (1991) The military, the nation state and the environment. *The Ecologist,* 21 (5), 220–25.

First Inspector's Report (nd; c. 1998) *Notice of Proposed Development by Ministry of Defence at Otterburn Training Area, Northumberland.* File number: N/P/R2900/222/97/1

Fisher, B. (1993) Seizing the opportunity in military base closures, *Urban Land,* 52 (8), 11–15.

Flint, C. (2004) (ed.) *The Geography of War and Peace.* Oxford University Press, Oxford.

Fonnum, F., Paukštys, B., Zeeb, B. and Reimer, K.J. (1997) (eds) *Environmental Contamination and Remediation Practices at Former and Present Military Bases.* Kluwer, Dordrecht.

Foot, W. (2001) Lecture on 'The Landscape of Defence, 1940', given by Database and Archive Manager of the Council of British Archaeology's Defence of Britain Project, *Context* (on-line), October 2001.

Fraser, G.M. (1971) *The Steel Bonnets: The Story of Anglo–Scottish Border Reivers.* Barrie and Jenkins, London.

Fuller Peiser and University of Reading (1999) *Development of the Redundant Defence Estate: A report to the Department of Environment, Transport and the Regions.* Thomas Telford, London.

Gallent, N. and Howe, J. (1998) Planning for aviation and diversification on small rural airfields in England and Wales. *Regional Studies* 32 (4), 365–381.

Gallent, N., Howe, J. and Bell, P. (1998) Happy Landings. *Town and Country Planning,* Jan/Feb, 32–3.

Gallent, N., Howe, J. and Bell, P. (1999) More Happy Landings. *Town and Country Planning,* July, 234–6.

Gallent, N., Howe, J. and Bell, P. (2000) New uses for England's old airfields. *Area,* 32 (4), 383–94.

Gentleman, A. (1998) Last of the peace women demand memorial. *Guardian,* 25 July, 1998.

Gerson, J. and Birchard, B. (1991) (eds) *The Sun Never Sets... Confronting the Network of Foreign US Military Bases.* South End Press, Boston.

Gillibrand, A. and Hilton, B. (1998) Resource accounting and budgeting: principles, concepts and practice – the MoD case. *Public Money and Management,* 18 (2), 21–8.

Glasby, G.P. (1997) Disposal of chemical weapons in the Baltic Sea. *The Science of the Total Environment,* 206 (2–3) 267–73.

Glassberg, A. (1995) Intergovernmental relations and base closing. *Publius: The Journal of Federalism,* 25 (3), 87–98.

Gonchar, K. and Opitz, P. (2000) Regional conversion in the Russian case. *International Regional Science Review,* 23 (1), 103–19.

Graham, S. (2002) Bulldozers and bombs: the latest Palestinian-Israeli conflict as asymmetric urbicide. *Antipode,* 34 (4), 642–9.

Graves, R. (1929, 1960) *Goodbye to All That.* Penguin, Harmondsworth.

Greenberg, M., Lowrie, K., Krueckeberg, D., Mayer, H. and Simon, D. (1997) Bombs and butterflies: a case study of the challenges of post Cold War Environmental Planning and Managmeent for the US Nuclear Weapons Sites. *Journal of Environmental Planning and Management*, 40 (6), 739–50.

Gregory, D. 1994. 'Discourse' *Dictionary of Human Geography*. Third Edition, Blackwell, Oxford.

Grint, K. (1997) Relatively green: sociological approaches to business and the environment. In Bansal, P. and Howard, E. (eds) *Business and the Natural Environment*. Butterworth-Heineman, Oxford, 83–101.

Grossman, Z. (2002) New US military bases. *Counterpunch*, 2 February, 2002.

Gruffudd, P. (1995) Remaking Wales: nation-building and the geographical imagination, 1925–50. *Political Geography*, 14 (3), 219–39.

Gruffudd, P. (1990) *Reach for the Sky: The Air and English Cultural Nationalism.* Nottingham University Department of Geography Working paper No. 7.

Gruffudd, P. (1991) Reach for the sky: The air and English cultural nationalism. *Landscape Research*, 16 (2), 19–24.

Guardian (2000a) Shrimps thrive on battlefield. *Guardian*, 12 April, 2000.

Guardian (2000b) Poles transform Soviet camps into capitalist beacons, *Guardian*, 26 August 2000.

Guardian (2001a) Moor guide drops explosive toilet tip. *Guardian*, 29 January 2001.

Guardian (2002a) British troops bound for Iraq conflict to be given suspect Gulf War syndrome drugs. *Guardian*, 16 December. 2002.

Guardian (2002b) (Guardian 19 July, 2002) listing of Harperly Camp, Co Durham.

Hall, P. and Markusen, A. (1992) The Pentagon and the gunbelt. In Kirby, A. (ed.), *The Pentagon and the Cities*. Sage, Newbury Park CA, 53–76.

Halvorson, J., McCool, D., King, L.G. and Gatto, L.W. (2001) Soil compaction and over-winter changes to tracked-vehicle ruts, Yakima Training Center, Washington. *Journal of Terramechanics*, 38 (3) 133–51.

Hansard (2003) Dr Lewis Moonie, Under-Secretary of State for Defence and Minister for Veterans, Written Answer, 18 March, 2003. *Hansard* Col. 624.

Hansard (1992) House of Lords debates: Otterburn Training Area. *Hansard* Vol. 541, col. 85, 8 December, 1992.

Hansard (1995) Nicholas Soames, Armed Forces Minister, House of Commons, 5 July, 1995. *Hansard*, 263, Col. 339.

Hansen, K., Skopek, T. and Somma, M. (1997) The fundamentals of local policy implementation in military base redevelopment. *American Review of Public Administration*, 27 (4), 377–97.

Harford, B. and Hopkins, S. (1984) *Greenham Common: Women at the Wire.* The Women's Press, London.

Hartley, K. and Hooper, N. (1991) Economic Adjustment. In Kirby, S. and Hooper, N. (eds), *The Cost of Peace: Assessing Europe's Security Options*. Harwood Academic Publishers, Reading, 199–223.

Hassink, R. (2000) Regional involvement in defense industry restructuring in Belgium and the Netherlands. *International Regional Science Review*, 23 (1), 81–90.

Heffernan, M. (1995) For ever England: The Western Front and the politics of remembrance in Britain. *Ecumene*, 2 (3), 293–323.

Heffernan, M. (1996) Geography, cartography and military intelligence: the Royal Geographical Society and the First World War. *Transactions of the Institute of British Geographers*, 21, 504–33.

Hill, C. (1998) *The Political Economy of Military Base Redevelopment: An Evaluation of Four Converted Naval Bases.* PhD thesis, Rutgers University, New Jersey.

Hill, C. (2000) Measuring success in the redevelopment of former military bases: evidence from a case study of the Truman Annex in Key West, Florida. *Economic Development Quarterly*, 14 (3), 265–75.

Hipperson, S. (undated) *Interview with Sarah Hipperson, Greenham Common Peace Campaigner.* Imperial War Museum Sound Archive Ref: 20900, IWM On-line exhibition on Greenham Common.

Hirst, R.A., Pywell, R.F. and Putwain, P.D. (2000a) Assessing habitat disturbance using an historical perspective: The case of Salisbury Plain military training area. *Journal of Environmental Management*, 60, 181–93.

Hirst, R.A., Pywell, R.F., Putwain, P.D. and Marrs, R.H. (2000b) Ecological impacts of military vehicles on chalk grassland. *Aspects of Applied Biology*, 58, 293–8.

Hodson, Y. and Gordon, A. (1997) *An Illustrated History of 250 Years of Military Survey.* Military Survey Defence Agency, Feltham.

Homer-Dixon, T. (1991) On the Threshold: Environmental Changes as Causes of Acute Conflict. *International Security*, 16 (2), 76–116.

Homer-Dixon, T. (1999) *Environment, Security and Violence.* Princeton University Press, Princeton.

Hooker, M. and Knetter, M. (1999) Measuring the economic effects of military base closures. *National Bureau of Economic Research Working Paper 6941.* NBER, Cambridge, MA.

House of Commons Defence Committee (1994) *First Report on the Defence Estate.* HC67i and ii, Vols I and II, HMSO, London.

House of Commons Defence Committee (1995) *Fourth Special Report: Government Reply to the First Report from the Defence Committee*, HC318, 1994–95, HMSO, London.

House of Commons Defence Committee (1998) *Eight Report: The Strategic Defence Review. Volume 1: Report and Proceedings of the Committee.* HC 138. The Stationery Office, London.

House of Commons Defence Committee (1999) *Defence Committee Annual Reporting Cycle: Ministry of Defence Performance Report 1997–98.* Volume I: Minutes of Evidence 10 February 1999. HC241, The Stationery Office, London.

Howkins, A. (1986) The discovery of rural England. In Colls, R. and Dodd, P. (eds) *Englishness: Politics and Culture 1880–1920.* Croom Helm, London, 62–88.

HQ Land Command (1995) *Striking A Balance: A Report on the Management of the Major Army Training Areas.* HQ Land Command, Wilton.

HQ Land Command (1997) *Striking a Balance '97*, HQ Land Command, Wilton.

HQ Land Command (1998) *Striking A Balance '98* HQ Land Command, Wilton.

HQ Land Command (1999) *Striking A Balance '99* HQ Land Command, Wilton.

Huck, M.C. (1997) US Army Military District of Washington: Implementation of a Historic Preservation Plan. *Cultural Resource Management*, 20 (13), 14–16.

Hughes, H. (2001) *Arms Conversion and Diversification*, United Nations Association UK, London. www.una-uk.org/Disarmament/armstrade/armsconverion.html.

Hugill, B. (1997) Britain is accused of poisoning paradise. *Observer*, 12 October, 1997.

I/MoD/1 (1997) Opening observations on behalf of the Ministry of Defence to the Otterburn Public Inquiry, 22 April, 1997, OPI document.

IABG: Industrieanlagenbetreibergesellschaft and BICC: Bonn International Centre for Conversion (1997) *Study on the Re-Use of Former Military Lands*. Federal Ministry for the Environment, Nature Conservation and Nuclear Energy, Bonn.

Isako Angst, L. (2001) The sacrifice of a schoolgirl: the 1995 rape case, discourses of power, and women's lives in Okinawa. *Critical Asian Studies*, 33 (2), 243–66.

Isserman, A. and Stenberg, P. (1994) The recovery of rural economies from military base closures: control group analysis of two decades of experience. *Southern Regional Science Association Meeting*, Orlando, Florida, April 1994, cited in Markusen and Brzoska, 2000.

Itô, Y. Miyagi, K. and Ota, H. (2000) Imminent extinction crisis among the endemic species of the forests of Yanbaru, Okinawa, Japan. *Oryx*, 34 (4), 305–16.

Jauhiainen, J. (1997) Militarisation, demilitarisation and re-use of military areas: the case of Estonia. *Geography*, 82 (2), 118–26.

Jauhiainen, J. (1999) The question of region in conversion. In Jelušic, L. and Selby, J. (eds) *Defence Restructuring and Conversion: Socio-cultural aspects*. COST A10, European Commission, DG Research, Brussels.

Johnson, W.G. (2002) Archaeological examination of Cold War architecture: a reactionary cultural response to the threat of nuclear war. In Schofield, J., Johnson, W.G. and Beck, C.M. (2002) (eds) *Matériel Culture: The Archaeology of Twentieth-Century Conflict*. Routledge, London, 227–35.

Johnson, W.G. and Beck, C.M. (1995) Proving ground of the nuclear age. *Archaeology*, May/June, 1995, 41–9.

Johnston, R.J., Gregory, D. and Smith, D.M. (1986) (eds) *The Dictionary of Human Geography*, Blackwell Oxford. Second edition.

Johnston, R.J., Gregory, D., Pratt, G. and Watts, M. J. (2000) (eds) *The Dictionary of Human Geography*, Blackwell, Oxford. Fourth Edition.

Johnston, R.J., Taylor, P.J. and Watts, M.J. (2002) (eds) *Geographies of Global Change: Remapping the World*. Blackwell, Oxford.

Junor, B. and Howse, K. (1995) *Greenham Common Women's Peace Camp: A History of Non-Violent Resistance 1984–1995*. Working Press, London.

Kade, A. and Warren, S.D. (2002) Soil and plant recovery after historic military disturbances in the Sonoran Desert, USA. *Arid Land Research and Management*, 16 (3), 231–43.

Käkönen, J. (1994) (ed.) *Green Security or Militarized Environment*. Dartmouth, Aldershot.

Kaldor, M. and Schméder, G. (1997) Introduction. In Kaldor, M. and Schméder, G. (eds) *The European Rupture: the Defence Sector in Transition*. Edward Elgar, Cheltenham.

Kelso, P. (2002) Aldermaston ready to don a green cloak. *Guardian*, 27 August, 2002.

Kippin, J. (1995) *Nostalgia for the Future: Photographs 1988–1994*. The Photographers' Gallery, London.

Kippin, J. (2001) *Cold War Pastoral: Greenham Common*. Black Dog Publishing, London.

Kirk, G., Cornwell, R. and Okazawa-Rey, M. (2000) Women and the US military in East Asia. *Foreign Policy in Focus*, 4 (9).

Kirsch, S. (1997) Watching the bombs go off: Photography, nculear landscapes, and spectator democracy. *Antipode*, 29, 227–255.

Kirsch, S. (2000) Peaceful nuclear explosions and the geography of scientific authority. *Professional Geographer* 52 (2) 179–92.

Kiss, J. (2000) Regional aspects of defense-industrial transformation in East-Central Europe. *International Regional Science Review*, 23 (1), 120–9.

Kitfield, J. (1998) The battle of the depots. *National Journal*, 30, 746–50.

Kohler, M., Hofmann, K., Volsgen, F., Thurow, K. and Koch, A. (2001) Bacterial release of arsenic ions and organoarsenic compounds from soil contaminated by chemical warfare agents. *Chemosphere*, 42 (4), 425–9.

Kuletz, V. (1998) *The Tainted Desert: Environmental and Social Ruin in the American West*. Routledge, London and New York.

Lacoste, Y. (1977) An illustration of geographical warfare: bombing of the dikes on the Red River, North Vietnam. In Peet, R. (ed.) *Radical Geography: Alternative Viewpoints on Contemporary Social Issues*. Maronfa Press, Chicago, 244–61.

Laka Foundation (1999) *Depleted Uranium: A Post-War Disaster for Environment and Health*. Laka Foundation, Amsterdam, Netherlands.

Law, R., Wolch, J. and Takahashi, L. (1993) Defense-less territory: workers, communities and the decline of military production in Los Angeles. *Environment and Planning C*, 11, 291–315.

Le Billon, P. (2001) The political ecology of war: natural resources and armed conflicts. *Political Geography*, 20 (5), 561–84.

Ley, D. (1983) *A Social Geography of the City*. Harper and Row, New York.

Liddington, J. (1989) *The Long Road to Greenham: Feminism and Anti-Militarism in Britain Since 1820*. Virago, London.

Lindsay-Poland, J. (2001) US military bases in Latin America and the Caribbean. *Foreign Policy in Focus*, 6 (35).

Lobeck, M., Pätz, A. and Wiegandt, C-C. (1994) Standortkonversion in Deutschland: Probleme und Handlungsansätze. *Berichte zur Deutschen Landeskund*, 68 (1), 57–84.

Lohmann, L. (1991) Who defends biological diversity? Conservation Strategies and the case of Thailand. *The Ecologist*, 21 (1), 5–13.

Loomis, D. (1993) *Combat Zoning: Military Land Use Planning in Nevada*. University of Nevada Press, Reno.

Lovering, J. (1990) Military expenditure and the restructuring of capitalism: the military industry in Britain. *Cambridge Journal of Economics*, 14, 453–67.

Lovering, J. (1994) The production and consumption of the 'means of violence': implications of the reconfiguration of the state, economic internationalisation and the end of the Cold War. *Geoforum*, 25 (4), 471–86.

Lovering, J. (1998) Opening Pandora's Box: De facto industrial policy and the British defence industry. In Delbridge, R. and Lowe, J. (eds) *Manufacturing in Transition*, Routledge, London, 151–68.

Lovering, J. (2000) Loose cannons: creating the arms industry in the twenty-first century. In Kaldor, M. (ed.), *Global Insecurity: Restructuring the Global Military Sector* Vol. III, Pinter, London, 147–76.

Lowe, P. (1983) *Environmental Groups in Politics*. Allen and Unwin, Boston.

Lowe, P., Clark, J., Seymour, S. and Ward, N. (1997) *Moralizing the Environment: Countryside Change, Farming and Pollution*. UCL Press, London.

Lowe, P., Murdoch, J. and Cox, G. (1995) A civilized retreat? Anti-urbanism, rurality and the making of an anglo-centric culture. In Healy, P., Cameron, S., Davoudi, S., Graham, S. and Madani-Pour, A. (eds) *Managing cities: The New Urban Context*. John Wiley and Sons, London, 63–82.

Luke, T. and Ó Tuathail, G. (2000) Thinking geopolitical space: the spatiality of war, speed and vision in the work of Paul Virilio. In Crang, M. and Thrift, N. (eds) *Thinking Space*. Routledge, London, 360–79.

Lukowiak, K. (1993) *A Soldier's Song: True Stories from the Falklands*. Phoenix, London.

Lukowiak, K. (2000) *Marijuana Time: Join the Army, See the World, Meet Interesting People and Smoke All Their Dope*. Orion, London.

Lulek, J.K., Szafran, B.A. and Lasecka, E. (1999) Levels of polychlorinated bi-phenyls in soil samples from some former Soviety army bases in Poland. *Abstracts of Papers of the American Chemical Society*, 217, 178-ENVR, Part 1.

MacEwen, A. and MacEwan, M. (1982) *National Parks: Conservation or Cosmetics?* Allen and Unwin, London.

MacEwan, A. and MacEwan, M. (1987) *Greenprints for the Countryside? The Story of Britain's National Parks*. Allen and Unwin, London.

Maguire, T.M. (1899) *Outlines of Military Geography*. Cambridge University Press, Cambridge.

Markusen, A. and Brzoska, M. (2000) The regional role in post-Cold War military industrial conversion. *International Regional Science Review*, 23, 3–24.

Markusen, A. and Park, S.O. (1993) The state as industrial locator and district builder: the case of Changwon, South Korea. *Economic Geography*, 69, 157–81.

Markusen, A., Hall, P., Campbell, S. and Deitrick, S. (1991) *The Rise of the Gubelt: The Military Remapping of Industrial America*. Oxford University Press, Oxford.

Matsuoka, M. (1997) Reintegrating the flatlands: a regional framework for military base conversion in the San Fransisco Bay area. *Capitalism, Nature, Socialism*, 8 (1), 109–24.

Mayer, K. (1995) Closing military bases (finally): solving collective dilemmas through delegation. *Legislative Studies Quarterly*, 20 (3), 393–413.

McCaffrey, K.T. (2002) *Military Power and Popular Protest: The US Navy in Vieques*. Rutgers University Press, New Jersey.

McDowell, L. and Sharp, J.P. (1999) *A Feminist Glossary of Human Geography*. Arnold, London.

McGowan, A. (1991) Editorial: the Complete cost of war. *Environment*, 33 (3) 2, 1.

McKee, M. and Berrens, R.P. (2001) Balancing army and endangered species concerns: Green *vs*. Green. *Environmental Management*, 27 (1), 123–33.

McMahon, C.A., Vintro, L.L., Mitchell, P.I. and Dahlgaard, H. (2000) Oxidation-state distribution of plutonium in surface and subsurface waters at Thule, north-west Greenland. *Applied Radiation and Isotopes*, 52 (3) 697–703.

Middleton, N. (1999) *The Global Casino: An Introduction to Environmental Issues*. Second Edition. Arnold, London.

Military Toxics Project (nd) *Depleted Uranium Factsheet*. Military Toxics Project, Lewiston, ME.

Mills, S. 1997. *Discourse*. Routledge, London.

Ministry of Defence (1991) *Options for Change*. Cm 1559, HMSO, London.

Ministry of Defence (1995a) *The Military Justification for the Development of Otterburn Training Area to Accommodate AS90 and MLRS Training*. MoD and RPS Clouston, Abingdon.

Ministry of Defence (1995b) *Otterburn Training Area: Options for Change Proposals: Explanation of the Proposals and non-technical summary of the Environmental Statement*. MoD and RPS Clouston, Abingdon.

Ministry of Defence (1996a) *In Response to Consultation: A new initiative by the Ministry of Defence. Otterburn Training Area Options for Change Proposals*. MoD and RPS Clouston, Abingdon.

Ministry of Defence (1998) *The Strategic Defence Review: Modern Forces for the Modern World*. Cm3999, TSO, London.

Ministry of Defence (2000a) *In Trust and On Trust: The Strategy for the Defence Estate*. TSO, London.

Ministry of Defence (2000b) *A Record Breaking Year*. MoD Press Release 063/00, 3 April, 2000.

Ministry of Defence (2000c) '"Operation Newt" A Great Success', MoD Press Release, 3 May, 2000.

Ministry of Defence (2000d) *Conserving the Balance – Training for the Millennium*. MoD Press Release 092/00, 16 May, 2000.

Ministry of Defence (2000e) *Strategic Environmental Appraisal of the Strategic Defence Review*. MoD, London.

Ministry of Defence (2000f) *MoD Puts Environment First: Strategic Environmental Appraisal*. MoD Press Release 190/00, 27 July, 2000.

Ministry of Defence (2001a) *2000–01 Performance Report*, Cm5290, TSO, London.

Ministry of Defence (2001b) *The Future of the Defence Diversification Agency: A Consultative Document*. MoD, London.

Ministry of Defence (2002) *Defence Industrial Policy: Ministry of Defence Policy Paper No.5*. Ministry of Defence, London.

Ministry of Defence and English Nature (1996) *Declaration of Intent between the Ministry of Defence and English Nature*. 26 June, 1996.

Ministry of Defence and Northumberland National Park (undated, c.1996) *Public Information Leaflet: Otterburn Training Area*. MoD and NNP.

Ministry of Town and Country Planning (1948) *Report on the Public Local Inquiry into the Effect on the Public Interest of the Proposal of the War Department to Use Land at Redesdale Ranges*. 30 June, 1948.

Minton, E. (1994) When Johnny goes marching home. *Planning*, 60 (11), 18–22.

Misrach, R. (1990) *Bravo 20: The Bombing of the American West*. John Hopkins University Press, Baltimore.

MoD/P/3 (1997) *Proof of Evidence, Landscape and Visual Impact. Ken Trew, RPS Clouston for MoD*. OPI Document.

MoD/R/3/1 (1997) *MoD Response to the Evidence of Northumberland County Council*. OPI Document.

Monmonier, M. (1995) *Drawing the Line: Tales of Maps and Carto-controversy*. Henry Holt, New York.

Morris, M. (1997) Gardens 'For Ever England': landscape, identity and the First World War British cemeteries on the Western Front. *Ecumene*, 4 (4), 410–33.

Morrison, M.L., Mills, L.S., Kuenzi, A.J. (1996) Study and management of an isolated, rare population: The Fresno kangaroo rat. *Wildlife Society Bulletin*, 24 (4), 602–6.

Municipal Journal (1995) Survey of districts following base closures 19–25.May, 1995.

Murdoch, J. and Ward, N. (1997) Governmentality and territoriality: the statistical manufacture of Britain's 'national farm'. *Political Geography*, 16 (4), 307–24.

Murdoch, J., Lowe, P., Ward, N. and Marsden, T. (2003) *The Differentiated Countryside*. Routledge, London.

National Audit Office (1987) *Ministry of Defence and Property Services Agency: Control and Management of the Defence Estate*. HC131, 1986–87, HMSO, London.

National Audit Office (1992) *Ministry of Defence: Management and Control of Army Training Land*. HC 218, 1991–92, HMSO, London.

National Audit Office (1998) *Ministry of Defence: Identifying and Selling Surplus Property*, HC776, TSO, London.

National Parks Review Panel (1991) *Fit for the Future: The Report of the National Parks Review Panel*. CCP 334, Countryside Commission, Cheltenham.

Navy Advancement (2003 www.navyadvancement.com. Web site giving information on US and overseas US naval bases. Visted 27 February, 2003.

Network Demilitarised (1994) *The Conversion of Military Sites: A Handbook Outlining a Commercial Audit Procedure to Assist the Re-use of Former Defence Establishments*. Wiltshire County Council, Trowbridge.

Network Demilitarised (1996) *Military Base Conversion: The Lessons from Experience*. Wiltshire County Council, Trowbridge.

Niedenthal, J. (2001) *For the Good of Mankind: A History of the People of Bikini and their Islands*. Second Edition. Bravo Publishers, Micronitor.

Niedenthal, J. (2002) Paradise lost – 'for the good of mankind'. *Guardian*, 8 August, 2002.

NPC/P/1 (1997) *Proof of Evidence of the Council for National Parks, presented by Vicki Elcoate and Amanda Nobbs*, OPI document.

NPC/P/3 (1997) *Proof of Evidence of the Northumberland and Newcastle Society, presented by Graham Coggins*. OPI document.

Ó Tuathail, G. (1996) *Critical Geopolitics: The Politics of Writing Global Space*. Routledge, London.

O'Loughlin, J. (1986) Political geography: tilling the fallow field. *Progress in Human Geography*, 10 (1), 69–83.

O'Loughlin, J. and van der Wusten, H. (1986) Geography, war and peace: notes for a contribution to a revived political geography. *Progress in Human Geography*, 10 (4), 484–510.

O'Sullivan, P. (1991) *Terrain and Tactics*. Greenwood Press, New York.

O'Sullivan, P. (2001) *The Geography of War in the Post Cold War World*. Edwin Mellen Press, Lewiston, NY.

O'Sullivan, P. and Miller, J.W. (1983) *The Geography of Warfare*. Croom Helm, London.

Oden, M. (2000) Federal defense industrial policy, firm strategy and regional conversion initiatives in four American aerospace regions. *International Regional Science Review*, 23 (1), 25–48.

Okazawa-Rey, M. (1997) Amerasian children of GI Town: A legacy of US militarism in South Korea. *Asian Journal of Women's Studies*, 3 (1), 71–102.

Otterburn Army Field Training Centre (1993) *Otterburn Training Area Strategic Estate Management Plan*. Unpublished OTA document.

Owens, S. (1990a) *Military Live Firing in National Parks*. UK Centre for Economic and Environmental Development, London.

Owens, S. (1990b) Defence and the environment: the impacts of military live firing in national parks. *Cambridge Journal of Economics*, 14, 497–505.

Palka, E.J. and Galgano, F.A. (eds) (2000) *The Scope of Military Geography: Across the Spectrum from Peacetime to War*. McGraw-Hill, Primis Custom Publishing, New York.

Parai, L., Solomon, B. and Wait, T. (1996) Assessing the socio-economic impacts of military installations on their host communities. *Defence and Peace Economics*, 7, 7–19.

Parkin, S. (1997) Environmental security: issues and agenda for an incoming government. *Royal United Services Institute Journal*, June 1997, 24–28.

Pearson G.S. (1992) Preface. In Carter, G.B. (1992) *Porton Down: 75 Years of Chemical and Biological Research*. HMSO, London. npn.

Peet, R. (1977) *Radical Geography: Alternative Viewpoints on Contemporary Social Issues*. Maronfa Press, Chicago.

Peet, R. (2000) Commentary: celebrating 30 years of radical geography. *Environment and Planning A*, 32 (6), 951–3.

Peltier, L. C. and Pearcy, G.E. (1966) *Military Geography*. D. Van Nostrand Co., Princeton NJ.

Pepper, D. and Jenkins, A. (1985) (eds) *The Geography of Peace and War*. Blackwell, Oxford.

Perani, G. (2000) Italian contrasts in regional military industrial conversion. *International Regional Science Review*, 23 (1), 91–102.

Peterson, M.M., Horst, G.L., Shea, P.J. and Comfort, S.D. (1998) Germination and seedling development of switchgrass and smooth bromegrass explosed to 2,4,6-trinitrotoluene. *Environmental Pollution*, 99 (1), 53–9.

Pettitt, A. (nd) *Interview with Ann Pettitt, Greenham Common peace campaigner*. Imperial War Museum Sound Archive Ref: 12745, IWM ON-line exhibition about Greenham Common.

Pilot Shack (2003) Information on military bases overseas from www.pilotshack.com/militaryBases-overseas.html. Visited 6 March, 2003.

Pitten, F.A., Muller, G., König, P., Schmidt, D., Thurow, K. and Kramer, A. (1999) Risk assessment of a former military base contaminated with organoarsenic-based warfare agents: uptake of arsenic by terrestrial plants. *Science of the Total Environment*. 226 (2–3), 237–45.

Poland, J.S., Mitchell, S. and Rutter, A. (2001) Remediation of former military bases in the Canadian Arctic. *Cold Regions Science and Technology*, 32 (2–3), 93–105.

Pratt, A. (1996) 'Discourses of rurality: loose talk or social struggle?' *Journal of Rural Studies*, 12, 69–78.

Preis, S., Krichevskaya, M. and Kharchenko, A. (1977) Photocatalytic oxidation of aromatic aminocompounds in aqueous solutions and groundwater from abandoned military bases. *Water Science and Technology*, 35 (4), 265–72.

PricewaterhouseCoopers (2002) *Department of Defence: The Economic and Social Impacts of the Royal Australian Air Force Base Richmond on The Hawksbury and Surrounding Region.* PWC, Sydney.

Prosser, C.W., Sedivec, K.K. and Barker, W.T. (2000) Tracked vehicle effects on vegetation and soil characteristics. *Journal of Range Managemen*, 53 (6), 666–70.

Public Accounts Committee (1983) *Fifth Report on Energy Efficiency.* HC106, 1983–84, HMSO, London.

Public Accounts Committee (1984a) *Eleventh Report on the Falkland Islands.* HC180, 1984–85, HMSO, London.

Public Accounts Committee (1984b) *Nineteenth Report on Energy Efficiency.* HC256, 1984–85, HMSO, London.

Public Accounts Committee (1987) *Ninth Report: Control and Management of the Defence Estate.* HC 191, 1986–87, HMSO, London.

Public Accounts Committee (1987) *Ninth Report: The Control and Management of the Defence Estate.* HC191, HMSO, London.

Public Accounts Committee (1989) Sixteenth Report *Control and Management of the Defence Estate.* HC 88, 1988–89, HMSO, London.

Public Accounts Committee (1993) *Thirty-Sixth Report: Ministry of Defence: Management and Control of Army Training Lands.* HC411, HMSO, London.

Public Accounts Committee (1999) *Tenth Report: Ministry of Defence: Identifying and Selling Surplus Property.* HC104. TSO, London.

Redhead, B. (1995) *The Inspiration of Landscape: Artists in National Parks.* Phaidon, Oxford.

Reichard, L. (2001) Military base in Ecuador shrouded in corruption. *Peacework*, December 2001–January 2002.

Renew (2002) Information from Parliamentary Question, 15 May, 2002, on wind power and MoD objections to turbines. Renew On-Line 39, Sept-Oct, 2002. www.tec.open.ac.uk

Riefler, R.G. and Smets, B.F. (2002) NAD(P)H: flavin mononucleotide oxidoreductase inactivation during 2,4,6- trinitrotoluene reduction. *Applied and Environmental Microbiology*, 68 (4), 1690–6.

Rocamora, J. (1998) The conversion of the US Subic Naval Base in the Phillipines: political and economic consequences. In Kaldor, M., Albrecht, U. and Schméder, G. (eds) *The End of Military Fordism: Restructuring the Global Military Sector.* Pinter, London, 287–311.

Rogers, A. and Viles, A. (2003) (eds) *The Student's Companion to Geography.* Second Edition. Blackwell, Oxford.

Rose, G. (1993) *Feminism and Geography.* Polity Press, Cambridge.

Roseneil, S. (1995) *Disarming Patriarchy: Feminism and Political Action at Greenham.* Open University Press, Buckingham.

Roseneil, S. (1999) *Common Women, Uncommon Practices: The Queer Feminism of Greenham.* Cassell, London.

Ross, A. (1996) The future is a risky business, *The Ecologist*, 26, 42–4.

Santos, A.F., Hofmann, C.T. and Bulawan, A. (1997) *Prostitution at the Bases: A Continuing Saga of Exploitation*. Paper to the International Planning Meeting on Women and Children, Militarism and Human Rights, 1–4 May, Naha, Okinawa, CATW Listserve, cited in Euler and Welzer-Lang (2000).

Schofield, J. (2001) D-Day sites in England: an assessment. *Antiquity* 75, 77–83.

Schofield, J. and Anderton, M. (2000) The queer archaeology of Green Gate: Interpreting contested space at Greenham Common Airbase. *World Archaeology* 32 (2), 236–251.

Schofield, J., Johnson, W.G. and Beck, C.M. (2002) (eds) *Matériel Culture: The Archaeology of Twentieth Century Conflict*. Routledge, London.

Scott, A. (1993) Interregional subcontracting patterns in the aerospace industry: the Southern California nexus. *Economic Geography*, 69, 142–55.

Scott, K. (2001) Moratorium sought on DU shell testing. *Guardian*, 21 February, 2001.

Scott-Clark, C. and Levy, A. (2003) Spectre Orange. *Guardian Weekend*, 29 March. 2003.

Seager, J. (1993) *Earth Follies: Feminism, Politics and the Environment*. Earthscan, London.

Sefarti, C. (2000) (ed.) *Government – Company Relationships in the Arms Industry*. European Commission, Brussels.

Services Sound and Vision Corporation (1993) *Train Green*. Army Training Video C1824VT, Crown Copyright.

Shapiro, M.J. (1997) *Violent Cartographies: Mapping Cultures of War*. University of Minnesota Press, Minneapolis.

Sharp, Baroness (1977) *Dartmoor: Report of a Public Inquiry into the Continued Use of Dartmoor by the Ministry of Defence for Training Purposes*. HMSO, London.

Shaw, B. (1999) *Smoking Guns: The Impact Area at Massachusetts Military Reservation*, Military Toxics Project.

Shaw, M. (1991) *Post-military Society: Militarism, Demilitarisation and War at the End of the Twentieth Century*. Polity Press, Cambridge.

Shields, D. (1996) Defence of nature's realm. *The Field*, July 1996, 92–5.

Shorrock, T. (2000) Okinawa and the US military in Northeast Asia. *Foreign Policy in Focus*, 5 (22), July.

Short, J.R. (1991) *Imagined Country: Environment, Culture and Society*. Routledge, London.

Shriver-Lake, L.C., Donner, B.L., Ligler, F.S. (1997) On-site detection of TNT with a portable fiber optic biosensor. *Environmental Science & Technology*, 31 (3), 837–41.

Siciliano, S.D. and Greer, C.W. (2000) Plant-bacterial combinations to phytoremediate soil contaminated with high concentrations of 2,4,6-trinitrotoluene. *Journal of Environmental Quality*, 29 (1), 311–16.

Sigmund, E. (1980) *Rage Against the Dying: Campaign Against Chemical and Biological Warfare*. Pluto Press, London.

Sinclair, I. (2002) *London Orbital: A Walk Around the M25*. Granta, London.

Solomon, B. (1996) The socio-economic assessment of military installations using an integer programming model. *Defence and Peace Economics*, 7 (1), 21–32.

Stephenson, T.W., Vaughan, M.R., Andersen, D.E., (1996) Mule deer movements in response to military activity in southeast Colorado. *Journal of Wildlife Management*, 60 (4), 777–87.

Stolpe, G. (1999) (ed.) *Proceedings of the Information Seminar 'Military Land and Conservation'*. International Academy for Nature Conservation, Vilm.

Sturdevant S.P. and Stoltzfus, B. (1993) *Let the Good Times Roll: Prostitution and the U.S. Military in Asia*. New Press, New York

Szasz, F.M. (1995) The impact of World War Two on the land: Gruinard Island, Scotland and Trinity Site, New Mexico as case studies. *Environmental History Review*, 19 (4), 15–30.

Thee, M. (1980) Militarism and militarisation in contemporary international relations. In Adbjorn, E. and Thee, M. (eds) *Problems of Contemporary Militarism*. Croom Helm, London, 15–35.

Tivers, J. (1999) 'The Home of the British Army': the iconic construction of military defence landscapes. *Landscape Research*, 24 (3), 303–19.

Trevelyan, G.M. (1934) *The Middle Marches*. Andrew Reid and Co., Newcastle upon Tyne.

Trinder, C. (2002) Postcard from Downunder. *Sanctuary*, 31, 13–16.

Turner, E.S. (2002) Our chaps will deal with them. *London Review of Books*, 24 (15), 13–14.

US Army (2003) www.yuma.army.mil/fy01economic.html Visited 6 March, 2003.

Uzzell, D. (1998) The hot interpretation of the Cold War. In *Monuments of War: the Evaluation, Recording and Management of Twentieth Century Military Sites*. English Heritage, London, 18–21.

Vanderbilt, T. (2002) *Survival City: Adventures Among the Ruins of Atomic America*. Princeton Architectural Press, New York.

Virilio, P. (1994) *Bunker Archaeology*. Princeton Architectural Press, New York.

Wainwright, M. (1998) Search begins for lost wartime defence ditches. *Guardian*, 29 September, 1998.

Walsh, M.R., Walsh, M.E. and Collins, C.M. (1999) Remediation methods for white phosphorus contamination in a coastal salt marsh. *Environmental Conservation*, 26 (2), 112–24. June.

Warf, B. (1993) The Pentagon and the service sector. *Economic Geography*, 69, 123–41.

Warf, B. (1997) The geopolitics/geoeconomics of military base closures in the USA. *Political Geography*, 16 (7), 541–63.

Warf, B. and Glasmeier, A. (1993) Introduction: military spending, the American economy and the end of the Cold War. *Economic Geography*, 69, 103–6.

Warner, F. (1991) The Environmental Consequences of the Gulf War. *Environment*, 33 (5), 6–9, 25–26.

Watson-Smyth, M. (1993) *Deserted Bastions: Historic Naval and Military Architecture*. Save Britain's Heritage, London.

Wegman, R. and Bailey, H.G. (1994) The challenge of cleaning up military wastes when US bases are closed. *Ecology Law Quarterly*, 21 (4), 865–945.

Weissflog, L., Wenzel, K.D., Manz, M., Klein, F. and Schurmann, G. (1999) Economic upheaval in 1990–93 and the ecological situation in central Germany. *Environmental Pollution*, 105 (3), 341–7.

Westing, A. (1988) The military sector via-à-vis the environment. *Journal of Peace Research*, 25 (3), 257–64.

Weston, S. (1989) *Walking Tall: An Autobiography*. Bloomsbury, London.

WGSG: Women and Geography Study Group (1997) *Feminist Geographies: Explorations in Diversity and Difference*. Longman, London.

Whitecotton, R.C.A., David, M.B., Darmody, R.G. and Price, D.L. (2000) Impact of foot traffic from military training on soil and vegetation properties. *Environmental Management*, 26 (6), 697–706.

Winter, J. (1995) *Sites of Memory, Sites of Mourning: The Great War in European Cultural History*. Cambridge University Press, Cambridge.

Winters, H.A. with Gerald Galloway, William Reynolds and David Rhyne, (1998) *Battling the Elements: Weather and Terrain in the Conduct of War*. Johns Hopkins University Press, Baltimore

Witzman, K. (1994) Land conversion and planning: looking back and ahead. *Raumforschung und Raumordnung*, 52 (4–5), 279–86.

Wood, D. (2001) *The Hidden Geography of Transnational Surveillance: Social and Technological Networks Around Signals Intelligence Sites*. PhD Thesis, University of Newcastle.

Woodward, R. (1998a) *Rural Development and the Restructuring of the Defence Estate: A Preliminary Investigation*. Research Report 98/5, Centre for Rural Economy, University of Newcastle.

Woodward, R. (1998b) *Defended Territory: The Otterburn Training Area and the 1997 Public Inquiry*. Research Report, Centre for Rural Economy, University of Newcastle.

Woodward, R. (1998c) 'It's a Man's Life!': soldiers, masculinity and the countryside. *Gender, Place and Culture*, 5 (3), 277–300.

Woodward, R. (1999) Gunning for rural England: The politics of the promotion of military land use in the Northumberland National Park. *Journal of Rural Studies*, 15 (1), 17–33.

Woodward, R. (2000a) Royal Dockyard at Chatham: History and Re-use. *Aquapolis*, 5 (1), 26–31.

Woodward, R. (2000b) Warrior heroes and little green men: military training and the construction of rural masculinities. *Rural Sociology*, 65 (4), 640–57.

Woodward, R. (2001a) In trust and on trust: the strategy for the Defence Estate. *Land Use Policy*, 18 (2), 93–7.

Woodward, R. (2001b) Khaki conservation: an examination of military environmentalist discourses in the British Army. *Journal of Rural Studies*, 17 (2), 201–17.

Woodward, R. (2001c) 'Local interests, regional needs or national imperative? The Otterburn question and the military in rural areas.' In J. Tomaney and N. Ward (eds), *A Region in Transition: North East England at the Millennium*. Avebury, Guildford, 199–217.

Woodward, R. (2003) 'Locating military masculinities: the role of space and place in the formation of gender identities in the Armed Forces.' In P. Higate (ed.) *Military Masculinities: Identity and the State*. Greenwood Press, London, 43–56.

Wright, P. (1995) *The Village That Died for England: The Strange Story of Tyneham*. Jonathan Cape, London.

Index

Printed and bound by CPI Group (UK) Ltd, Croydon, CR0 4YY
18/07/2022
03136723-0003